WITH THE
8TH SCOTTISH RIFLES
1914–1919

LIEUT.-COLONEL H. M. HANNAN

O.C. 1/8TH SCOTTISH RIFLES

Killed Gallipoli, 21st June, 1915

WITH THE
8TH SCOTTISH RIFLES
1914-1919

BY

COLONEL J. M. FINDLAY
D.S.O.

BLACKIE AND SON LIMITED
50 OLD BAILEY, LONDON; GLASGOW, BOMBAY
1926

First Impression, January, 1926
Second Impression, March, 1926

Printed and Bound by Antony Rowe Ltd

Dedicated to the Memory of
LT.-COL. H. MONTEITH HANNAN
and all other
FALLEN COMRADES

Preface

This book was originally intended to be an official history of the 8th Scottish Rifles during the Great War, but when I found that the records were not complete, and when from time to time it was represented to me by various friends that a personal method was more likely to make the book interesting and acceptable to its prospective readers, I decided to abandon its official form.

I admit that I was further influenced to make the story informal by the fact that I found it easier to express myself in that way, after more than one attempt to keep it impersonal and official. Moreover, it left me free to make any observations and criticisms (if I so desired) which would have been out of place in an official record.

At the same time I have endeavoured to maintain the historic accuracy of events, by having it revised by officers who could corroborate details, and by obtaining narratives of certain portions of the history when I was not there from officers who were with the battalion during such periods. But memory is a faulty thing, and if, in spite of precautions, there are any important omissions or errors I ask the forgiveness of those concerned.

I am indebted to Lieutenant-Colonel R. N. Coulson, D.S.O., for the narrative of the latter days in Gallipoli (Chapter III), to him and to Major W. T. Law for the material for the early days in Egypt (Chapter IV), to Lieutenant-Colonel R. D. Hunter, D.S.O., and Captain W. Whigham Ferguson, M.C., for the story of the " Great Push " in the autumn of 1918

(Chapter IX), and to Lieutenant-Colonel D. S. Carson, O.B.E., for portions of Chapters I and II.

I am also indebted to Captain Sir Steven Bilsland, Bart., M.C., Major A. Bankier Sloan, R.A.M.C., Lieutenant-Colonel R. N. Coulson, D.S.O., Colonel R. Murray White, D.S.O., and Captain J. B. Ramsay, for placing at my disposal their collections of photographs.

For kindly help in other ways I wish also to thank Major-General E. S. Girdwood, C.B., C.M.G., Brigadier-General A. H. Leggett, C.M.G., D.S.O., Colonel W. R. Maxwell, V.D., Lieutenant-Colonel A. D. Ker, T.D. (2/8th Scottish Rifles), Lieutenant-Colonel J. M. Hannan (3/8th Scottish Rifles), Major H. A. MacLehose, Major J. T. Tulloch, M.C. (H.L.I.), Captain E. R. Boyd, a coterie of ex-officers consisting of Captains C. Eric Findlay, M.C., W. S. Scott, Sir A. Steven Bilsland, Bart., M.C., Lieutenants G. J. Innes and H. G. Carswell, M.C., and others, who furnished me with some " personal " incidents; the Editors of the 52nd Divisional History and Captain J. B. Ramsay, M.C., 7th Scottish Rifles, for permission to use the latter's most excellent maps and plans; the Editor of the 34th Divisional History for similar kind permission; the Editor of the 5th Highland Light Infantry History for corroborative references and plans, and Messrs. Jackson, Wylie & Co., for the block of W Beach, Gallipoli.

The Battalion is indebted to the following officers and friends, whose generosity has made the publication of this book possible.

General Andrew L. Macfie.
Colonel Warden R. Maxwell.
Colonel J. M. Findlay, D.S.O.
Colonel Johnstone Macfie.
Lt.-Col. R. N. Coulson, D.S.O.
Walter W. Blackie, Esq.
Mrs. J. Robertson Blackie.
Capt. Sir Steven Bilsland, M.C.
Capt. E. R. Boyd.
Lt.-Col. D. S. Carson, O.B.E.
Capt. Neil Caw.

Capt. J. P. Cuthbert, M.C.
Mrs. F. Findlay.
Mrs. J. Findlay.
Capt. C. E. Findlay, M.C.
R. C. Greig, Esq.
Mrs. H. Monteith Hannan.
Lt.-Col. J. M. Hannan.
Capt. Richard Humble.
G. J. Innes, Esq.
Lt.-Col. Alan D. Ker.
Major W. T. Law.

David M'Cowan, Esq.
Mrs. J. B. Macindoe.
Dr. Norman Macnair.
Major Hamish A. MacLehose.
Capt. Nelson Mitchell.
J. A. Ralston Mitchell, Esq.
Ronald W. Mowat, Esq.
Richard Niven, Esq.
Peter Rintoul, Esq.

Wilson Robinson, Esq.
James Scott, Esq.
George Sloan, Esq.
Capt. W. N. Sloan.
Major A. B. Sloan, R.A.M.C.
A. B. Sloan, Esq., M.D.
Major A. S. L. Young.
Alfred A. Young, Esq.

One word more. It would be interesting to know if there are any other battalions or units which can claim to have had such a varied experience during and after the war as this Battalion. It saw service in France and Flanders, Gallipoli, Egypt and Palestine, Mesopotamia (Trench Mortar Battery), and in the Army of Occupation in Germany.

J. M. FINDLAY, *Colonel.*

October, 1925.

Contents

APPENDICES

Plates

Plates

Maps in Colour

Table

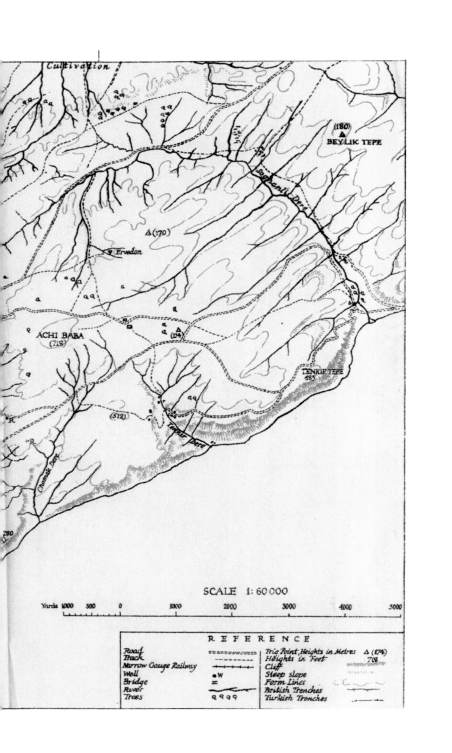

Cultivation

(180)
▲
BEYLIK TEPE

Baghanli Dere

△(170)

🌳 Eredon

ACHI BABA
(718)

△
(174)

TENKIR TEPE
585

(512)

R

Chanak Dere

Tenkir Dere

280

SCALE 1: 60000

Yards 1000   500   0   1000   2000   3000   4000   5000

REFERENCE

Road	Trig Point Heights in Metres △ (174)
Track	Heights in Feet 718
Narrow Gauge Railway	Cliff
Well ●W	Steep slope
Bridge =	Form Lines
River	British Trenches
Trees ९ ९ ९ ९	Turkish Trenches

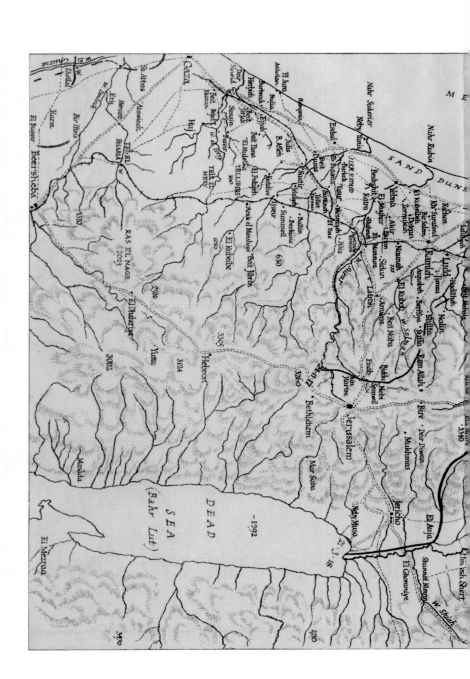

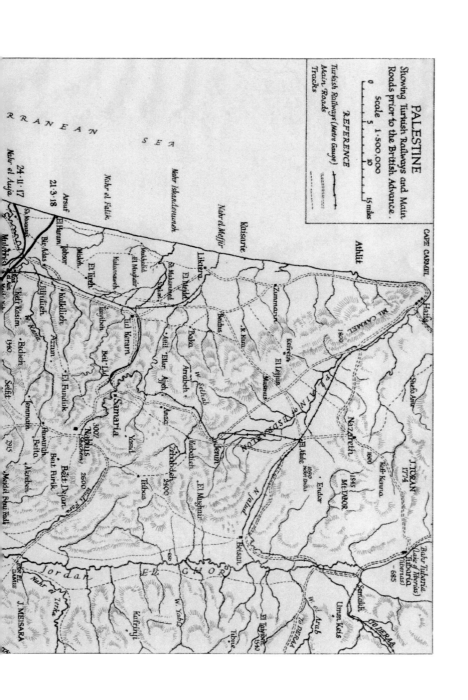

PALESTINE

Showing Turkish Railways and Main
Roads prior to the British Advance.

Scale 1·500.000

0   5   10   15 miles

REFERENCE

Turkish Railways (Metre Gauge)
Main Roads
Tracks

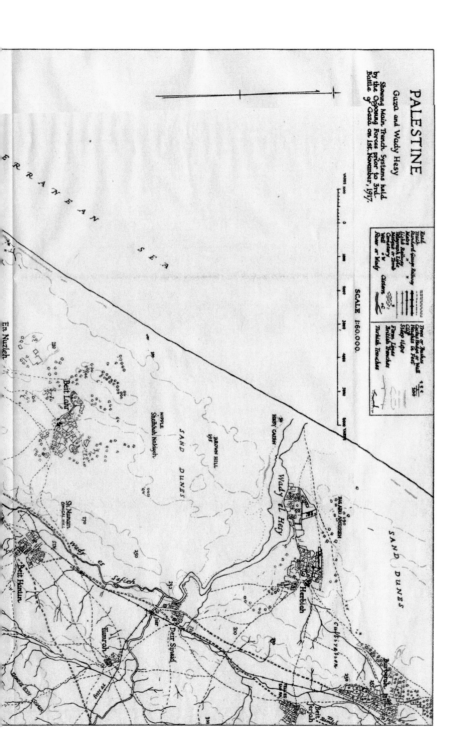

PALESTINE

Gaza and Wady Hesy

Showing Main Trench Systems held
by the Opposing Forces prior to 3rd
Battle of Gaza on 1st. November, 1917.

SCALE 1:60,000.

WITH THE
8TH SCOTTISH RIFLES
1914—1919

CHAPTER I

Mobilization and Training

Great Britain went into the war to honour a "scrap of paper". One wonders how many dissentient voices there were in the Cabinet when that decision was arrived at. One perhaps cynically wonders now whether it was a wise one, though it was the only one which could honourably be taken. It was a momentous decision for every man, woman, and child in the country, and generations yet to come will suffer, even as we are doing, from its far-reaching effects. At the time it is safe to say that no one realized its incalculable consequences—probably no one cared; of its inevitability few outside naval and military circles were convinced.

For years there had been a gathering cloud on the horizon, discernible to seeing eyes. Some prophesied its dispersal, and others went their way quietly preparing for the catastrophe; but when it suddenly burst upon us its violence rendered breathless even the most redoubtable pessimist.

To most of us our future enemies seemed rather a domesticated lot, associated in our minds with German bands, sausages, the goosestep, and schooners of beer. Even the few who had read the doctrines of German military writers never imagined for a moment that the brutal maxims and rules of warfare enunciated by them would be put into practice by the whole nation. Within the space of three days, with the rapidity of lightning, the masks were torn off, and we were confronted with the grim actuality of these doctrines.

The change from Peace to War has a marked influence upon the mental outlook of every soldier over and above the transformation of his material circumstances, be he Regular, Reservist, or Territorial.

The Regular, although accustomed to discipline at all times, now finds it suddenly stiffened; while the Reservist, after some years of civil life, is again brought into contact with it in its sternest form. To the Territorial also the rigid discipline that is a necessary condition of war comes as a rude shock to his former ideas of values. His friend " Mac ", who possibly merely by reason of a sharper razor and an aptitude for retaining his pull-through wears three stripes on his arm and stands in comparative freedom as a supernumerary behind him on parade, now becomes in place of a sparring partner and boon companion, an ogre possessed apparently with the powers of life and death, who has quickly realized his powers, and whose every word must be " sprung to ".

It was, however, in the New Armies especially that discipline was hard to arrive at, but ere long there was engendered a new sense of proportion, the realization of which put many a man's patriotism to an immediate test. The millionaire in the ranks, the ranker officer, the head of a business subordinated to his junior clerk, these were examples of the contrasts and anomalies to be found in every regiment. Never were the words of our national poet, " A man's a man for a' that ", more fully justified.

The 8th Scottish Rifles mobilized for war on 4th August, and, with the 5th, 6th, and 7th Scottish Rifles, made up the Scottish Rifle Brigade, soon to be known as the 156th Infantry Brigade, 52nd (Lowland) Division. The Division was under the command of Major-General G. G. A. Egerton, C.B. The Brigade was commanded by Brigadier-General S. W. Hare (late K.R.R.C.), with Captain E. S. Girdwood (Scottish Rifles) as Brigade-Major.

On the previous Friday we had just completed our annual training at Gailes, and it is certain that nobody had the remotest idea of the upheaval to industry, to society, and to ordinary routine of life which we were to experience during the next few years. We knew, of course, in a vague way, the serious things a possible war portended. We had sent off, before camp training was completed, various guards to Scapa, to Lochgelly Oil Works, to Arran, and other places, and we thus realized its imminence. I shall never forget the envy with which those told off for these duties were regarded by the other less fortunate members of the battalion, and the pride and self-conscious importance of the parties as they marched off to entrain. I think we all looked forward to mobilization, and went into the affair lightheartedly and eagerly as though setting out on a great adventure.

The bustle, the confusion, the difficulties of organizing, of procuring and fitting clothes, of enrolling new men during that first week of mobilization, with half the battalion billeted at Head-quarters and half in the Night Asylum, will be to those who remember it a memory something between a bad dream and a scene from Hogarth. As far as I remember, the battalion on mobilization was about 600 strong; within two days it could have been over 1000 strong.

We soon had our full complement of officers who, as they joined, were told off temporarily to those jobs which they seemed best fitted to fill. As an instance of how short-sighted and untrue our appreciations of the situation were, I recollect that 2nd-Lieutenant Carson, who, as an accountant by profession, had been detailed to go over and balance the pay sheets of the men absent on special defence duties, anxiously asked the Adjutant if he would be on this job for the rest of the war!

Upon the C.O. and the Adjutant, Captain G. C. Bramwell, naturally fell the brunt of the organization, and both Colonel Hannan and he were for many days literally snowed under by a pile of correspondence, orders, and instructions issued by the War Office, Scottish Command, and Division. I personally was detailed to purchase horses for Brigade Head-quarters and the battalion—about 100 all told, riders, heavy and light draft, and pack-animals, with all the necessary saddlery, harness, and wagons. It was a somewhat thankless job; everybody seemed to be buying horses—Gunners, Engineers, Yeomanry, A.S.C., not to mention other infantry battalions, and though a census had been taken within the previous year and districts and firms allotted to horse-purchasers, it was impossible to adhere to the allocation, as some firms had ceased to exist, and others had not the type of horses required, so that one had finally to take what one could get. I have a distinct recollection of the scathing remarks which I overheard (perhaps it was so intended) as to my purchases; had I ever flattered myself on my knowledge of horses, which I did not, my self-esteem would have experienced a rude shock. However, I managed to get my purchases completed in about five days, and then commenced the business of sorting out and assembling harness, classifying and allotting horses. Law was appointed Transport-Officer with, I think, Carson to assist him, and they tackled the work heroically, together with Transport-Sergeant Livingstone, who had few men of any experience under him. Certainly, we none of us had our troubles to seek, and things were not made the easier by the hospitality of the men's friends, who, with misguided but real approval, were at all times ready to toast their patriotism. It was a harassing time, and everybody was thankful when we received orders from Brigade at the end of a week, for the move to the Falkirk-Larbert area. The 8th was to move to Larbert, whither I was sent in advance with a billeting party to arrange for its housing.

The distance to Larbert is some 23 miles, and it was decided that we should march there. Unhappy decision! Normally, and especially when we had just completed our training, the march would not have stretched the men's capacity over much. But I suppose that in spite of all efforts to keep the men fit during the week in Glasgow, the ten days' interregnum from training had softened them, and this was no doubt accentuated by unwonted conviviality. Sufficient to say, at any rate, that on a hot day, with new boots, the march was a very trying one, and our entry into Larbert was hardly of the " conquering hero " description. There was an epidemic of blistered feet in the battalion for a week after.

The billeting accommodation in Larbert was good, and the distribution as follows, I think. The big factory of Messrs. Dobbie Forbes, Ltd., housed four companies, the school another three, and the Town Hall one, with Battalion Headquarters at the Station Hotel, where also, to begin with, the officers messed together. The officers were billeted in various hospitable houses in and around the town, and I hope that all our hosts and hostesses realized how grateful we were, and how we appreciated their kindness and hospitality.

Man is an adaptable animal and we soon settled down to a life of strenuous training. We were not destined, however, to remain long as a battalion at Larbert. About a fortnight after our arrival there, we had a Brigade route-march, during which the Brigade had half-an-hour's fall-out in a large field a few miles out towards Airth. While there, the Brigadier, who had previously sent a chit to Os.C. battalions, asking them to ascertain how many of their officers and other ranks were willing to volunteer for foreign service, came round each battalion to find out the response. As far as our battalion was concerned, it is comforting, even at this distance of time, to remember that all the officers and over 90 per cent of the other ranks unhesitatingly stepped forward in reply. The volunteering in the Brigade was not, however, so uniformly good, and it was decided by the War Office to form one Service Battalion out of those who had come forward for active service in the Brigade, to be composed of drafts from each unit, leaving the rest of the battalions to form reserves for it. In consequence of this reduction, recruiting for the Brigade and for the formation of reserve units was unfortunately stopped for a month or two, at the very time when recruits were coming forward most enthusiastically. Indeed, several ex-officers of the 8th joined New Army battalions instead of their own old unit. It can be well understood that this was a lasting handicap to us, and the effect of it was felt by battalions right up to the very end.

The Service Battalion thus formed was composed of eight companies; of these, the 8th provided three companies and the officers for four companies and the Transport-Officer, Lieut. D. S. Carson; the 6th three companies (one officered by the 8th); and the 5th and 7th between them two companies. It will be realized, of course, that in all units a considerable number of volunteers were unable to be taken; in fact, two battalions could have been formed, but only one was permitted. Lieut.-Colonel R. Jeffry Douglas commanding the 5th Battalion was given command; he chose Kennedy of his own unit as second in command. I was Junior Major without a company, and Billie Croft was Adjutant. Douglas asked me to be Mess-President, and I had one triumph in this line. I actually got the messing down to an average of 1s. 6d. per diem, and for one week it was as low as 1s. 3d. I don't claim that the lads were over-fed, judging from what was left over and from their remarks; still they did quite well, and I don't approve of over-feeding. A Mess-President doesn't get much credit if he keeps down the bills, but he soon hears if he doesn't keep up the food.

The service battalion ousted the 8th from Larbert, and after a day or two to settle down, we again got into the way of strenuous training. I remember we did a good deal of night work, and some special instructors in musketry and platoon-training came to us from the Gordons.

My recollections of that service battalion are happy in many ways. It was a fine battalion; everyone keen and hard-working. Jeff Douglas and his Adjutant were both able fellows, and of course one was proud that considerably the largest quota of it was contributed by the 8th.

A soldier's life is full of change, and scarcely three weeks had passed when this gallant service battalion was split up, and each battalion again had its contingent relegated to itself. Those of us who had been with the service battalion were at first naturally sick about the change, and the return to the 8th, who had been sent to Grahamstown, the northern part of Falkirk, made one feel that all one's hopes of proceeding on foreign service at an early date were frustrated. Still, it was a great thing to get back to one's own battalion, and when we heard (as we did quite soon thereafter) that each battalion was to go out as a unit, we were not only reconciled, but full of enthusiasm and satisfaction that we would be with our own fellows.

We found that our battalion had taken up its Head-quarters in a school in Grahamstown Road, and that the various companies were in schools or halls close by. Looking back on it, everyone was, I think, tolerably comfortable, with the exception of one man, a hefty miner, who had recently joined up in Charles Mowat's company, and who one day complained to the Orderly-Officer at dinner that " Ah have nae axe tae grind, but ah canna thole the po powri ". By the latter he was understood to mean " pot pourri ", and to refer to the stew.

At the end of September, Ker, who was Senior Major, was given command of the 2/8th Scottish Rifles, which battalion was to furnish our reserves. At this time, also, six young officers were posted to the battalion by the War Office without any reference to the C.O. Their names were Aitken, Aucott Bannen, Cameron, Craigie, and Ferguson, and they all did their duty nobly. " Wee Fergie " subsequently served overseas with the battalion for more than three years and did gallant work, earning a M.C. and bar and Croix-de-Guerre. Aitken did good work with a M.G. Company, receiving the M.C.; Cameron also did well, and was awarded the O.B.E., while Craigie, badly wounded in Gallipoli, went off to the Scottish Coast Defence Cyclists, and Aucott, though only for a short time with 1/8th Scottish Rifles, proved his worth, and later earned the M.C. and bar.

October, November, December, 1914, and January, 1915, passed quickly in hard training, and hard swearing at our fate that we would never get to the front, as we supposed. To our great chagrin, in November, the 5th Scottish Rifles were sent off on their own to France. The following month the 6th Scottish Rifles also departed for France. They were lucky— always a strong battalion, they were then the strongest in the Brigade, and were chosen to make up a Brigade in the Highland Division, in place, I think, of a battalion which had some epidemic of sickness. There were thus left only the 7th Battalion and ourselves. To complete the Brigade, I think in April, 1915, there eventually came into our area the 4th and 7th Royal Scots from Edinburgh and Leith respectively, and these two battalions—loyal and staunch friends—remained with and completed the 156th Brigade until the end.

Those months were accompanied by a succession of those rumours without which no war is complete. In fact, if one were asked to say what was the prevailing atmospheric condition of the war, more especially at home, one would say " rumour ". We breakfasted and dined off it, and no Headquarters was worthy of the name whose signallers could not provide the canteen and Officers' Mess with a daily crop. As an example of the extent to which the credulity of the battalion was taxed, it was even reported one day in mess that Captains Boyd and Macindoe had retained their seats on their newly-acquired chargers throughout the whole morning's parade.

What fun and chaff there was throughout the battalion over those company chargers when they arrived, and in mess all the fellows who had not to ride them gave advice to those who had. One remembers too the first of the few battalion drills we had. It was held in the Gasworks field, and synchronized with the arrival of the said chargers, which thus appeared on parade for the first time. The battalion, impressed by the array of cavalry in its forefront, was trying to look its best and was prepared to do justice to the occasion. After the command " Tell off by companies " had been duly executed, the cautionary " The battalion will advance " was given, whereupon a certain Company-Commander—no names, no pack drill—began an apparently involuntary retrograde movement through the serried ranks of his company, while his mount, after finally getting rid of him by lying down and rolling, quietly trotted off and commenced lunching operations on a friendly and neighbouring hedge. Everyone was put in great good humour by this heartening sight of another's afflictions, and the parade in consequence was one of the best we ever had from the point of view of good and attentive drill.

The hills behind Falkirk in the morning and the Gasworks

field in the afternoon were the chief scenes of our activities. On the former we attacked and defended every conceivable position in every conceivable way. The amount of energy expended in these attacks, retirals, and night manœuvres was amazing, and was only equalled by the eagerness of the rush every Monday evening for the front stalls in the local Grand Theatre. There the stars did not require a compass to march to, and they seemed more attainable and hardly less bright than the twinkling but cold and distant luminaries by whose aid our " young idea " were taught to march at night.

On the Gasworks field Sergeant-Major W. Fox held sway, and a more indefatigable and efficient sergeant-major it would have been impossible to find. He had a curious assortment of material to mould into the shape of soldiers. On one occasion someone, who shall be nameless, turned repeatedly to the left when he should have turned to the right, and the sergeant-major, exasperated beyond endurance, yelled at him: " Good God, man, do you not know your 'Right'?"

" Naw."

Sergeant-Major: " But, blast you, I have just told you a dozen times which is your right."

" Aye, but ye see ah'm left haundit."

Other excellent drill instructors who were to be seen daily, at morning and afternoon parades, on the Gasworks field were Sergeants W. Paton and J. Maclachlan. The former was blessed with a fine voice, knew his job, and was of a cheery and apparently unconcerned disposition. The latter had a happy faculty of rendering pliable even the most unwilling and obstinate recruits and defaulters. We often used to think he must be sick of the sound of the Defaulters Bugle Call, while the soldiers' words which accompany it: " You can be a defaulter as long as you like, so long as you answer your name ", seemed to be interpreted rather too literally by some members of the battalion.

At times Company-Commanders were occupied, like the policeman in *The Pirates of Penzance*, with " crime " and the orderly-room work which this entails. The fact that the battalion was so near its home centre, Glasgow, tended to increase the crime of " Absence without leave ", whilst the treating to which all were subjected when they went home materially helped this by casting a temporary oblivion over the recipients, causing them to forget their duties elsewhere. Monday after Monday the following dialogue became almost a matter of routine at each company orderly-room.

" Well, Private M'Turk, here you are again.   You are charged with being drunk and absent without leave.   Were you drunk?"

" No, sir."

" But the Sergeant says you were drunk."

" Ach! he disnae ken, sir, what drunk is."

" How much had you?"

" Just a hauf, sir."

" Half what, half a barrel or half a bottle, or what?"

" No, sir; just a hauf a gless.   Ye see, sir, the wife's just gaun to hae a child, and——"

Captain, interrupting: " Well, you'll have to explain that to the Colonel, I can't deal with you.   Next man, Sergeant."

But in spite of all the trouble and worry caused by the frequent delinquencies of men who, once on active service, proved themselves over and over again to be the hardiest and best of soldiers and good comrades, I think I am right in saying that there was no battalion in the countryside whose company officers and men were on better terms with each other.

A vast amount of time, too, was spent—wasted, some of them thought—in teaching junior officers and men the principles of rifle fire, the trajectory of the bullet, the theory of gravitation, and a deal of stuff which seemed to be a long way over the heads of even some of the instructors, and therefore beyond the grasp of men, many of whom did not appear to understand the meaning of the simplest every-day words.   One Company-Commander after a long dissertation on the flight of a bullet, asked one of his men what course a bullet took after leaving the rifle.   After much probing he elicited the disconcerting news that it described a circle.   It is perhaps a pity that this description is not a correct one.   If it were, the problem of the League of Nations would be solved, and their work would be confined to doling out ammunition to fractious and quarrelsome parties, who would be told to get on with it. Again, at the rifle range a shockingly bad performer was asked, after repeated misses, what part of the target he was aiming at:

" Aboot a yaird to the richt o' the bul, sir."

" What do you call a yard?"

" Aboot twa feet, sir."

" Good heavens, man, do you not know what a yard is?"

Silence!

" What's an inch, then?"

" A widna like to say, sir."

After this mysterious and chaste reply, which, had the question been whether his girl affected garters or suspenders, could not have been uttered more coyly, the noble and gallant Captain retired a beaten man.

Some of the companies were rather handicapped in training through shortage of officers. Very soon after we went to Falkirk specialist jobs began to crop up, and Company-Commanders had to detail officers to fill these posts. Lieut. Ebenezer Maclay was Machine-Gun Officer, with Dick Humble as his whipper-in. During the early days of the war the value of machine-guns, of which there were then only two to each battalion, was not generally understood by infantry commanders. Even the experience gained from the Russo-Japanese War had not borne fruit, except in Germany, with the result that their employment was less frequent and their mobility less appreciated than it ought to have been. In taking up a position the usual procedure was to site everything and everybody else, and then say: " Where shall we put these damned machine-guns?" Before the war had been in progress six months, however, machine-guns were at a premium, and infantry companies which were not near them felt unprotected. Talking of siting reminds one of the complicated problems that faced field and company officers in those early days when taking up a position. The company officer would be given a portion of the battalion frontage and told to site his trenches. Having attended, open-mouthed, a lecture on the subject by an expert just back from France, he would give effect to the opinions he had heard expressed by choosing a position on the reverse slope of a hill a little distance below the crest. In a few minutes the Colonel would come along and say: " By Jove, I don't like this position of yours; you've got no field of fire! Move down to the foot of the hill and then you will have shelter from shell-fire and be able to mow down the enemy if they come over the crest." While this move was in progress up would gallop the Brigade-Major. " Where the hell are you fellows going to? You could be blown to blazes there by howitzers. You must get on the forward slope of the hill, and site your trench on some natural feature below the crest." The company officer, thinking what an infernal fool he had been not to think of howitzers before, and wishing to goodness he had had the luck to be found in the right place by the Brigade-Major, hurriedly moves his company into what appears to be a natural feature on the forward slope and gives the men a five minutes' smoke. The only match in the company has no sooner been passed round, than the Brigadier appears slowly over the crest of the hill, and stands there regarding the situation generally. Out go all the Woodbines, and the entire company is found engrossed in making range cards, with the exception of the pioneers, who get busy with the siting of a latrine. The Brigadier riding slowly forward to the officer commanding the company would say: " Good morning, Church." Looking around, he would appear to consider the position, and then say quietly: " Nice view you've got here, but rather dangerous, don't you think? Very difficult to say, of course, but I think that if you are going to be on this side of the hill you ought to be right bang at the foot of it. Grand field of fire, and it would not be easy for the enemy to pick out trenches well placed along the base of the hill. Here, your men cannot fire downhill with accuracy, and would have to expose themselves to do it at all. I think I'd move down there if I were you. Good morning."

A few minutes afterwards, the message would come that companies were to march back to their quarters independently, and the company would wend its way back to Falkirk pondering many things in its heart.

Lieut. Gerald Moore and 2nd-Lieut. Carson had charge at varying times of the Battalion Scouts, and reached such a state of efficiency that it was currently reported that they knew every " pub " between Linlithgow and Bonnybridge. One day the scouts were being instructed in sending back messages and reports of what they had seen, and Moore, after emphasizing the frequent value of negative information, asked them to imagine themselves to be reporting on an enemy position, and to write an example of negative information. One of the reports was worded somewhat as follows: " The enemy's left flank is guarded by a field of turnips, but there are no turnips in it."

Captain Willie Law who, by reason of a natty and horsey appearance, combined with the ability to maintain nonchalantly in his mouth the straw without which no self-respecting custodian of horses is complete, had hitherto been our Transport-Officer, and who had acted so efficiently that he caught the eye of Brigade, was now summoned from the stable to the staff to deal with higher and weightier matters.   In his place came Lieut. W. D. Hannan, a worthy brother of our Colonel's, and it was not long before he learnt all the tricks of the trade. I always remember him coming into mess one day shortly after we had had an issue of mules along with brand-new equipment and saddlery, with which, at first sight, he and Transport-Sergeant Mackenzie had been delighted.   On endeavouring to fit the harness to the mules, however, it was found that the harness and pack-saddles had evidently been made for elephant transport, and Hannan found the Sergeant almost in tears, and using most awful language in his efforts to make the harness fit.   He had laughingly said to him: " Cheer up, Sergeant, there is always a fly in the ointment," to which Mackenzie replied: " Yes, sir, but this yin's a ruddy bluebottle."

About this time, in December I think, in consequence presumably of information, it was considered that an enemy landing on the East Coast of Scotland was within the sphere of probability, and I recollect some of the senior officers of the Brigade went off on a reconnaissance to the ground south of Edinburgh, which was the area allotted to the 156th Brigade to defend in such an eventuality. I remember noticing that the southern entrances to Edinburgh were barricaded, sandbagged, and in portions, wired. No preparations had been made to put the outlying country in any state of defence, nor did any action on the part of the Navy seem to be taken into consideration. Our place of concentration certainly was a mile or two beyond these barricades, but even that seemed too close to the capital. However, as everyone knows, the enemy happily never succeeded in eluding the vigilance of the Navy, so these preparations were never put to the test.

In January we began to get awfully sick of things; everything appeared to be against our going on foreign service. We even envied the troops who had been sent to India, poor devils! Units here and units there seemed to be chosen, whilst we, one of the finest battalions extant, as we considered ourselves, were left firmly fixed at home. Towards the end of the month I was ordered to take a party of about 200 strong to Torphichen to carry out a musketry course. While there the men were billeted in a comfortable little hall in the village, while we officers were most hospitably entertained by Mr. Wood, of Wallhouse, and his niece, Miss King. We spent there a useful and happy ten days.

In February we were ordered to the Tay Defences to relieve the 4th Black Watch, ordered on foreign service. We went off and relieved them, the C.O. taking up his Head-quarters with two companies in Dundee, whilst I was sent in command of the remaining two companies to Broughty Ferry. By this time the battalion had been organized into four companies of 250 strong, instead of eight companies of 125 strong. The officer in command of the 4th Black Watch at Broughty Ferry was Major Alexander. He went out with the 4th Battalion, did well, got the D.S.O. and a " stop-at-home " wound, went to the Ministry of Munitions, and became eventually Brigadier-General Sir William Alexander. [1]

Broughty Ferry was a good place, and considering how fed-

---

[1] Now M.P. for Glasgow Central.

up we all were about our non-removal to a sphere of active operations, it was a happy change, and one appreciated by the men. The two companies at Dundee had a poor time, having constantly to furnish guards whenever they were required down at the docks. So much so that the Commanding Officer had seldom sufficient men with whom to do any decent training. At Broughty Ferry, however, we managed to carry on quite good training. There was a prohibited area round the Fort which had to be guarded and patrolled at night. I am afraid that a long sojourn had made the previous battalion somewhat slack in their guards, and when we came along and were stricter, the inhabitants complained. Those, for example, who lived within the prohibited area had to have night passes. I suppose the Black Watch knew them all, but we did not, and it occasionally happened that a late comer at night had no pass, whereupon he remained in the guard-room until identified. Such occurrences had a stimulating effect upon the memory of other dwellers in the prohibited area; they soon all remembered to produce their night passes.

Barry Range is only about 20 minutes by rail from Broughty Ferry and 35 minutes or so from Dundee, and while on the Tay Defences the battalion profited by the proximity to the Range, and all ranks were put through a musketry course— most excellent and most valuable, as was proved later in the war; incidentally, we had some good games of golf on the course there. The people in Dundee and Broughty Ferry were kindness and hospitality itself to us, and grateful are our remembrances of them. At Broughty Ferry we were made honorary members of the mess at the Fort, which was garrisoned by the Tay Garrison Gunners, commanded by Lieut.-Colonel Thomson, a forcible, bluff and hearty Gunner, who was in charge of the local defences, and who with his local knowledge was of great assistance to me on many occasions. The local defences had been prepared (though not by him) principally to prevent a raiding party gaining access to the Fort, and to delay a landing-force proceeding to Dundee. A series of posts were fortified upon the high ground north of Broughty Ferry, but apart from the one at Castle Roy, they appeared to be badly sighted, and to have little or no mutual support, nor could they have been of any use against an enemy landing close to the Fort. Perchance they were there to inspire the local populace with a feeling of security.

Training was somewhat interfered with by the necessity for garrisoning these posts, but nevertheless progressed fairly well. I recollect one great route-march, when for a mile or so we had to traverse a road about three feet deep in snow. To see everybody floundering about in the snow afforded the men much more amusement than annoyance, and so discomfort was forgotten; and many were the jokes and shouts of laughter when any unlucky wight came a cropper, which it was quite easy to do. " Ye'll hae tae change yer breeks when ye get hame, Jock." " I'll hae to change mair nor ma breeks, an' I didna wash ma ithers last week, fule that I wis!" " That'll learn ye, Jock, tae wash them on Saturdays accordin' tae orders." The habits of cleanliness inculcated by the discipline of soldiering have strange aids now and then.

It was at Broughty Ferry that Phil Brown, my groom, earned his dismissal from my service. The episode, though it was public and serious from a disciplinary point of view, was most amusing. One peaceful Sunday morn—that is peaceful and sunshiny between the snow showers—Brown and his crony, Paddy Cassidy, both well-known characters and Irishmen, had apparently been refreshing themselves to the extent of considerable hilarity, and it occurred to one of them (evidently in a sunshiny interval) that it would be a grand thing to have a bathe in the sea. No sooner said than done. Together they commandeered a rowing boat, which was lying handy below the esplanade on the beach, pushed it into the water, without oars, and jumping aboard, commenced to undress. It happened to be the hour when the douce folk of Broughty Ferry took their after-kirk stroll along the esplanade, on the landward side of which were the billets and mess in which we were quartered.

The process of undressing and the shouts and noise and laughter which it was necessary to indulge in, either from native incapacity to do anything quietly, especially when

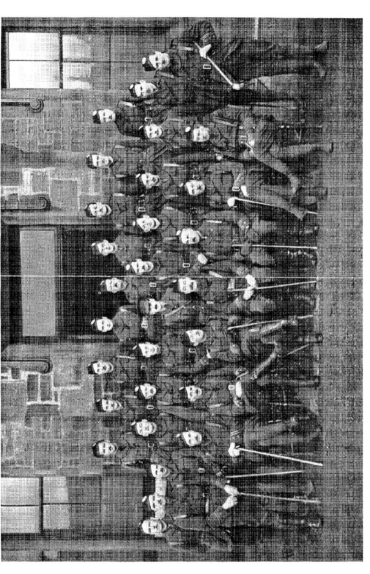

Capt. W. T. Law (standing)

OFFICERS OF 8TH SCOTTISH RIFLES AT TRAINING QUARTERS, FALKIRK, 1914

Capt. F. T. Young (standing)

Front Row: Capt. J. W. H. Pattison, Major R. N. Coulson, Major J. M. Findlay, Lt.-Col. H. M. Hannan, Jr., T.D., Capt. C. J. Bramwell (Adjutant), Capt. J. M. Boyd, Capt. C. A. Dunn Macindoe.

Second Row: 2nd-Lt. D. S. Carson, Capt. C. J. C. Mowat, 2nd-Lt. T. L. Tillie, Lt. H. M'Cowan Capt. W. C. Church, Capt. A. R. Sloan, M.D., R.A.M.C. (T.), Capt. H. A. MacLehose, Lt. R. C. B. Macindoe, Lt. A. C. Moore, Lt. A. D. Templeton, 2nd-Lt. J. W. Scott.

Back Row: Lt. E. Maclay, 2nd-Lt. R. Humble, Lt. J. T. Findlay, Lt. W. N. Sloan, Hon. Lt. and Qr.-Mr. H. Bowen, 2nd-Lt. T. Stout, Jr., 2nd-Lt. A. R. Tillie, 2nd-Lt. W. S. Maclay, Lt. G. H. Crichton

inebriated, or from the fact that they realized that they were the cynosure of all eyes, naturally drew the attention of everyone to themselves. To the horror, no doubt, of all beholders, they divested themselves of their garments, and after some more pantomimic display, plunged into the icy water. More yells and shrieks. By this time another snow-shower had started, and so had my Provost-Sergeant, with two assistants in another boat (this time *with* oars). Armed with these they succeeded in rescuing Brown and Cassidy from probable pneumonia, but to certain retribution of a disciplinary nature.

About the middle of April, 1915, the battalion returned to Falkirk, being relieved by a unit of the Welch Regiment on the Tay Defences. We knew then that we were destined for the Dardanelles, and a very strict medical examination was one of the necessary preliminaries—owing to this 70 other ranks were rejected as unfit, and a few others were hurriedly fitted out with dentures to enable them to cope with " hard tack ", &c. We spent about a month in fitting out, weeding out, completing everything in the way of equipment, to war-scale, making wills, and getting embarkation leave. Just previous to our return to Falkirk, our Brigadier, Brigadier-General S. W. Hare, was taken away from us to command the Fusilier Brigade of the 29th Division, also destined for the Dardanelles. We were very sorry to lose him, but later on had the luck to come under his command in the 3rd and successful Battle of Gaza. Brigadier-General Scott-Moncrieff took over command. He was a charming man, who, alas, was killed along with so many other good fellows, in the Brigade's first action in Gallipoli.

CHAPTER II

Gallipoli—28th June, 1915

On 17th May, 1915, the battalion left Falkirk for Devonport. The right-half battalion departed at 1700 hours, Colonel Hannan, with the Adjutant, Captain Bramwell, in command, and the left half at 1800 hours under my command. We all arrived at Devonport on the morning of the 18th, and embarked on H.M.T. *Ballarat*,[1] a requisitioned P. & O. Joint-Liner. The battalion transport did not leave Falkirk until the 21st, arriving in Devonport on the 22nd, and embarking on H.M.S. *Shropshire* on the same day. As has been mentioned, the transport had recently been put under the command of 2nd-Lieut. W. D. Hannan, the Commanding Officer's young brother, who had already seen war service in France with the 5th Scottish Rifles, and had been granted a commission and posted to the 8th. Three other officers went with the battalion transport, Captain E. T. Young, Lieutenants A. D. Templeton and A. F. Rogers; they eventually joined the battalion at Mudros on 31st May, but the transport personnel with horses and vehicles were disembarked at Alexandria, and moved to a camp in Aboukir Bay where they spent nine exasperating months of inactivity until they once more joined the battalion at Kantara in February, 1916.

There is not much to chronicle about our voyage to Mudros, the port on the island of that name, which was the " jumping off " ground for troops landing in Gallipoli. We had a very comfortable, quiet journey; nobody was permitted to go ashore at Gibraltar or at Malta, and at that time the submarine menace did not trouble transports except very occasionally. The

---

[1] The *Ballarat* was afterwards a victim of the Submarine offensive, and was torpedoed in 1917, while carrying Australian troops in the Indian Ocean.

Commander of the *Ballarat* was called Hanson. He was a very fine chess player—had taken on champions at the game. Lynes (3rd Officer) was Troop Officer. He arranged games and looked after the comfort of the troops aboard.

We arrived at Mudros on the 29th May, and anchored first in the outer harbour; at 1600 hours we steamed right in to the inner bay. Mudros is one of the most wonderful natural harbours in the world. It has sufficient depth of water all over to anchor, I suppose, the whole British Navy. I forget how many ships of all shapes and sizes we counted one day, some hundreds anyhow. It is approached by a narrow channel which enters from the sea at one angle, and which opens to the harbour at another, from the shores of which the ground rises on either side to such effect that ships passing outside at sea, unless they knew of the harbour, would have no idea of its possibilities in the way of berthing and concealing craft. The channel was made still narrower in those days by a buoyed gate extending over half of the original entrance. Our Mediterranean fleet used to use the harbour for their regattas.

One day Cecil Macindoe, Dai Carson, Hamish MacLehose, Charles Mowat, and myself went ashore to visit the salubrious village of Mudros. En route to the village we rashly invested in some khaki shorts, for which we parted with a vast hoard of good coin. Mudros is a filthy hole, and the Greeks are thieves, without a redeeming quality that we could discover. That day we climbed the hill above the town to try to see Helles, but, instead, we had a view of some Greek soldiers practising the attack. Much criticism by us, of course! It was a very hot day, and we were glad to get back and have some " lemonade ". Another day, when the wind blew hard, one of the lighters which had come alongside to take off the equipment of a Casualty Clearing Station was overloaded and capsized, distributing all its precious mercies to the deep. We organized salvage parties, launched the boats, and retrieved a considerable portion of the equipment. I think we rather enjoyed it, though the officer commanding the C.C.S., one Kelly, did not. He blessed the 8th Scottish Rifles however.

The Camp Commandant ashore about this time was having

great difficulty in guarding the wells, keeping the Australians in hand, and preventing the Greeks pilfering around generally. Colonel Hannan was ordered to send a police piquet of two officers and 100 other ranks ashore to reinforce his guards. Lieut. W. N. Sloan, with 2nd-Lieut. R. M. Pattison, commanded this detachment, and their tales afterwards of the week they spent trying to carry out the duties allotted to them, did not give one a favourable impression of the condition of things ashore at that time.

After a fortnight of weary waiting, during which we passed the time in physical training, swimming, and sailing, we at last got our marching, or rather sailing, orders. Battalion Head-quarters and the companies under Captains MacLehose and Macindoe and the half of Captain J. M. Boyd's company[1] were detailed to go in the *Osmanieh*, one of the Khedivial Line boats, while I, with a company (Captain Church's), was told off to Trawler 328, with instructions that as we would probably arrive first, we were to act as an advance party for the rest of the battalion. With what eagerness we all changed ships, hurrying aboard the smaller craft lest by any chance an order cancelling our departure should come in before we started. Some of us in our anxiety even harboured secret fears that Gallipoli would be taken and our troops be in Constantinople before the luckless 8th Scottish Rifles got there. The only fly in the ointment was that we had to go off and leave Major Coulson on the *Ballarat*, as he had a severe attack of sciatica. I have seldom seen a more depressed face in my life than his as we steamed away without him.

My recollection of our passage on the trawler to Helles is that we left the *Ballarat* at about 1800 hours on 13th June, and arrived alongside the *River Clyde* by V Beach about 2300 hours. We were lucky in getting ashore without being subjected to a shelling—usually a nightly, just-for-luck, periodic occurrence for this old sea-horse. Having formed up, we started off under the guidance (save the mark!) of a youth sent for the purpose, who had himself only arrived the day before, in the hope of finding the spot where we were to bed down

[1] The other half was doing guard duties at Mudros.

GALLIPOLI: X BEACH, LOOKING NORTH

for the night. After wandering about for four hours or so,
during which I had to dispense with the services of our ineffectual guide, we came across, by good luck, the Brigade-
Major, Captain E. S. Girdwood. He led us to a dump of
picks and shovels, which were distributed, and we proceeded
to dig ourselves into our first downy beds on the peninsula.
It was then dawn. We hadn't been digging long when an enemy
aeroplane came over, spotted us digging, and in a few minutes
thereafter we tasted our first dose of shell-fire. 'Twas poor
stuff, but we took cover all right, and then carried on digging.
We were in full view of " John Turk " where we were, but
we weren't much troubled by shelling (at any rate not as we
knew it afterwards), and we soon made ourselves trenches and
holes in the ground to live in. This, be it understood, was to
become eventually the Rest Camp for the troops at Helles.

The C.O. and the remainder of the battalion left Mudros
Harbour about 7 o'clock in the evening, and I leave it to one
who was with that portion of the battalion to carry on.[1]

" As the *Osmanieh* moved slowly through the maze of shipping
in the harbour, thousands of soldiers and sailors lined the
rails or swung themselves into the rigging of the ships as we
passed, and cheered us on our way. To a shipload of Australian
sick and wounded some of our fellows yelled out the stock
phrase at that time: ' Are we downhearted? No!' and when
some Australian wag shouted back: ' Well, you damned soon
will be ', our chaps, though taken aback, were incredulous.
As the ship passed out through the winding harbour entrance
darkness came down and everyone retired below deck to have
a feed, with butter and such kindred comforts, the like of which
was not to be seen again for some considerable time. In fact
the meal on board the *Osmanieh* was so good that one of the
sergeants of C Company left his entire set of false teeth behind
in this gastronomic El Dorado, and landing on the Peninsula
without them, very soon had to retire to hospital in consequence.
Whether his teeth, in emulation of John Brown's soul, kept
munching on, is not known.

" Notwithstanding these attractions below every one felt

----

[1] Lieut.-Colonel D. S. Carson.

that the top deck was the place to be. This, if ever, was a
nox noctium, each moment of which was to be fuller than a
cycle of the past. Here we were on the threshold of the door
leading to the Great Adventure, though what lay on the other
side none of us could say and few of us even considered. All
we thought of was that at last the results of our nine months'
hard training were to be put to the test, and our discipline and
fortitude tested on the anvil of modern war. Thus, very soon,
we all crowded up from below and gathered in groups on the
upper deck or pressed for'ard into the bow, the men eagerly
leaning over the bulwarks peering into the darkness as though
an earlier solution of the future might thereby be attained.
There, in the darkness and stillness and the mysterious proximity
of the unknown, the commingling of the thoughts of so many
minds seemed to give silent birth to that great sense of comrade-
ship which, fertilized by later events, grew to a maturity which
still endures. The atmosphere of that calm star-lit summer
night, unbroken by any sound except the gentle lapping of
the Ægean waters against the ship's side as she softly rose
and fell in her passage through them, exuded romance, and
if the sirens from some unseen island in the darkness had
suddenly burst into song no one would have been surprised.
Expectation was in the air, yet what to expect! Gradually as
we drew nearer our goal thought gave place to the actualities
of immediate events, and the C.O. and Adjutant, who were
regarded as omniscient, were bombarded with questions.
Would we be in time to march into Constantinople? Were
the harems subject to early closing? Would there be any
Turkish Delight left for the 8th Scottish Rifles? Should we
ask the ship's captain to send a wireless to Sappho apologizing
for not calling and asking her whether she was still ' burning '
and if she still ' loved and sung '? But all the time we kept
listening and listening! We had been told that the sound of
firing could be heard a long way out at sea, and if there was
still firing we might yet be in time. At last, amid great
excitement, the tongues of war were faintly heard in snatches
above the chunking of the propeller; soon the rattle of musketry
and the rat-tat-tat of machine-guns became distinct and

coherent, and only the booming of big guns was needed to complete the chorus. As we approached Cape Helles we could see every now and then Very lights shoot into the sky, hover for a few illuminating seconds in dead silence, and go out amid a roar of defensive and, as we soon found out, nervous Turkish rifle fire. What an entry into war! Can you picture it? We had literally sailed into it, and suddenly seemed to have drifted out of the peaceful calm of sleeping Nature, where the majesty of night made life feel eternal, into this little patch of concentrated activity where life seemed very temporal. Yes! we had sailed in luxury and comfort right into it, and over seas traversed through the ages by Greek, Persian, and Roman warriors of history and legend, and by the countless gods and goddesses of mythology; and in some undefinable way we felt associated with them. Perhaps we even felt towards them something of the complacency with which the old Paisley buddy, whose son had achieved immortality by having a few doggerel verses accepted by the local paper, regarded our Avon Poet when she exclaimed: ' Whaur's yer Wullie Shakespeare noo?'

" But soon all was bustle and activity: our ship which for some time past had been zigzagging about for fear of submarines came to a dead stop, and lighters ranged alongside into which we tumbled as quietly and as quickly as possible. Within twenty minutes we were alongside other lighters which were hard and fast on the beach called Lancashire Landing, and from them we jumped ashore where we lay receiving orders and counter-orders till a few hours after daylight, when we joined the other half of the battalion which had landed earlier.

" It would be impossible to convey here a picture of the perplexity with which our C.O. received the multitude of ambiguous and conflicting orders which came to him in rapid succession during this short period, and as we lay there on the beach we sensed in the atmosphere, like a chilling fog, the lack of that grip and the absence of that real command which in all forms of warfare are so essential to success and which efficiency in other matters can in no way replace. We had all been trained to believe that we were going to form part of a machine which ran with the utmost efficiency, control, and energy, and when, at the outset, we found the efficiency and control wanting, our confidence received a set-back.

" Gallipoli Peninsula, which forms the western or European shore of the Dardanelles, is a tongue of hilly land about 53 miles long dividing the Ægean Sea from the Straits. At its wider part it is nearly 12 miles across, but for the last 5 miles its southern extremity, which is the part with which we have to deal, tapers gradually from a width of 4½ miles to 1½ miles at Cape Helles. The approach to the Cape from the sea is extremely beautiful. Away on the left of the panorama is the lofty-peaked island of Imbros, and eastwards, across the wide sweep of the dark blue Ægean Sea, the long irregular yellow coast-line of the Peninsula is seen on the horizon, its highest point, 1100 feet, falling gradually in apparently gentle undulations to its extremity at Cape Helles. For as far as the eye can see the beach seems narrow and shelving, with abrupt sandy cliffs rising 100 to 300 feet above the sea, and at the top merging into a wide sandy-coloured, scrub-covered plateau, for the most part uncultivated, but dotted about with clumps of pine and fig trees. Farther to the east again, across the sparkling and fast-running waters of the Dardanelles, towers the mountainous and scrubby coast-line of Asia Minor, very steep in the Straits themselves, with scattered villages here and there on the hillsides, but gradually decreasing as it approaches the open sea and the Turkish fort and promontory of Kum Kale.

" The terrain on the Peninsula itself changes considerably on a closer acquaintance. One finds that the sandy cliffs rising up from the narrow beach are broken at intervals by deep ravines, bone-dry except during the winter rains, when they become rushing torrents. These ravines do not always join the shore-line at right angles, but frequently run parallel to it for a considerable distance before finally breaking through to the beach. The natural strength of the coast-line is thus greatly increased by these tortuous ravines which break the front of an attacking force, and in which, owing to their rugged

GALLIPOLI: W BEACH

and deeply broken and pitted sides, snipers and machine-guns can lie successfully concealed and immune. On reaching the plateau and turning northwards up the Peninsula one seems to be looking over a gently undulating, little-cultivated, and gradually-rising plain, which finally culminates, without any noticeable interruption of the even surface of the ground, in a gently sloping innocent-looking hill called Achi Baba. In actual fact, on very short acquaintance one finds that after the first mile the surface of the ground is extremely rough and uneven, broken up by innumerable nullahs and water-courses of varying depth with no decided or identifiable watershed. These water-courses follow such devious ways that in a few hundred yards they may have pursued all four points of the compass."

.   .   .   .

By 14th June the whole of 156th Brigade was ashore, and was attached to the 29th Division, Major-General H. de B. de Lisle commanding.

The battalion soon made themselves as comfortable as possible under the circumstances, and settled down to live in this sort of rabbit-warren known as Torres Lines. We were not left long undisturbed, as the Rest Camp was heavily shelled on the morning of the 15th June from Asia, the battalion suffering several casualties. All the officers were ordered to make visits to the front-line trenches by day and by night. I remember when I went up one night to the Hants battalion with a batch of officers, we got up to a company commanded by a charming fellow who looked fagged to death; when we arrived he was trying to get a few minutes' sleep, only to be disturbed by us. He was going to show us round, but I insisted that he should remain and try to get some rest, and we went round the line ourselves. It began to rain, a somewhat unusual occurrence there at that time of the year, and after going round (one can't see much in the dark) we took cover and slept for an hour or two just before dawn. Captain Barlow [1],

[1] Later, in 1916, I met Captain Barlow in El-Arish, where he was Political Officer, having actually been there when war broke out. He was afterwards given command of 5th Argyll and Sutherland Highlanders, who with 5th King's Own Scottish Borderers and the 8th, formed the 103rd Brigade of the reconstituted 34th Division in 1918. He was killed alongside of us on 30th July of that year at the taking of Beugneux.

by now somewhat refreshed by a couple of hours' sleep, then
showed us a forward sap and one or two points in the front
line which had particularly to be looked after.

As we came down from the trenches that morning just
after dawn, we came across a burying party of the Essex Battalion, under a Major with whom we had some converse.
His job was an unsavoury one, made necessary by the un-
thorough methods of the Turks, who paid scant respect to
their fallen comrades. I remarked that while one could made
no mistake in realizing the proximity of the dead, it was somewhat difficult, I imagined, to spot the actual place of each.
" Sometimes it is, and sometimes it isn't," he replied. " Look
at what you are sitting on just now." I looked, and there upon
the parapet of the communication trench I saw a hand, un-
noticed before, being of the same colour as the background,
sticking out in a suppliant manner as if its owner was beseech-
ing release. " We'll have to re-bury this one," said he, and we
were glad to leave him to his task.

Our chief hardships were, of course, the great heat, shortage
of water, and the swarms of flies. Add to these the stench of
half-buried bodies which we experienced in the front line,
and you have a pretty fair idea of our distasteful experiences.
Moreover, we had come from fairly decent food ex *Ballarat*
to bully and biscuits. It would have been a very good thing
had we gone through a sort of hardening process, not only
in diet but in physical training, during the fortnight when
we were lying in Mudros Harbour, but it would have been a
difficult thing to compass. Apart from the fact that the fare
for all meals was arranged under contract between the Government and the P. & O. Joint Line (and, of course, it was up to
us to see that the Government got their money's worth), I
am sure that a curtailing and simplifying of the rations would
have been regarded as a great hardship upon the men who
at any moment were to be ordered to face great privations and
death. As for the hardening from a physical point of view, one
could do little aboard ship, and it was only possible occasionally
for one company at a time to go ashore. When they did get
there anything sufficiently energetic to be of much use was

precluded by the great heat. Nevertheless, one has only to read accounts of other portions of the Gallipoli campaign, particularly of the landing at Suvla in August, 1915, to realize that better physical fitness alone might have turned the campaign from a tragic failure into something like a success.

On the night of 18/19th June, 1915, the battalion relieved the Essex Battalion of the 88th Brigade of 29th Division in the portion of trenches opposite to that part of the Turkish line called H 12 and H 12 a, which was distant from our line about 150 to 175 yards.

Along nearly all our front was a well-defined ridge running between the two lines, which, more or less, followed and hid the Turkish trenches from us, and vice versa. On our immediate right our trenches ran back, and I think also, to a certain extent, on our left, so that had defilading traverses not been built at certain points, the portion of our trenches held by us could have been enfiladed from both flanks, as the Turkish trenches, which had once been their second or third line, conformed more or less to our alignment. The significance of this will be seen when I come to describe the action of 28th June.

I don't think that I shall ever forget that move up to the trenches on the night of the 18/19th. One must realize that in order to relieve a battalion in the front line, the relieving unit (if it came from the Rest Camp where we were) had to move up across country in full view of the enemy as far as a place called Pink Farm, where commenced the long and deep communication trench called the Southern Mule Track. Even at that time one could have marched troops up most of it, in fours, and it was sufficiently deep to screen its contents from Turkish eyes. To arrive there with the minimum of casualties, however, companies had to move across the open in small parties, by half-platoons or platoons, at 50 or 100 yards distance, and in the evening it will be comprehended that it was very easy to lose touch with troops both in front and in rear. On this occasion I was ordered to go with Nos. 1 and 2 Companies, so I pushed them off by platoons, bringing up the rear of No. 2 Company myself, with a machine-gun section under Humble. Darkness falls very quickly there, and touch was lost not only with the leading company on the way to Pink Farm but also with the front platoon of No. 2 Company. I managed to collect No. 2 Company, less its leading platoon, which had kept in touch with No. 1 Company, and we pushed on. Almost immediately we found ourselves in Krithia Nullah, which contains a noisome, stinking, sluggish stream croaking with frogs. This, though it was too far to our right, I knew at any rate would take us up to the Eski lines (our third line of resistance). A lively action seemed to be in progress on our front, and hundreds of " overs " whistled past our devoted heads. At this point, Humble, who had been carrying a machine-gun tripod for one of his men who was weak with dysentery, seemed almost played out. I relieved him of the tripod (a machine-gun tripod is no light weight to carry), and we eventually arrived scathless at the Eski lines, and farther on, at the top of a communication trench leading to the front line, I let the men rest (and the tripod too) and pushed along to find out what was happening. I soon came across the Commanding Officer of the 5th Royal Scots, Lieut.-Colonel Wilson, who was himself in the front line with his battalion, on the right of the 88th Brigade. A bit of a scrap was going on, and he said he was expecting reinforcements at any moment. On the spur of the moment I offered him my company and machine-guns. However, like a wise man he refused my offer, expecting his own reinforcements at any moment, and anyhow, he could carry on. On reflection, I realized what a hole my impetuous offer might have landed me in had any action been in progress on the Essex front, and had the remainder of my battalion completed their relief while I remained embroiled elsewhere. I returned to my merry(?) men, and shouldering again that infernal tripod, I took them along the trench amid the curses of the disturbed garrison, and after a last weary lap, we arrived at the Essex part of the line, only to find that not one of the rest of the companies of our battalion had arrived. Here it was comparatively quiet, and we lay down in the reserve trench and slept till dawn, when the remainder of the battalion arrived. They had had a nasty time and suffered considerable casualties before getting to the Southern Mule Track, and the Command-

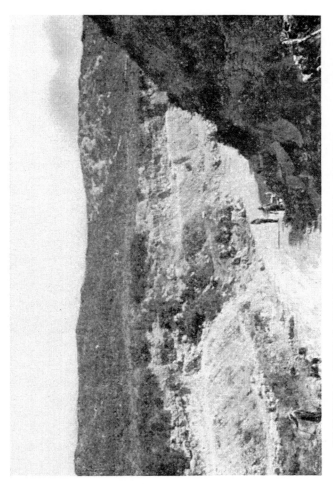

GALLIPOLI: GREAT GULLY, JUST BELOW "BOOMERANG" TRENCH

ing Officer, who with No. 3 and 4 Companies had come up to No. 1, had been ordered by 88th Brigade to lie doggo and take what cover could be found until just before dawn, when they could slip into the Southern Mule Trench and proceed with the relief.

The first time spent by a battalion in trenches is naturally one of considerable over-anxiety. We knew we had relieved good men, that an attack was possible at any moment; and the feeling that we had to prove ourselves put all of us on our mettle. The result was that vigilance was keyed up almost to breaking point. Trench discipline and routine, a matter of course to more seasoned troops, bore hardly on both officers and men. Sentries were prone to imagine things. Officers were apt to make it a point of honour not to sleep at all during the night. At this time, too, men were unhandy at getting fires going to cook meals and make tea, &c., and in the evening large ration and water parties had to toil for miles to bring up these necessities, thus considerably depleting each company. But man is an adaptable animal and after a few days we became accustomed to things, and officers and men got to know their jobs, and we began to think of something offensive to do to the Turks.

It was the Turk, however, who first succeeded in dealing a blow at us, the lamentable result of which, from the battalion's point of view, was incalculable. On the early morning of the 21st, the French, a mile or so on our right, were carrying out an attack on a fairly broad front. At about 0600, the Commanding Officer, Bramwell and myself were watching the action from an uncovered O.P.[1] alongside of Battalion Head-quarters about a quarter mile from the front line. After about five or ten minutes the C.O. said, " Look here, we had better get below; we might easily be sniped here. Let's have breakfast." Back in our dug-out, we had barely started breakfast, when a furious burst of fire could be heard from the direction of the fight, and Colonel Hannan went up again to see what was doing. A minute or so afterwards we heard a thud and a moan, and leaping out we saw the Commanding Officer lying crumpled

---

[1] O.P. = Observation Post.

up on the ground; when we reached him we found that he was severely hit and insensible. Bramwell and I laid him down more comfortably, and spoke to him. We sent for the Doctor, but he could do nothing, for the Colonel had been shot through the neck.[1] Looking back now I can well remember the awful feeling of loss, both to the battalion and myself, which came over me, the loss of a real friend, the loss of someone to appeal to in a difficulty, the loss to us all of a very generous-hearted gallant gentleman, cut off just when he was about to prove the mettle of the men whom he had been training for the previous nine months. We had had, of course, some casualties from shell fire on our way up to the trenches, and in our so-called rest trenches, but this brought us so abruptly face to face with the terrible suddenness of death that we were staggered for the time being. I remember Bramwell saying to me: " Well, my friend, it's up to you now." It was fortunate for me I had to buckle-to and carry on. I had no time to think about anything but the immediate requirements of the battalion.

After two more days in trenches, quiet as far as offensive action is concerned, we moved back on the 24th June to our Rest Camp, being, I think, relieved by the same battalion which we had relieved. As I brought up the rear of the battalion, returning down the Southern Mule Track, I remember that we met Generals Egerton and De Lisle with some of their staff. The former asked how we had got on, and said how sorry he had been to hear of Hannan's death, and expressed his sympathy with me and the battalion. The latter evinced nothing but impatience about it, and the contrast struck me at the time.

On the 25th Sloan and Pattison, who had been sent ashore at Mudros for Guard duties, arrived and were full of the chaos and ill-discipline of the troops there, and the thieving propensities of the country folk. A few convalescent Australians no doubt contributed to the liveliness of things and gave colour to their strictures. On the afternoon of the 27th, Bramwell

[1] Later on, when in hospital at Malta, I heard that the sniper who killed the colonel was himself done in by an Australian sniper. They told me that the sniper must have shot Colonel Hannan from 1100 yards distance.

and I attended a conference at 52nd Divisional Head-quarters. Brigadier-General Scott-Moncrieff was there, and Girdwood our Brigade-Major, and, I think, Major Charles MacLean, D.A.Q.M.G., and Walsh, the G.S.O.I.; also, of course, the other Commanding Officers of our Brigade. General Egerton talked to us generally on the conduct of the campaign and local conditions, and then more particularly about our participation as a Brigade in the next day's attack. (The Brigade was still attached to the 29th Division.) Thereafter the Brigade-Major dictated to the assembled Commanding Officers and Adjutants the orders for the attack next day, which I now incorporate in these notes.

ORDERS FOR ATTACK—JUNE 28th, 1915

BRIGADE ORDERS BY
BRIGADIER-GENERAL W. SCOTT-MONCRIEFF,
COMMANDING 156th BRIGADE

(1) The 156th Brigade has been detailed to attack trenches H 12 a, H 12, H 11, and the ravine north-east of H 11 as far as the communication trench at the bend of the ravine. The 87th and 86th Brigades and Indian Brigade are attacking the trenches on the left of H 11.

(2) The 156th Brigade will take over that portion of the front line trenches from the junction of these trenches with H 12 inclusive—" Turkey " Trench exclusive, at present held by 88th and 86th Brigades.

(3) 8th Scottish Rifles will occupy from junction with H 12 for a distance of 300 yards to their left, and the support and reserve trenches immediately in rear. 7th Royal Scots will occupy from left of 8th Scottish Rifles for a distance of 150 yards to their left, and support and reserve trenches immediately in rear.

4th Royal Scots will occupy from left of 7th Royal Scots to the Turkey Trench exclusive and the support and reserve trenches immediately in rear.

The 7th Scottish Rifles will occupy the trenches immediately in rear of reserve trenches of front line, and will be in Brigade Reserve.

(4) During the night 27/28th June, O.C. companies will see personally that every man has steps cut in the front of the parapet. Verbal instructions have been issued on this subject. They will also see that all wire or other obstacles are removed from the front of their parapet. The R.E. attached will assist in this work.

Instructions for the Attack.

(5) All watches will be set under Divisional arrangements.

(6) An artillery bombardment on the objective Turkish trenches will take place on 28th June from 9 a.m. to 11 a.m. During the bombardment all troops except the necessary look-outs must keep down under complete cover, and absolute silence will be maintained.

(7) By 8 a.m., 28th June, the assaulting party, consisting of 8th Scottish

Rifles (less two companies), 7th Royal Scots (less one company), 4th Royal Scots (less two companies), will be in position in front line. Each man of assaulting party will carry 200 rounds of ammunition, 1 equilateral piece of tin tied with string loops round the shoulders, 2 sandbags through the belt, entrenching implement, iron ration, full water-bottle. No pack or entrenching tools will be carried.

(8) The supporting party, consisting of 1 company, 8th Scottish Rifles, ½ company, 7th Royal Scots, 1 company, 4th Royal Scots, will be in position in the front line by 10.30 a.m. They will carry, in addition, entrenching tools in proportion of 1 pick to 3 shovels, the latter being tied across the back.

(9) The Reserve party, consisting of 1 company, 8th Scottish Rifles, ½ company, 7th Royal Scots, 1 company, 4th Royal Scots, will move into the support trenches, which will have steps cut in the parapet. Planks will be laid across the front trenches. The Reserve party will carry the same as the supporting party. They will move forward 75 yards in rear of supporting party.

(10) Bombing parties consisting of 1 officer, 3 throwers, 6 carriers, and 3 bayonet men will be detailed by 8th Scottish Rifles and 4th Royal Scots, and will be placed on the outer flanks of the supporting companies.

(11) One machine-gun will accompany each battalion. The remaining four guns will be under the orders of the Brigade Machine-Gun Officer at the Kink in our front line.

(12) Two S.A.A. dumps have been formed: one on the right of the 8th Scottish Rifles and one at the Kink in the front line. A centre has been formed north of 12 Tree Copse (Essex Regiment Head-quarters). Battalion-Commanders will insure that all ammunition carriers know the exact spots of these dumps.

(13) Each battalion will be provided with 2 screens, red with white diagonal on one side, khaki on the other. These will be erected by day in rear of our trenches (red side to rear) to indicate to artillery that supporting fire is requested.

By night Battalion Head-quarters will keep six Very pistols and will indicate the request by clusters of six lights simultaneously. These demands must not be made without sufficient cause. The Very pistols are only meant to supplement telephones if the latter are out of order.

The Assault.

(14) No firing, only the bayonet to be used. The objective of the 8th Scottish Rifles will be H 12, H 12 a, and portion of H 12 north of H 12 a. That of the 7th Royal Scots will be those portions of H 12 and H 12 a from the dotted line west of *H* in H 12 a to the left kink in H 12. That of the 4th Royal Scots will be the Ravine from its junction with J 11 to its junction with northern communication trench leading to H 12—H 11 and H 12 opposite this original front.

Each company will be allotted the position of their objective, and will take compass bearings thereon. The supporting companies will follow the assaulting parties to their immediate front, and will aim at the same objective, compass bearings being taken. The reserve parties will similarly follow the supporting parties.

(15) At 11 a.m. precisely (watches having been previously set under Divisional arrangements) the companies detailed will spring to the assault on the order "Attack" by Company-Commanders, which will be repeated by Platoon- and Section-Commanders. The supporting party will follow 75 yards in rear of the assaulting party, and the reserve party 75 yards in rear of supporting party.

3 Sappers will accompany each assaulting company, the remainder of the company R.E. will follow the reserve party, and will be allotted to units under verbal instructions issued to O.C. London Field Company, R.E.

As each trench is captured it is to be put in a state of defence by parties detailed beforehand from the support and reserve. All communication trenches leading from the enemy towards captured trenches will be occupied and barricaded by parties detailed beforehand from support and reserve parties, about 50 yards ahead of captured trenches. These parties, together with a few skirmishers pushed forward from the assaulting party, will form a covering party under which the work of consolidation can be carried out.

(16) All troops are reminded that the care of the wounded falls to the Field Ambulance. NO fighting troops are to accompany wounded to dressing stations.

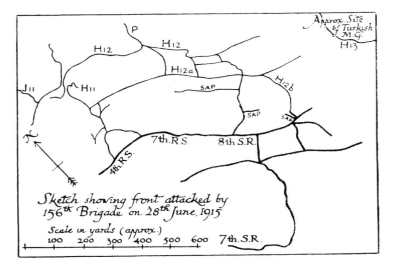

Sketch showing front attacked by 156th Brigade on 28th June, 1915

Scale in yards (approx.)
100 200 300 400 500 600 7th. S.R.

(17) In no case are officers or others in the front trenches to be in possession of Brigade or Battalion orders or of any maps.

(18) Reports to where communication trench joins the support trench.

Dictated to C.O.'s and Adjutants, 2.30 p.m., 27th June.

Additional Instructions for 28th June.

(1) Water-carts to be filled and sent to Eski Lines by midnight. No water to be drunk till after assault is over.

(2) All bayonets to be fixed by 10.57 a.m.

(3) 24 hours' rations to be carried on leaving camp.

NOTE.—Order No. 18 was cancelled later. Brigade Head-quarters remained about 800 yards in rear on the main communication trench (Mule Track).

The conference over, I returned to the battalion, and calling all the officers together carefully went over the orders upon which I framed my own, and which, owing to the shortage of time, could only be verbal. The two assaulting companies were to be No. 1 Company (Captain MacLehose) and No. 3 Company (Captain C. Dunn Macindoe), with No. 2 Company (Captain J. M. Boyd) as supporting company, and No. 4 Company (Captain E. T. Young) as reserve company. The two bombing parties which were to proceed up the saps on the battalion's right and centre were to be under the command of Lieut. G. A. Moore and 2nd-Lieut. R. M. Pattison respectively. The machine-gun section which was to remain with Battalion Head-quarters was under 2nd-Lieut. E. Maclay, and was to accompany Battalion Head-quarters as it moved up the left bombing sap after the assault. Battalion Head-quarters previous to the attack was at a point in the communication trench, 400 yards behind the front line, just where a lateral communication trench joined it. After the successful assault Battalion Head-quarters was to move forward to the new position at the junction of H 12 and H 12 a, and reports were to be sent there. All officers seemed thoroughly to understand their orders, and that night our relief of the Essex Battalion came off up to time. It will be noticed from Brigade Orders that a piece of tin was to be fixed between each man's shoulders; its glint in the sun was to be an indication to the Gunner O.P.'s as to how far the front line had advanced. If I remember aright, once objectives were reached these tins were to be planted on the parados facing our rear so that the gunners could see them.

I do not think that many of us got much sleep on the night of 27/28th June—I know that to me the night was slow in passing—but dawn came at last, cool and beautiful, with a hint of the coming heat, and the dried-up sparse scrub had been freshened by the night's dewfall. One was impressed by the good heart of all ranks, but, whether it was premonition or merely the strain of newly acquired responsibility, I could not feel the buoyancy of anticipated success. I remember going round the line in the early morning and finding that there was some difficulty about the planks which the support and reserve companies had to put across the front trenches to facilitate passage, but these eventually arrived in time. The artillery bombardment which took place from 0900 to 1100 was, even to a mind then inexperienced in a real bombardment, quite too futile (the shortage of shells and guns was criminal), but it drew down upon us, naturally, a retaliatory shelling which caused some casualties amongst the battalion before they moved forward at all. One was Captain J. M. Boyd,[1] O.C. No. 2 Company, whose right leg was smashed, and who never returned to the battalion.

As 1100 approached, leaving my Signalling-Officer, 2nd-Lieut. T. Stout, at Battalion Head-quarters, where, until all objectives were taken, all companies knew that messages would be received, Bramwell and I made our way up to the front line; both of us felt, I think, that our place was there, doing what we could to cheer the men going over the top. We divided our front into two, I took the right and Bramwell the left. How slowly these minutes from 1055 to 1100 passed! Centuries of time seemed to go by. One became conscious of saying the silliest things, all the while painfully thinking " it may be the last time I shall see these fellows alive "!

Prompt at 1100 the whistles blew, and up and over went Nos. 1 and 3 Companies, followed almost immediately by No. 2 Company. Five minutes after they had started they were practically wiped out, and No. 4 Company from the support trench had also suffered severely even before they reached our front trench. As I have said, there was a ridge running between our line and the Turks' front line, having crossed which every advancing man was subjected to a deadly fire from right, front, and left, and it was when each successive wave advancing topped this rise that line after line was enfiladed and mown down. Very few men reached the Turkish trenches, and those who did were either killed or wounded, with the exception of one or two men who managed to crawl back to our trenches during the night.

---

[1] Captain J. M. Boyd, after a long illness and recovery, joined the R.A.F., with whom he did good work, eventually becoming Lieut.-Colonel.

From where I was I could see the men advancing up to
the ridge, but once over it they were hidden from me, so that
I did not know whether they had reached the enemy trenches,
but I felt in my bones that they had not been successful, and
I remember, after seeing the right of the battalion going over,
coming back to Bramwell and saying: " Bramwell, it's a wash
out," and he agreed with me. Nevertheless, I decided to send
a message to Brigade Head-quarters for reinforcements. On
the assumption that we might reach our new Battalion Head-
quarters, Bramwell and I then pushed our way up the sap,
which for a short distance concealed us, but got shallower
as we went along, until first our heads, then our shoulders,
and then the most of our bodies were exposed. One or
two of my runners, and Tom Stout and his signallers now
accompanied us; we soon arrived at Pattison's bombing party,
which I had sent up this sap. He had been killed, and those
of his men that were left were lying flat; they could not get
on as the sap rose a few yards in front of them to the ground-
level, and the leading man was lying in only about 18 inches
of cover. In any case they were still some 50 yards from the
enemy trenches. Bullets were spattering all around us, and
we seemed to bear charmed lives, until just as we arrived at
the rear of this party Bramwell fell at my side, shot through
the mouth. He said not a word, and I am glad to think that
he was killed outright. He was a fine man who could be trusted
in difficult situations. Everybody liked him, for himself and
for his soldierly qualities. One felt that he would have gone
far. Two of the men carried him back. Some of Stout's signallers had also been hit, but we still moved forward, and I
made up my mind that the only thing to be done was to collect
what men there were and make a dash for it. I told this to
Stout, and stooping down to pick up a rifle I was shot in the
neck. At the moment I didn't feel much, but when I saw the
blood spurt forward I supposed that it had got my jugular
vein. I stuck a handkerchief round my neck and tried to get
on, but I was bowled over by a hit in the shoulder. I tumbled
back over some poor devil, and for a minute or two tried to
collect myself. Up came young Stout and said: " I am going

GALLIPOLI: FIRING-LINE TRENCH IN "THE VINEYARD"

to try to carry you back, Sir," but I wouldn't let him. I was obsessed by the idea that our job was to get forward to our new Battalion Head-quarters to establish communication with all companies if they had reached and taken their objectives, and I told Stout to send another runner for reinforcements. A few minutes later he came back and took me by the shoulders and some other good fellow lifted me by the feet, and together they got me back some ten yards, and though a bullet got me in the flesh of the thigh, I was now comparatively sheltered while they were still exposed. It was then that a splinter of shell blew off Tommy Stout's head, and the other man was hit simultaneously. Gallant lads! God rest them!

By this time it cannot have been more than 1130, though an age seemed to have passed. Perforce I remained where I was; my senses were quite alert. It was insufferably hot, and I recollect having a drink of water, and giving one to a boy called Reid, who lay mortally wounded alongside me. Perhaps about an hour afterwards, I was aroused by a young officer of the 7th Scottish Rifles (which battalion had been in reserve), who came along and asked me what to do. I asked how many men he had got, and he replied " only my platoon ". I told him to go back and get his Commanding Officer to push on with his whole battalion. He went away, and we all remained lying there in that sap, sometimes conscious, sometimes blessedly unconscious. The heat as we lay there was appalling, but things were gradually getting quieter; what we longed for was coolness. Reid, poor lad, was by this time in agony, he had been shot in the stomach, and all I could do for him was to give him a little more water. Sometime during that after-noon, I heard afterwards, a scrub fire was kindled between the enemy lines and ours; it was never known whether the fire was caused accidentally or designedly, its awful results were, however, the same—a terrible culmination of the morning's tragedy.

The day wore on into the interminable night, broken by the moans and agonizing cries of the wounded and dying, till dawn came coolly and quietly. In a moment of conscious-ness, I realized I was looking at a Turk who had appeared round a corner of the sap. We gazed at each other, and he went away. One of my own poor fellows was lying dead alongside of me. The Turk returned and again looked at me, and again disappeared. A second afterwards I saw a bomb hurtling through the air, evidently thrown by him; it seemed to be coming straight for me, and with a great fear in my heart I managed to pull myself up, my knees to my chin, and my left arm cuddled round them. The bomb—it was one of those not very powerful cricket-ball ones which the Turk used—landed at my feet, and bursting, bespattered my left leg and arm and portions of my thighs. It seemed, however, to galvanize me into action, and another bomb coming over, I managed to roll over on to the other side of the dead lad and all its charge lodged in him. Somehow I then succeeded in getting to my feet and staggered back down the sap for a few yards over the shambles of dead bodies lying there, until I fell down. Another bomb came over, landing short, and I got up again and got farther back down the trench. By this time the sap was becoming deeper and was clear of bodies, and I tottered still nearer our lines. I then came across a little lad of my battalion lying with an awful wound in his chest, but alive and conscious. He asked me to help him, I feebly grinned and said: " Can you get on your feet?" To my surprise he managed it, and imbued for the moment with superhuman strength we staggered together down the sap, still pursued by bombs which miraculously always seemed to fall just short. Then we came to a barricade of sandbags eight feet high, for at this point the sap was deep. My heart sank, what could we do? We both pulled at a sandbag at one side, and by the mercy of God (I say it in all reverence and thankfulness) it came away and brought down along with it a dozen or so of its mates above. How we slipped over I do not recollect, but we did, and ten yards farther on, through a look-out hole in another barricade, some of the Essex people saw us and came out and took us in. They gave us nectar to drink, I mean stewed tea. Soon we were carried through tortuous communication trenches down to the battalion aid-post, where we found Hamish MacLehose. (I remember one of the good souls who took an end of the improvised stretcher was Cleveland Donaldson, then in the Camerons and attached to the Essex; he was afterwards killed.) Alec Sloan did what he could for us at the battalion aid-post, and we were carried down to the C.C.S., and after attendance there, to the beach, I forget which, where after hours of waiting in a broiling sun lying in the open, we were at length lifted into a tender by means of a pulley and crane, from which each stretcher case was hoisted into a hospital ship. Somebody gave me a whisky and soda, which I enjoyed, but like the tea, it remained not long. I can only imagine that I got that drink because it was thought that I was too far gone for it to matter much. I had seven major wounds besides a considerable number of minor bespatterings from the bomb. I remember quite distinctly explaining graphically to the night-nurse how a man in a cot near by was a Turk coming down the sap throwing bombs at me, and then feeling somehow that I ought not to tell her in case she might think me delirious!

I don't recollect anything of our voyage or who of our wounded were on board. At Malta by means once more of the pulley and crane we were landed at the quayside, where we were allotted to our various hospitals. At the Convent of the Blue Sisters at Sliema where I presently found myself were Hamish MacLehose, Willie Sloan, and Dick Humble. At first Hamish MacLehose, who was considered to be lightly wounded, used to come round and see us and write letters for us, until his wound got serious with arrested sepsis. We have all good reason to remember gratefully the great kindness of doctors and nurses and the Sisters of the Convent, though the everlasting clucking of the poultry in their adjacent farmyard got on our disordered nerves, already much tried by the heat. Later on one or two N.C.Os. of the battalion visited me from other hospitals in Malta, and gave me a little information about the events of the 28th of June. Afterwards by dint of interrogating officers and men whom I came across during my time in hospital, or at home, or again on my return to the battalion a year later, I was able to glean small, sadly small, items of news about various officers and men reported killed or missing. How Cecil Macindoe, who was adored by his men, most gallantly led his company; how Dai Carson of that company was one of the very few who reached the Turkish trenches before being knocked out; how Gerald Moore and his bombing party reached and held their sap-heads; how Eric Young, Willie Church, Charles Mowat, Jack Findlay, and Ronald Macindoe, were seen to fall at once, leading their platoons; how others like Hew M'Cowan, Billie Maclay, Templeton, managed to get a little farther forward before fate overtook them. The N.C.Os. played up to the officers in the most devoted manner: C.S.Ms. Donald Hunter, Jock Buchanan, J. Wilson, and Sergt. J. Gilmour—all of whom (with the exception of Wilson, who was so badly wounded that he was never really fit for service again, though he managed to join the battalion later) afterwards earned the D.C.M.—are names which I remember to be specially worth mentioning. I wish that I could do verbal justice to all those gallant fellows who did so nobly on that fatal 28th June. The great fact which will ever remain in my mind about that day, is the absolute faith of all the men in the devotion and bravery of their officers and N.C.Os., and that, of course, implies the like qualities in themselves.

On the morning of the 29th June, there were left but three officers, Captain A. B. Sloan, R.A.M.C., Lieutenant E. Maclay, M.G. Officer, and Lieutenant and Q.M. H. Bowen, and about 70 other ranks who had been collected, the pitiful remnant of a fine battalion.

The action of the 28th June was undertaken with a view to pushing forward and straightening out the left of our line, and from Gully Ravine to the sea on the left it succeeded. It was upon this locality alone that there was any artillery bombardment. Our failure to take the H 12–H 12 a system was due to the lack of this, and not to inexperienced troops, as might be perhaps supposed, for the 88th Brigade of the 29th Division, composed of units which had been on the Peninsula since the landing, were launched upon the same objectives the same day, and also failed with heavy losses to take the position. Thereafter no further attacks were pro-

jected upon this valuable point d'appui, which remained in
Turkish hands until the end.

In his *Gallipoli Diary* Sir Ian Hamilton, writing of our
attack on H 12, says: " One thing is clear: if the bombardment
was ineffective, from whatever cause, then the men should not
have been allowed to break cover ". He further comments
" the exact facts (re artillery support) were not known to me
until long afterwards " (*Gallipoli Diary*, Vol. I, p. 355). Even
now, ten years after the event, when one has acquired a truer
perspective, the thought of the futile loss of these gallant men
on the 28th of June makes one sick at heart. The 8th losses on
that day were 25 officers and 448 N.C.Os. and men (see
Appendices Nos. II and VII), old and valued friends, the best
of comrades, who have left a void which can never be filled.
Only four of the officers who were casualties in the action ever
returned to serve with the battalion, namely Carson, Humble,
Rogers, and myself. And what makes the loss of these comrades the more bitter is that no real recognition of their gallantry
and devotion was ever officially given for the heartening of
their friends at home. For despite the two congratulatory
letters printed at the end of this chapter, which were only
known within the depleted Brigade, the Special Order of
29th June published by the Commander-in-Chief on the
battle completely ignored the 156th Brigade, and when Sir
I. Hamilton's official dispatch of 26th August, 1915, was published, it contained only the statement " but the remainder
of the 156th Brigade were unable to get on ". No more.

Our *Divisional History* says (p. 73): " The result was that
the words were most cruelly interpreted by a certain war-
correspondent, who incidentally was so far misinformed as to
assign the bulk of the losses to three units in the 86th Brigade.
Another war-correspondent referring to the Cameronians
(Scottish Rifles) imagined, or was wrongly informed, that they
' had failed to make good their holding '. Every trench captured by the Scottish Rifles and every unit of the 52nd Division
on Gallipoli was held by them. The H 12 trenches were not
captured simply because corpses cannot walk forward, and no
man there got forward more than a few dozen yards without

being killed (or wounded). There never was any question of them failing ' to make good their holding '. Naturally, everyone in the Division, and the Scottish Rifles in particular, felt keenly the misrepresentation and the official silence."

I cannot add anything to this graphic paragraph, save to say that one war-correspondent did his best to make amends (see Appendix No. IX).

The same prodigal losses on a still greater scale in France would seem to have been necessary to bring home to the politician safe at home that men cannot take the place of guns and shells. But when has any British campaign been adequately equipped at its start? We in Gallipoli suffered more from the lack of guns and shells than the Armies in France; we were farther away, and it was a case of " out of sight, out of mind ". Supplies and matériel were held up also, because there was no unanimity in the Cabinet as to the strategic importance of the command of the Bosphorus. It did not seem to occur to those responsible for launching the expedition that they were in honour bound to pursue it wholeheartedly. Even allowing for the universal shortage of guns and shells which prevailed at the time, there still remains much of apathy and negligence which one cannot forgive. An occasional pious hope was breathed in our direction that the campaign might be a success, but the material help needed to insure its success did not come in time.

To GENERAL EGERTON,
            52nd Division.

H.W. 418. 1/7/15.

Sir Ian Hamilton wishes me to reiterate the congratulations I conveyed to the 156th Brigade immediately on their return from the trenches. Please express to all officers, N.C.Os., and men of 156th Brigade, the C.-in-C.'s congratulations on their fine attack which has brought so great distinction on their Brigade, and on the 52nd Division.

GENERAL HUNTER-WESTON.

To G.O.C.,
    52nd Division.

29/6/15

    General de Lisle wishes to express how much he valued the help given to the 29th Division in yesterday's attack by the 156th Brigade. The attack by the 156th Brigade was almost entirely successful—the 4th and 7th Royal Scots succeeded in every detail in the tasks imposed upon them. The 8th Scottish Rifles met with enormous resistance owing to the fact that our artillery had not prepared the Turkish position in front of them *quite so successfully as in other places*. The 8th Scottish Rifles were very gallantly led. This position was unsuccessfully attacked twice by the 88th Brigade (29th Division) with great gallantry. General de Lisle does not blame the 8th Scottish Rifles at all for their failure. He much regrets the death of Brigadier-General Scott-Moncrief.

G.O.C., 29th Division.

    The italics are mine. It has been well-established that there was no artillery preparation. We are indeed grateful that he does not blame us.

CHAPTER III

Gallipoli—Evacuation

By Lieut.-Colonel R. N. Coulson, D.S.O.

After the terrible casualties of the battalion on 28th June, a composite Scottish Rifles battalion was formed of the 7th and 8th, the former of which had also suffered serious losses. The Commanding-Officer was Major W. T. Bird of the 7th, a gallant and capable officer, who took it into action on 12th July, and himself on that occasion made the great sacrifice. His Adjutant was E. Maclay,[1] the only combatant surviving officer serving with the 8th. The battalion War Diary has the following entries in connection with this action:

"*July 11th.* Two parties, each of 1 officer and 25 other ranks, left at 1530 to act as garrison of redoubt near Achibaba Nullah. Battalion moved up on the evening to reserve trenches at Backhouse Post. 155th and 157th Brigades held the forward trenches. Orders for attack were issued by Division—156th Brigade to be Divisional Reserve. (These orders were destroyed in conformity with an order that no orders or maps were to be taken into the firing line.)

"*July 12th.* Attack by 155th and 157th Brigades. The combined British and French artillery bombarded the Turkish trenches intermittently from 0430 to 0730, when the assault was made. Before the assault, the Scottish Rifle Battalion was moved up to Eski Line and remained there until about 1100, when it was called on to proceed to the firing line on the left of the French. About 1530 No. 1 Company went over the open and captured the trench in front, barricading it on the right of a sap leading forward, thus assuring No. 2 and 3 Companies' advance on the left of the sap. No. 1 Company then went up the sap which brought them in touch with the Royal Scots. During the night of 12/13th July the Turks counter-attacked three times but were repulsed with heavy casu-

---

[1] Killed later on in France when with the Scots Guards.

GALLIPOLI: REST CAMP, CAPE HELLES

Looking towards Achi Baba

alties. Trench then consolidated. Great difficulty experienced in getting sandbags owing to enormous demand—Bandsmen J. M. Doull and J. Smith were awarded the D.C.M. for clearing wounded and dead from a dangerous sap, and making a passage to the captured position.

"*July 13th.* Continued to consolidate position. In the early morning a large body of Turks were seen advancing, apparently to surrender, but as they carried arms with fixed bayonets, the order was given to fire and they were shot down. Battalion returned to Backhouse Post, being relieved by R.N. Division."

On the 21st July, Captain W. A. Davenport (West Yorks) was posted to the command of the composite battalion, and in the course of a month thereafter many officer reinforcements arrived. 2nd-Lieutenants C. France, L. W. Thom, J. Walker, K. B. Craigie, W. J. Westland, S. N. Aucott, W. J. Aitken, C. E. Findlay, W. S. Scott, F. W. J. Burns, J. E. Bannen, W. H. Carslaw, W. Dow and H. B. Dunn, had all come by the end of August, though no signs were forthcoming of the early advent of reinforcements of other ranks.

From the middle of August to 19th September the battalion remained in trenches on the right of Krithia Nullah, taking turn about with the other battalions in the Front, Local Reserve, and Eski Lines.

On the 11th September, Major C. Macfie (late Adjutant, 6th H.L.I.) took over command from Captain Davenport, to be relieved later by Major J. R. Simpson, H.L.I., who, in turn, was succeeded by Lieutenant-Colonel W. B. C. Bridge, H.L.I., who did a great deal to pull the battalion together. He infused it with a common *esprit de corps*, and stiffened up discipline, which had suffered after the actions of 28th June and 12th July.

During these autumn months, patrolling of the narrow " No Man's Land " was carried out nightly, and every effort made to harass the enemy. On one occasion a small reconnoitring patrol of two men of the battalion were out during a good deal of machine-gun fire and shelling. Hearing moans out in " No Man's Land ", without a thought of self, C.S.M. Donald Hunter dashed over the parapet of the front-line trench to the rescue, and under a hot fire succeeded, with the aid of the remaining member of the patrol, in bringing in the wounded man.   For his gallantry he was awarded the D.C.M.

The weather now began to show signs of coming winter. It became colder at nights—for that matter, during the day also—rain fell more frequently, and troops began to experience mud in the trenches.

On November 15th the battalion took part in a successful attack by the 156th Brigade.   The telegraphic dispatch given below received from the General Officer Commanding the Mediterranean Force announces the success of the action, although only meagre results were achieved considering the casualties incurred.

SIEGE WARFARE IN GALLIPOLI
TURKISH TRENCHES CARRIED

November 17th, 1915.

" 52nd Division carried out a very successful attack on the Turkish Trenches on 15th instant, for which careful preparations have been in progress for considerable time.   Three mines were exploded successfully under enemy trenches in the neighbourhood of Krithia Nullah at 3 p.m., and the infantry pushing forward immediately after, captured about 160 yards of trench on east of Nullah and 120 yards on its west.   Captured trenches were at once consolidated and bombing parties pushed on up communication trenches and erected barricades.

" Simultaneously with the assault, our artillery opened on enemy's reserve support trenches, two 14-in. Monitors and H.M.S. *Edgar* co-operating, and fire was maintained until position was reported consolidated at about 6 p.m.   Enemy's batteries replied heavily but very erratically, and did little damage.   Turks in neighbouring trenches, who fired heavily, were caught by machine-gun, rifle fire and bombs, and suffered considerably, their fire becoming very wild.   No attempt at counter-attack was made until night of 16/17th, when it was easily repulsed.   Our casualties were under 50 killed and wounded.   Over 70 Turkish dead seen in captured position, and wounded prisoner reports that over 30 were buried by explosion of one mine.   Units employed were 4th and 7th Royal Scots, 7th and 8th Scottish Rifles, and Ayrshire Yeomanry, all of the 156th Brigade."

With regard to the above dispatch it is of sad interest to note that the casualties of the Brigade in this action were:

			Officers		Other Ranks
Killed	..	..	3	..	22
Wounded	..	..	2	..	85
			5		107 [1]

More than half of these belonged to the battalion.

This was the first time that in a telegraphic dispatch from the front the units engaged were specifically mentioned. The new departure was very generally welcomed. It was very gratifying to those in these Scottish regiments which had made the successful advance, to receive without delay the credit which was their due. It is also likely that the announcement acted as an incentive to recruiting in Scotland.

The battalion marched to Rest Camp on 21st November for a well-earned rest. Owing to cold and fatigue and the strain of the recent action, dysentery, paratyphoid, and jaundice were rife, and out of a battalion strength of just over 300 some 20 to 30 men per day were being sent to hospital. These numbers were truly alarming, and the M.O., Captain A. W. Cassie, actually put in a report that he considered the battalion unfit for further work in the trenches unless it were given a rest. Fortunately he was wrong; pluck and endurance enabled the men to carry on till the evacuation, nearly seven weeks later.

On the evening of 28th November heavy rain fell, which turned to sleet, and next morning six inches of snow was lying on the ground. By 8 a.m. on 29th the battalion was on the move again to the front line, and was duly grateful to the snowstorm, in that it prevented the Turks seeing the move and shelling the troops as they crossed the open. The three miles move up to the line was, at that time, the limit of the men's powers, and strong fellows, who at home could carry their full kit for 20 miles, had now to halt and rest every few hundred yards. By midday bright clear frost set in, which gradually increased in intensity, till during the night the ther-

---

[1] Compare these with the dispatch figures.

mometer fell to 12° F. At Helles the troops were somewhat protected from the full effects of the blizzard, but at Suvla, where there was no shelter, there were thousands of casualties.

The firing line at this time was held strongly with an average of nearly one man to every two yards of fire trench. Owing to the severe weather the tour of duty at night was only one hour, and while this made certain that the sentries would be on the alert, it meant that these men never obtained even two hours' sleep at a stretch. This combined with the cold and exposure aggravated the debilitated condition of the troops.

The intense frost had another unexpected effect, which might have proved even more serious. It tended to jam the action of the men's rifles. Oil got into the bolts and became thickened with the cold, to such an extent that when the trigger was pressed the striker could only come forward slowly and would not explode a cartridge. Fortunately a supply of paraffin was at hand, and once the bolts were washed out with this they became serviceable again.

Work during the day consisted chiefly of improving trenches, many of which had originally been occupied by the Turks. In consequence the former parados became the parapet. The Turks had an objectionable, and, to say the least of it, insanitary habit of burying their dead in the parados. Our unfortunates had the task of making new fire bays. This necessitated digging in the old parados and removing the remains of brother Turk which had lain there in a hot climate for several months. More need not, I think, be said.

On 1st December the first reinforcing draft arrived— 3 officers, 2nd-Lieuts. R. Humble of the 8th (who had been wounded on 28th June), A. T. Coltart, and W. Murdoch of the 7th, and 78 other ranks. One can imagine how welcome was even a small draft such as this. They remained in Rest Camp until the battalion was relieved in the trenches, which came about on 9th December.

The battalion was on this occasion housed, for the first and only time on the peninsula, in decent dug-outs. These, it is true, were only splinter proof, each being 9 feet long by

7 feet wide, but at any rate the men could stand up in them and get decently warm at night.

" Rest Camp ", to which several references have been made, was remarkably ill-named. Digging fatigues were performed daily, and the whole camp was under observation from Achi Baba, and shell fire came from not only that hill and Krithia, but also from the coast of Asia across the Straits, from a gun called Asiatic Annie. Shells from the latter direction pitched into us from behind, and gave an unpleasant feeling of insecurity. The Turks were now receiving from Germany and Austria more guns and shells, both of a much superior quality. Formerly many of their shells failed to explode, but now they were much more effective. Bulgaria about this time joined forces with the Central Powers, who, thus reinforced, allowed Turkey to draw upon them more freely for their munitions.

On 19th December, as an extension of the advance already made by the 156th Brigade on the 15th November, an attack was launched by the 157th Brigade on G 11 A, a trench which crossed the ground between the two branches of the Krithia Nullah. The battalion was in the line to their left in the " Rue de Paris " immediately west of the above nullah, and although not taking part in the action, it came under the Turkish barrage and had an unpleasant hour or two.

On the 22nd a move was made back to Rest Camp, where a new area had been allotted to the unit. This was absolutely water-logged, and the men, tired as they were, had to dig and drain holes in which to sleep. All ranks spent a most unhappy night, but next morning was beautifully fine and kits could be dried in the sun.

On Christmas Day, 1915, Major R. N. Coulson took over command of the composite battalion from Lieut.-Colonel Bridge, who had received a Staff appointment. Major Coulson had arrived about a month before from hospital in Egypt, whither he had had the bad luck to retire, owing to severe sciatica, almost as soon as the battalion arrived at Mudros.

On the early morning of 9th January, 1916, the evacuation of Cape Helles was successfully completed. The 156th Brigade provided the final garrison of the 52nd Division's portion of the

5

front, and to the battalion fell the great honour of supplying the final garrison of the firing line, along with parties of the 6th and 7th H.L.I. The garrison got away without any casualties. Anzac and Suvla had been evacuated on the last days of 1915, and it was by a stroke of good fortune that the troops at Helles succeeded in getting off with no casualties. So ended the heroic tragedy of the Dardanelles Campaign. How nearly it succeeded! That it did not was due to no fault of the gallant troops who unceasingly responded to all demands made upon them. The strategic conception of the expedition was brilliant. It is generally admitted that success would have shortened the war by two years or so, but the premature movements of the Fleet two months before any soldiers were sent to co-operate, thus eliminating the element of surprise, lukewarm and questioning support at home, no thought-out plan, the constant demand from the Western Front for men and munitions, the difficulties of transport, the fierce opposition of the French to any risk of weakening the Western Front, combined to defeat what might have been a magnificent coup.

The actual method of carrying out the evacuation required considerable preparation and detailed planning. Lieut.-General Sir Charles Munro, along with Major-General Lynden-Bell as his Chief Staff Officer, was responsible for it, and as a military manœuvre it was magnificently organized and carried out.

Orders were issued to the troops at Helles informing them of the brilliant evacuation of Suvla and Anzac, which had been effected on the night of 19/20th December, with the loss of only some half-dozen guns, and practically no casualties. They were told that, though the temporary evacuation of these places had been necessary, to them had been allotted the honour of maintaining the ancient traditions of the service, and the holding of Helles till such time as a fresh effort could be made in the ensuing spring.

So well were the orders conceived that the troops, inwardly envying those who had got away from the peninsula, felt that they were in for a stiff job, and never for a moment had any idea that in three weeks' time they also would be evacuating Gallipoli.

Information was allowed to leak out that reinforcements were on their way from Egypt, and definite news reached the battalion that the transport men were rejoining the unit.

Higher command did some excellent work in this way, and completely deceived the Turks. Egypt was full of spies, and naturally the movement of the transports and other details must have been reported to the enemy. So far did this stratagem go that the Divisional transport was embarked, and was only turned near Mudros after the evacuation had actually taken place.

On 24th December the Turks attacked the centre of the line, but fortunately the defence was too strong and none of them succeeded in getting beyond the British wire, in spite of the fact that the enemy's bombardment was heavier than had previously been felt. This failure must have given them food for thought, and satisfied them that at that date at any rate no evacuation had taken place. On 29th December the battalion moved up to the line, and when there received the good news that the 155th Brigade had taken G 11 a and completed the task which the 157th had commenced on the 19th.

Information now reached us that our Corps was to be relieved by the 9th Corps. This seemed too good to be true, and when in addition on the 31st we were advised to reduce our kit and send off surplus stores, owing to the possibility of a shortage of transport when the new corps arrived, we began to suspect that after all there was going to be an evacuation of Helles. It was not, however, till 3rd January that confidential instructions about the evacuation were received by the Commanding Officer, and these were not passed on to the Company Officers till a day or two later.

The problem of withdrawing troops and stores from Cape Helles was one of extraordinary difficulty. The front line extended for something over three miles, and the nearest distance from it to a suitable beach was about three miles and a half. The withdrawal itself might not have been so difficult had the country been undulating, but every portion of the route to the beaches was like a glacis slope, and under direct observation from Achi Baba. It was not as if the evacuation was going to be an unexpected thing to the enemy. He had already seen the withdrawals at Suvla and Anzac, and had to be deceived as to our intentions. To add to the difficulties there were no proper piers and everything had to be loaded on lighters, and these towed out to the ships at night.

As we now know, the evacuation of the front line was intended to be completed at 12 o'clock on the final night, so it was necessary to accustom the Turks to a cessation of fire from this hour till " stand to " in the morning. This was the more important, as it had been the custom for our sentries to fire four rounds per hour at the Turkish trenches. On the first night of the cessation of fire, 30/31st December, the Turks sent over patrols to find out what was happening, but this had been expected and some of their men were caught. After a night or two the enemy appeared to become quite used to the new conditions. By day appearances were kept as normal as possible, cookhouse fires were kept burning, odd fatigue men were employed to walk about the Rest Camp, carts were driven about, dummy water-carts were set up, and troops were even landed at the beaches. Gradually, however, by shipping at night, the number of troops was reduced and a mere skeleton of an army left.

The work on the beaches was nerve-racking, as the Turks shelled them continuously by night. One gun in particular at Chanak across the Straits was hated by everyone. Its flash could be plainly seen and a sentry who was posted to watch for it would blow a whistle. A tense silence of some moments elapsed, then the shell could be heard approaching and at the end of 30 seconds it arrived. Men were supposed to go to ground when the whistle blew, but many did not and casualties were numerous.

On the final night it was all important to deceive the Turks and make them think the trenches still occupied, and many were the expedients employed. A simple device for the automatic discharge of rifles was one of the best. A loaded rifle, with the stock sawn off to render it unserviceable, was fixed to the parapet. A fine wire passing over a nail, as a pulley, was attached at one end to the trigger, while from its other end was suspended an empty tin. Above this tin was fixed a petrol can filled with water, but having a small hole in it. The water gradually dripped from the hole into the suspended tin. As the tin became heavier the strain on the wire increased until it finally pulled the trigger and fired the rifle. The time of discharge could, of course, be varied by altering the size of the hole in the petrol can. This method was also employed with Very's pistols so that flares were shot up over the Turkish lines after our departure. Bombs having long fuses attached were carried out towards the Turkish trenches and these safety fuses were lit by the last men to leave our trenches.

Turkish aeroplanes were very active at this time, and one of their pilots who was circling over Achi Baba suddenly dived for our line and flattening out passed right along Plymouth Avenue, which we were then occupying, at a height of only about 100 feet. We fortunately had dressed up dummy figures with blankets to represent men sleeping on the fire-steps in the support line as by this time there were very few troops left. The dummies must have deceived the observer in the enemy plane. The Turks undoubtedly suspected that evacuation was going to take place, but had no idea as to when. A proof of this was their big attack on the trenches to the left of our line on the afternoon of 7th January, the day before the final troops left. Again our luck was in, as the time chosen for the attack coincided with the relief of one Brigade by another and both were actually in the trenches. The Turks sustained a heavy reverse and lost many men. They were caught under a heavy fire, and few if any got beyond our wire.

The Divisions holding the line at the finish were (from right to left) the R.N.D., 52nd, 29th, and 13th. General H. A. Lawrence, our Divisional Commander, was in charge of the local military arrangements for the embarkation at Helles, and our Brigade, the 156th, was selected to cover the withdrawal of the 52nd Division. Parts of the 6th and 7th H.L.I. were attached to it for the occasion. At this time the Brigade strength was hardly that of a battalion.

Everything humanly possible was done to ensure that no one should lose his way on the final night. All officers and a proportion of the N.C.Os. followed the route right down to the sea, and in the battalion every man was made to go several times from his post in the line to the battalion rendezvous.

It was considered likely that we should be attacked on the final night before we had gone very far, and the lines of defence selected were the Redoubt Line, the Eski Line, and a new line immediately covering the beaches.

All trenches not actually required were carefully blocked, and arrangements made to close the communication trenches with barbed wire as soon as the final parties had passed the various controls. Trip bombs and various other booby-traps were arranged ready to be set by the last troops to leave.

In spite of the worn-out condition of the men, it gave one a thrill to realize their absolute steadiness. Men who had been a bit nervous, stiffened up when the time came and were marvellously cool; sentries no longer imagined they saw movements in the dark in front of them; and generally every man did his job, realizing that the safety of the whole force depended on absolute obedience to orders. The feeling was pretty general that there wasn't much chance of the covering force getting away, and that its job was to make the withdrawal of the rest secure, no matter what happened.

A wonderful system of controls had been established at points on the routes by which the various parties had to go. These controls were connected to Divisional Head-quarters by wire, and each consisted of an officer, some sappers, and a telephonist. The parties coming down from the line were of an exact number, and the officer in charge of each had to report to the control officer. The latter only allowed the party to pass him at the time scheduled and after counting and reporting it to Brigade Head-quarters. The timing worked out extraordinarily well, and there was no congestion at any point.

On the morning of the last day, 8th January, all men belonging to the battalions in the line, who were the least unfit, were marched to the Rest Camp before daybreak, and they and those who were already at Rest Camp were embarked on the evening of this day. There now remained, therefore, only those actually selected to hold on to the finish.

At 8.30 p.m. on 8th January the first parties, including Battalion Head-quarters, left the battle positions. These parties were 60 per cent of the force selected to hold the line on the last day. Not till 11.45 p.m. did the final parties, the remaining 40 per cent, leave the line, and they had to double down a good part of the way to keep up to the scheduled time.

The actual numbers of the composite Scottish Rifles battalion on 8th January were:

	Officers	Other Ranks	Total
At Rest Camp	1	26	27
Party which left the line at 4 a.m. . . .	11	132	143
First party which left the line at 8.30 p.m.	7	88	95
Final party which left the line at 11.45 p.m.	3	62	65
On control duty	2	10	12
On duty at Brigade Head-quarters . . .	—	6	6
	24	324	348

Orders were issued that on the last night no packs were to be carried, and that all surplus kit was to be rendered unserviceable and left behind. The men seemed to be possessed with the demon of destructiveness and took a perfectly vicious delight in cutting up such things as beautiful rubber thigh boots, which had only reached us a week before. They, at any rate, were determined that nothing should be left to the Turks.

When leaving the line there was hard frost, and all ranks wore two sandbags tied on to each foot to muffle the sound of the feet on the hard trench floor. The quietness of movement was extraordinary, and seldom can so many men have marched off with so little noise. At Divisional Rendezvous men were told off into parties of 100 each and marched in fours, with 50 yards between parties. All went well till the zigzag road above V Beach was reached. Here there was a block, which was particularly unfortunate as the big Chanak gun commenced operations. The first shell fell about 100 yards from the battalion among some corrugated iron roofs and made no end of a clatter. The men were wonderfully cool, not one quitted the ranks, which says a good deal for them, as they had to stand in close order in pitch darkness under nervous tension, see the flash of the gun and wait the 30 seconds till the shell arrived, with the full knowledge that it would fall near them. Seven shells arrived while the battalion was at this part of the road, but fortunately there were no casualties.

The landing-stage was eventually reached, and was found to consist of three old steamers, sunk stem to stern, and having gangways between them; the final one had been a French cruiser. It seemed strange to walk along their 'tween decks in the darkness. From the end of the jetty a " beetle " was boarded. These were large motor lighters, so called from their shape, which had been specially constructed for the Suvla landing and held 500 men when filled below and above deck to their fullest capacity. Without delay the beetle put out into the bay, where, owing to the strong wind, the sea was rapidly rising. At about 1 a.m. on the 9th, our beetle ran alongside H.M.S. *Prince George*, and all clambered safely on board. The Navy were kindness itself, and we only heard next morning that the crew had gone without their dinners in order to give the troops a meal. There was a feeling of thankfulness at being on board a British ship again, but this not without many a thought for those of the rear party, whom we had left behind, and for whose safety we were more than anxious. A few minutes after the ship had weighed anchor a dull thud was felt, but no one told us what it was, and it was only when Mudros was reached that we learned that the *Prince George* had been struck by a torpedo, which fortunately for us failed to explode. The Turks duly reported in their communiqué on the evacuation that they had torpedoed and sunk a British battleship with 1200 troops on board. Their numbers were correct, but luckily not the main fact.

The battalion was put ashore at Sarpe pier, West Mudros, within a short march of a camp which had been pitched by an advance party from Brigade Head-quarters.

It was a glorious morning, and it was difficult to realize that we were safe and could walk about in the open without any danger from shells, and that at night a real tent would be over our heads.

In the afternoon the final party of 65 officers and men rejoined, having performed their task of holding the line to the very end, and by good discipline, not to speak of good fortune, had been spared for another campaign.

The evacuation orders which follow are of interest:

To SCOTTISH RIFLES. SECRET BM 806.

Though definite instructions have not yet been received from the 52nd Division for detail of the final evacuation, the following will be of assistance to O.C. units for estimating their numbers, &c.

(1) In all future orders Y night will mean the last night before evacuation; Z night will mean night on which evacuation will take place.

(2) On Y night the evacuation of sick and wounded will be carried out as usual. On Z night, from an hour to be stated, all evacuation will be done by Field Ambulance bearers.

(3) Stretchers and R.A.M.C. bearers will be at Control Stations. Bearers will have instructions not to leave their stations. Any wounded will be brought to *the bearers* by men in trenches. On the march down troops will have to assist R.A.M.C. bearers in carrying wounded on stretchers for short reliefs. If all stretchers are full any extra wounded will have to be carried by their comrades until reserve stretcher posts are reached. These positions will be detailed later.

(4) Regimental stretcher bearers can be used as rifles or sent down when R.A.M.C. take over bearer duty. O.C. units can therefore count on their regimental stretcher bearers for rifles for last night.

(5) The method of evacuation can now be outlined. Each line held, i.e. Firing Line, Local Reserve Line, Eski Line, and Observation Hill, will be evacuated in two parties.

1st Party.—All details mentioned in para. 2, 156th Brigade Order No. 26, except a proportion of R.E. in Firing Line and Local Reserve Line, to assist control officers in setting mines, trip bombs, &c., and about 25 per cent of garrisons.

2nd Party.—About 25 per cent of garrisons followed by control parties and R.E. not in above. O.C. units will therefore have to detail commanders for the second parties.

(6) Numbers of 2nd parties will be:

FIRING LINE: 6th H.L.I., 25 officers and other ranks; 7th H.L.I., 40 officers and other ranks; Scottish Rifles, 40 officers and other ranks.

LOCAL RESERVE: Royal Scots, Parson's Road east of Central Street, 10 officers and other ranks; west of Central Street, 10 officers and other ranks. Royal Scots, Redoubt Line, 25 officers and other ranks.

ESKI LINE RESERVE: Royal Scots, 25 officers and other ranks.

OBSERVATION HILL: 6th H.L.I., 5 officers and other ranks; 7th H.L.I., 5 officers and other ranks.

(7) Regimental M.Os. and their orderlies (included in numbers for Brigade Head-quarters para. 2, 156th Brigade Order No. 26) will not necessarily march with their Battalion Head-quarters. Control Officers are being instructed that Regimental M.Os. and their orderlies will march anywhere in the columns where they can best attend to their work. One M.O. Royal Scots will be at No. 8 Control Station. Number of executives in Battalion Head-quarters will therefore be 2 officers, 3 orderlies, and 3 signallers.

(8) First parties will march at an hour to be stated. Second parties will remain in their positions, and those in Front Line carry on sniping, &c., until they are timed to move. They will also set in motion any automatic rifles, bombs, &c., before leaving.

(9) These second parties will have to hasten down to the Divisional Rendezvous, as the time-table which is being prepared will allow the second parties less time than the first parties. Therefore only the best and fittest men should be detailed for these parties.

(10) The positions allotted to units for Z night in 156th Brigade Order No. 26, will probably be taken up on Y night or during Z day, when numbers superfluous to those required will be sent down to Rest Camp.

	(Signed) W. H. DIGGLE, Captain,
4/1/16.	Brigade-Major, 156th Brigade.

B.M. 816   Copy No. 4

156th INFANTRY BRIGADE ORDER No. 27

7/1/16.

Reference Maps R.N.D., New Sector, 8th A.C. Com. M.S. 29.

(1) The final stage of the evacuation will be carried out in one day instead of two. Date will be notified.

(2) The numbers of troops to hold each line on the last day, given in 156th Brigade Order No. 26 of 2/1/16, para. 2, hold good with the following amendments.

(i) LOCAL RESERVE LINE, Parson's Road between Regent Street and Oxford Street. (a) East of Central Street for " 50 officers and other ranks, Royal Scots ", read " 25 ". Delete " 1 R.E. officer."

(ii) REDOUBT LINE and PORT ARTHUR. For " 100 officers and other ranks Royal Scots " read " 75 ".

(iii) OBSERVATION HILL will not be held.

(iv) In Front Lines and Local Reserve Lines 3 R.E. out of the 5 enumerated in each case will be attached to the Control Stations which their lines will pass, to assist in blocking trenches, setting up trip bombs, &c.

Time will be notified when the final dispositions are to be taken up, and the mode of evacuation of men superfluous to numbers required.

(3) Troops are detailed to pass Control Stations as follows (see para. 2, 156th Brigade Order No. 26).

FIRING LINE: Right Subsector, Nos. 1 and 4 Stations; Centre Subsector, Nos. 2 and 5 Stations; Left Subsector, Nos. 3 and 6 Stations.

LOCAL RESERVES LINE: (1) (a) No. 4 Station; (b) No. 5 Station. (2) No. 6 Station.

ESKI LINE RESERVE via Central Street to No. 7 Station. All troops Nos. 7 and 8 Stations to Divisional Rendezvous. All officers in command of parties on passing a Control Station will inform the officer in charge of the number of men, unit to which they belong, and where they have come from.

(4) Troops will be withdrawn on the last night as follows:

At 1730: (a) All troops in Local Reserve Line; (b) all troops on Eski Line, *except* 50 officers and other ranks Royal Scots, 2 machine-guns and teams, and M.G.O.

At 2030: All troops in the Firing Line *except* (*a*) Right Sector, 45 officers and other ranks 6th H.L.I., 1 machine-gun and team, and M.G.O. (*b*) Centre Sector, 65 officers and other ranks 7th H.L.I., 1 machine-gun and team, and M.G.O. (*c*) Left Sector, 65 officers and other ranks Scottish Rifles. Those troops remaining will maintain the normal fire action against the enemy from 2030 to 2345.

At 2200 two machine-guns and teams from Front Line (1 from each Right and Centre Sector) under M.G.Os. with 4 men per gun to assist carrying down.

At 2130, 25 officers and other ranks Royal Scots from Eski Line, and 2 machine-guns and teams and M.G.O. from Eski Line.

At 2345: (*a*) Remaining troops in Eski Line; (*b*) all remaining troops in Front Lines. They will move off quickly and silently through their Control Stations to Divisional Rendezvous.

Nos. 1, 2, and 3 Control Station parties will follow the last troops from the Front Line. Nos. 4, 5, and 6 Control Station parties will follow Nos. 1, 2, and 3 Control Station parties respectively. Then will follow No. 7 Control Station party, and last of all No. 8 to Divisional Rendezvous. All parties of troops should, if possible, have an officer in front and another in rear.

(5) The possibility of attack must never be forgotten by commanders. They must be prepared to hold any of the lines of defence at once. Observation Hill has been prepared as a rallying position if necessary. Any attack taking place must be at once reported to 156th Infantry Brigade Headquarters. On no account must small attacks be allowed to delay progress of embarkation.

(6) On arrival through Control Stations at Divisional Rendezvous, troops will be formed into parties of 100 under an officer. They will be marched to " A " forming-up place, just west of Sedd el Bahr Fort (vide map attached), halted, closed up, and await orders. If necessary there will be a " B " forming-up place, 100 yards south of Cemetery for W Beach.

(7) If infantry meet any artillery on the road during withdrawal, infantry will give way to the artillery.

(8) The A.P.M. 52nd Division will be responsible for guiding troops from Divisional Rendezvous to forming-up place, and Embarkation Staff responsible for guiding from forming-up places to beaches.

(9) Instructions for embarkation are issued as an Appendix.

(10) Stretchers and bearers (R.A.M.C.) will be posted as under:

No. 1 Control Station			6 Bearers	3 Stretchers
,, 2	,,	,,	8 ,,	4 ,,
,, 3	,,	,,	6 ,,	3 .,
,, 4	,,	,,	2 ,,	1 ,,
,, 5	,,	,,	2 ,,	1 ,,
,, 6	,,	,,	6 ,,	3 ,,
,, 7	,,	,,	2 ,,	1 and 1 officer
,, 8	,,	.,	16 ,,	28 and 2 officers
			and S.M.O. 156th Brigade and Orderly	
,, 9 (Divisional Rendezvous)			45 Bearers	56 Stretchers and 5 officers

A stretcher and bearers will accompany each party of 50 men throughout, and embark with it and any wounded they may be carrying. They will receive their march orders from Control Stations from Officers in charge of Control Stations. 2 Ambulance wagons will be at Divisional Rendezvous for the use of 156th Infantry Brigade. All ranks are to be warned that on no account are wounded men who can walk to be accompanied by other men to the rear.

(11) Time will be given out at 0800 and 1600 on the final day, when watches will be synchronized.

(12) 156th Infantry Brigade Head-quarters will be established at Divisional Rendezvous at 1700 on last night, and will embark with the last troops of the 52nd Division. Messages can be sent to 156th Brigade Headquarters through any Control Station.

(Signed) W. H. DIGGLE, Captain,

Issued at 1030.   Brigade-Major, 156th Infantry Brigade.

Copy No. 1 to 6th H.L.I.
   „   2 „ 7th H.L.I.
   „   3 „ Royal Scots
   „   4 „ Scottish Rifles   } By Orderly.
   „   5 „ 1/3 Kent R.E.
   „   6 „ 52nd Division
   „   7 „ retained
   „   8 „   „

Dictated to all Control Station officers.

SECRET.—APPENDIX TO 156th BRIGADE ORDER No. 27.

On arrival at Divisional Rendezvous troops will be formed up by the Brigade-Major, 156 Brigade, into parties of about 100 each under an officer.

This officer must ascertain what troops he has under his command, and be prepared to report the exact numbers of all ranks of his party at forming-up place.

From forming-up place parties will be led to the beach and to lighters, each holding about 400 men. To ensure that lighters are properly packed, 1 officer of each party will be stationed at the foot of the lighter gangway below deck to see the lower deck properly filled up, 1 officer at the top of the gangway to pass men down rapidly, and a third at the point where men board the lighter. If three officers are not available for these duties, senior N.C.Os. will be detailed by O.C. Party.

The senior officer in charge of each lighter will be responsible for the rapid unloading of the lighter. Officers will therefore on embarking at once ascertain who is the senior on board. The senior officer of the *first* lighter to come alongside any ship will act as staff officer to that ship.

The senior officer on board will be O.C. Troops, and will see that the ship is unloaded as quickly as possible.

(Signed) W. H. DIGGLE, Captain,

Brigade-Major, 156th Infantry Brigade.

7/1/16.

INSTRUCTIONS TO TROOPS ENTERING EVACUATION AREA

(1) No packs are to be carried. Any left behind must be destroyed. No packages to be taken.

(2) After embarking any Mills bombs are to be thrown into the sea.

(3) O.C. parties of 100 leaving Divisional Rendezvous will have states given them showing the number and composition of parties. These states will be handed to Embarkation Station Officer at gap in wire fence on the road to " Forming-up Place ".

(4) Maps and documents are to be destroyed.

(5) Blankets are to be destroyed. They may be used to deaden noise on floor of trenches.

(6) Spare bombs are to be buried.

(7) If necessary to re-land, troops proceed to forming-up places and await orders.

(8) In case of attack after dark and Turks drive us from Front Line, firing line will rally and hold Redoubt Line and Parson's Road till 2345 when evacuation will continue.

(9) All men must know we embark at V Beach.

(10) Secret instructions read to officers.

8/1/16.

RICHARD N. COULSON, Major,
Commanding Scottish Rifles Battalion.

CHAPTER IV

Egypt—Battle of Romani

The Scottish Rifle Battalion remained at Mudros until 1st February, when it embarked for Alexandria in H.M.T. *Briton* (strength, 20 officers, 6 warrant officers, and 358 other ranks), arriving there on the 3rd, and moving to Abbassia near Cairo on the 5th. Here they found about 200 officers and men awaiting them, some from hospital, but most of them from the 3rd-line battalion at home. Soon after, more reinforcements to the unit arrived, 8 officers and 148 other ranks, and the composite battalion now included 50 officers and 659 other ranks. It moved to Ballah on 16th, and on 21st February the battalion was re-organized into 1/7th and 1/8th Scottish Rifles again, Captain J. G. Romanes (late Adjutant, 7th Royal Scots) being appointed to command the 7th, and Major R. N. Coulson the 8th.

Here at Ballah we had our first experience of E.P.I.P. tents (European Private Indian Pattern). These are rectangular (about 16 feet by 12 feet), having two centre poles and a bamboo ridge pole. The roof is double, with an air-space between, and overhangs the sides by a foot. The material for both roof and walls is quilted cotton, and owing to this construction the resulting tent is wonderfully cool. Only four or five were issued to each unit.

On 6th March the battalion marched to Kantara, some 7 miles off, on the east side of the canal. This, its first experience of camel transport, was a trying one. Acting on instructions, all loads were duly made up ready for the camels to march to them and " barrak "[1] for loading, but, to anyone who knows, that is only a beginning. Loads have next to be roped

---

[1] i.e. to make a camel sit down.

OUR SECOND IN COMMAND, MAJOR R. N. COULSON
AND
LIEUT. HARRY BOWEN, QUARTERMASTER

One of the best friends the Battalion ever had

on the camel in such a way that they will not be shaken off when it gets up and walks, and this is no light task for the uninitiated. The men were, of course, absolutely new to these proceedings, and on this occasion expected a good deal of work from the camel boys. It is true that the camels were loaded eventually, but only after fully two hours' work. Later at Mahemdiyeh, after some practice, the battalion actually loaded up its transport complete, ready to move off, in six minutes! The march over soft sand was very trying to troops unaccustomed to it, and it was a thoroughly exhausted body of men that reached Kantara. Next day by the arrival of Lieut. W. D. Dulieu and four other officers, the battalion strength was made up to 23 officers and 340 other ranks.

The officers now with the battalion were:

Major (Temp. Lieut.-Colonel) R. N. Coulson.
Captain Neil Caw.
Captain A. B. Sloan, R.A.M.C.
Captain W. S. Wilson, C. of E. Padre.
Lieut. and Adjutant W. D. Dulieu.
Lieut. and Q.M. H. Bowen.
Lieut. D. D. Bannerman.
Lieut. L. W. Thom.
Lieut. W. D. Hannan.
Lieut. R. Humble.
Lieut. A. F. Rogers.
2nd-Lieut. W. W. Ferguson.
2nd-Lieut. W. J. Aitken.
2nd-Lieut. H. Lawson.
2nd-Lieut. J. A. MacLaren.
2nd-Lieut. T. A. Herd.
2nd-Lieut. R. J. Allan.
2nd-Lieut. C. E. Findlay.
2nd-Lieut. W. S. Scott.
2nd-Lieut. J. M. Nicholl.
2nd-Lieut. V. C. A. M'Leod.
2nd-Lieut. A. Cameron.
2nd-Lieut. J. K. Scotland.

At this time, Kantara, which is on the Suez Canal, about 30 minutes' run from Port Said, was not the great canvas city which it became a year or so later. Then, as subsequently, it was the base through which everyone going up the line to the troops in the forward zone had to pass, and where, whether going or returning, one seemed to be unnecessarily and annoyingly detained. Even then it was a busy place; every nation and branch of the service seemed to be there, English and Scottish, New Zealanders and Australians, Indians and Egyptians, Dagos and other scallywags, all intent upon their own occupations, useful and otherwise. The railway to the frontier, which eventually reached Jerusalem, was commenced in the beginning of April, and was being laid at the rate (roughly) of a kilo per day. Later on the pace of its construction was doubled, but owing to the rails being laid on sand nearly all the way to the frontier there was always the chance of some portion being made impassable by sand drifting over it, or sand-ballasting under the rails being blown away, and the pace of the train had perforce to be slow. It was, however, a great feat of primitive railway construction, and with all its disabilities and discomforts absolutely essential, of course, to the conduct of operations. It is marvellous to think how that single line of railway served an army of 200,000 men more than 200 miles from its base.

The battalion remained at Kantara until Sunday, 23rd April. Lieut.-Colonel Coulson employed this time in smartening up the drafts, not to mention the veterans of Gallipoli who also required " refresher " instruction. Close-order drill, handling of arms, open-order work, outpost schemes, the attack, night work by compass, punctuated with working parties for fatigues and trench digging, kept them all fully and necessarily occupied.

23rd April is memorable for the surprise attack by the Turks on the English Yeomanry near Katia, and for the brilliant defence of Dueidar by the Royal Scots Fusiliers of the 155th Brigade. That evening the battalion and the 4th Royal Scots with the 156th Brigade Machine-Gun Company moved out by train and took up an outpost position in the dark at Pelusium, covering railhead. During the night the shattered remnants of the Yeomanry retired through our lines. Later the 7th Scottish Rifles joined us, and the Brigade (less the 7th Royal

CAMELS DRINKING AT THE WELLS MADE AT ROMANI DURING OUR ADVANCE

Scots) remained till 11th May in the vicinity of " Young's Hill ", a sandy eminence immediately to the south of and covering the railway at about the 30th kilometre from Kantara. Yeomanry and New Zealand and Australian Light Horse performed the duties of protective cavalry. On 11th May the battalion marched out and took up an outpost position at Sabket-el-Romani, about a mile and a half in advance of the new railhead, while the remainder of the Brigade marched to Mahemdiya.

On the march the battalion was allotted 110 camels as transport for baggage and water. The water allotment at this time was 200 gallons, and on their arrival at the outpost position after a trying hot day, this amount was depleted by 30 precious gallons on urgent representations from the Glasgow Yeomanry, who at that time were doing cavalry outpost duties for us. The battalion remained on this outpost position till 17th May, during which time the heat was terrific and well earned the title " Hell's Gate " for the place. A shade temperature of 127° Fahrenheit was actually registered. During this time the men were employed in digging, wiring, and protective duties; water was very scarce, being rationed at ½ gallon per man per day for all purposes, and the men suffered severely from its want and from the devastating heat. Only those who have had experience of the desert in summer can realize what this allowance of water meant, and the men's tongues became so swollen by evening that they could hardly speak. Doctors told us at the time that the Egyptians in the hot weather drink nearly three gallons of water a day.

On the 17th May the battalion marched from Romani to Chabrias, which is near the sea. That march to Chabrias, though only three and a half miles, came as a climax to the trials of Hell's Gate. Owing to some mistake, the 4th Royal Scots, who should have relieved us shortly after dawn, when the march could have been accomplished in comparative coolness, did not arrive till 1000, when it was beginning to be hottest. There was no breeze, and no shade tempered the pitiless heat of the sun which concentrated its burning rays upon the marching men. Rifle barrels became searingly hot. The

6

march would have been bad enough if there had been any
water to revive the vitality of men parched by more than a
week of the very scanty water ration—but there was none;
the day's rations of food and water having been sent direct
from Railhead to Mahemdiya. After the first mile or so the
men started to fall out, some delirious, some staggering like
drunken men, some unable to speak and black in the face
from thirst. The last mile was strewn with those who had
succumbed. The doctor told me he never experienced a worse
time during the war (he himself went sick). Eventually in one
way or other, all the casualties were carried into Chabrias, but
many had to go to hospital, and some dozen or so were never
fit for further war service. On this particular day sixty camels
in our area died through being worked in the heat, and stringent
orders had to be issued to prevent their use during the hottest
hours.

Romani and the area Chabrias–Mahemdiya are some forty
kilos from Kantara, Chabrias being on the shore side of
Romani, and a branch railway line from there of about three
or four kilos in length was ere long constructed. It was decided
that a strong defensive position should be made here, on the
line Katib-Gannit-Chabrias. A series of sand dunes round
Katib Gannit dominate Romani to its east and south-east,
and of these Katib Gannit is the highest. These are continued
on the north side of the railway into the Chabrias defences,
which have their left resting upon the sea. The distance from
the sea to Gannit is about four miles due south, and the line
of defence ran back from there westward for one and a half
miles to Et Maler. It was a strong position, but in May, 1916,
the chain of fortified works which were being prepared for all-
round defence were not in a very advanced stage of construction.
Including the Chabrias defences there were twenty-three fortified posts, few of which were completed by the 4/5th August,
the date of the battle of Romani, which will be described later.

It was with the Chabrias defences that the battalion was
chiefly concerned; in their occupation o' nights as garrisons
for various posts, and in their construction by day. The chief
relaxation of this camp was the sea bathing, which, subject to

the necessary work being carried on, was encouraged, and enjoyed by all ranks.

On 23rd May I embarked from Devonport, and after varying vicissitudes of fortune in the way of obstructionist R.T.Os., &c., eventually reached the battalion on the 17th June. At this time there was a serious amount of carelessness on sentry duty, and a number of the men had to be court-martialled for " sleeping on his post "—one of the most serious crimes on active service. I had great sympathy with the men—they had had a very trying time. They had not yet recovered from the march to Chabrias, and the great heat since then, combined with the necessity for working hard at the defences, gave them no chance to recuperate. Tired men, they had to go on outpost duty with the knowledge that the enemy was thirty miles away and that our cavalry was between. It was a sore temptation to yield to an overwhelming desire for sleep. The 8th at the time was largely composed of new drafts, and there had been but little leisure to pull them and the rest of the battalion together. Crimes of this kind had to be rigorously stamped out, however, and they *were* stamped out.

The B.G.C. when I arrived was General Koe, but he departed two days afterwards. He had been struggling against illness for some time, and had at last to give in. Lieut.-Colonel G. B. Wilson from one of the 155th Brigade Battalions then temporarily commanded until the arrival, to our great delight, of Brigadier-General E. S. Girdwood, who had been Brigade-Major of our Brigade in Gallipoli, after which he went to Salonica, became Colonel of the Staff, and now came back to his old Brigade as its commander. His staff at this time consisted of Captain E. D. Tollemache (Coldstream Guards), Brigade-Major; Captain W. T. Law (8th Scottish Rifles), Staff-Captain; Captain J. W. H. Pattison (8th Scottish Rifles), Brigade Machine-Gun Officer; Captain W. T. Copestake (7th Scottish Rifles), Brigade Signal Officer.

During these hot days at Chabrias we worked in the mornings from 0600 to 0930 hours, and from 1530 to 1900 hours, thus avoiding the great heat in the middle of the day. Our work consisted of digging and wiring the defences, the occupation of them at night, and, at the same time, of company and specialist training as far as was compatible with the work on the defences. Water and rations were regular, and the former was now more plentiful than hitherto. In fact, part of our work was the construction of a tank for the storage of that precious commodity. Bathing parades were also in the daily programme, and now and then camels were provided, so that we could practise loading them, a very necessary and certainly a difficult art to acquire. The degree of difficulty depended upon what one was loading. Water and ammunition were simple enough, and so were blankets after the men got accustomed to rolling them properly, but when it came to cooking utensils, officers' kits, messing and bivouac gear, orderly-room paraphernalia, &c., the question of balancing articles upon each side of the primitive wooden saddle in the rope net, which often broke, became a serious one and was the source of more bad language, I imagine, than has ever been heard since the Children of Israel crossed the Sinai Desert. How often has one seen a carefully piled-up load slip over as soon as the camel rose to its feet! If a camel's load overturned or fell off on the march, the camel of course had to fall out to be reloaded, and had to catch up the column at its next halt. How we used to curse these camels, but in their aloof unfriendly way they served us well. We could not have done without them, and many a time the arrival of our transport, travelling an hour or two's march behind us, was hailed with thankful cheers. What wonderful loading tables Coulson used to prepare for me! He was in his element. The only crab was that having been allotted a certain number of camels (say eighty), it quite often happened that only perhaps seventy-three arrived, thus necessitating the readjustment of the loads and perchance the jettisoning of somebody's treasured articles, and always the upsetting of the loading tables. An excellent example is given opposite.

During June two drafts arrived for the battalion; on the 7th one of 2nd-Lieut. J. T. Neilson and forty-six other ranks from 3rd line, and on the 17th 2nd-Lieut. N. R. Edwards and thirty-eight other ranks. They were soon absorbed, and

ROMANI: LOADING FANTASSIES ON CAMELS

Each fantass held from 10 to 15 gallons according to size—Two large fantassies constituted a camel's load (about 350 lb. as a maximum)

1/8 BATTALION SCOTTISH RIFLES
MOBILE COLUMN TRANSPORT CAMELS

6/12/16

Camels	Article	Detail	Packages per Camel	Weight per Camel. (Pounds.)	Officer	Remarks
4	WATER	8 15-Gallon Fantassies.	2	360		
3	S.A.A.	12 Boxes Mk. VI. / 2 Very Pistols, 1 in. / 1 Very Pistol, 1½ in. / 3 Parachute Lights. / 2 Boxes Bombs (24). — Very Lights, 25 di. 1 in.; 3 Red.; 3 Green.; 5 di. 1½ in.	5	350		4 Boxes S.A.A. and 1 Box Bombs or Very Lights as top load.
2	BLANKETS	1 Blanket per man at 4½ lb., 270 lb. / 1 Bivouac Stick per 2 men at 1 lb., 30 lb.	4	300		Blankets rolled in bundles of 15 round 6/8 Bivouac Sticks.
2	BAGGAGE	Officers' Shelters, Valises, Mess Stores, and Equipment, C.Q.M.S.	—	360		
1	COOKS	8 Dixies (at 9 lb.), 72 lb.; Fresh Meat, 120 lb.; Vegetables, ½ lb., 30 lb.; Potatoes, ¼ lb., 30 lb.; Tea, ⅙ oz., 4½ lb.; Sugar, 3 oz., 22½ lb.; Milk, ¼ tin, 6½ lb. Total, 225¼ lb.	—	319	— Servants not included. / Staff and Head-quarters / Transport, Orderly Room / Each taken as 120 men. / W, X, Y, Z Companies.	Fresh Meat ration when carried. If not space may be used at discretion of Company - Commander + Cooking implements.
1	TOOLS	25 Shovels at 3½ lb., 77½ lb. / 1 Pick Axe, 8 lb.; 4 Bill Hooks, 8 lb. } 93½ lb.	—			
1	S.A.A. MK. VII	4 Boxes Mk. VII.	4	320	2nd-Lt. MacLaren	Loaded by Lewis-Gun Sections + 6 ponies.
5½	—	4 Companies as above.	—	—	—	All loaded under Company arrangements.
2	SANITARY	Latrine Seats at 15 lb.; Cresol Drums at 9 lb.; Fluid.	—	—	Sergt. M'Robbie	
1	PIONEER AND ARMOURER	14 Shovels at 3½ lb., 49 lb.	—	—	Staff-Sergt. Stally	
1	M.O.	Stretchers.	—	—	Capt. Sloan	+ 1 Pony.
1	SIGNALS	—	—	—	2nd-Lt. Innes	
3	WATER	6 Fantassies.	2	360	Sergt. Paton + 6 Fatigue Party	
1	COOKS, H.Q.	—	—	—	Sergt. Cook	
2	Q.M. STORE	—	—	—	Q.M.S.	
2	TRANSPORT	—	—	—	T.O. / L/Cpl. Duffy + 4 Fatigue Party	
3	STORES	—	—	—	Head-quarters	
2	BAGGAGE	—	—	—	Provost Sergt. and 6 Fatigue Party	Officers' Valises and Personal H.Q. Staff blankets includes O.R. Staff.
2	SHELTERS	—	—	—		
1	ORDERLY ROOM	—	—	—	O.R. Sergeant and Orderlies	
1	BRIGADE	—	—	—		
74						R. N. COULSON, Major.

the increase of numbers was not apparent. It seldom was, unless a really good-sized draft appeared.

On 8th and 9th July the battalion entrained for Kantara en route for Alexandria, where we were going to have a long-promised rest, but at Kantara we were held up, and on the 19th at 2300 hours we entrained back again for Chabrias, 348 strong, leaving behind the last two drafts. Arriving back at Chabrias at about 0100 the next morning, I reported to G.O.C. 157th Brigade, under whose command I had been ordered to put the battalion, our own B.G.C. having gone with us to Kantara and still remaining there. I was given instructions that we were to occupy a position between the railway (branch) line and the southern end of the Chabrias defences and dig in. This we did, but immediately on our front was Hill 80, the occupation of which by the enemy would have entirely dominated not only our position but also a portion of the Chabrias and Romani defences. Fortunately Colonel Waller, the C.R.E., came round next day and he agreed that this hill ought to be occupied by us; after representation to Division, he succeeded in getting Egyptian labour for the immediate formation of two " lunettes " on the forward slope of Hill 80. These hastily constructed redoubts were occupied by the battalion on the night of 21/22nd July—a company was allotted to each " lunette ", with the remainder of the battalion about a quarter of a mile in rear in reserve.

On 22nd I received orders to rejoin the 156th Brigade at Romani, and we entrained about 1330 hours, having waited for the train in the heat of the sun from 1000 hours. We arrived at Romani half-an-hour afterwards, and marched to a camp half a mile away, where tents had been already pitched for us by Brigade. We appreciated the thoughtfulness of this, having been out in the blazing sun during the three previous days.

We were now in Divisional Reserve and carried on training for some days at Romani. We did some practical attack and defence schemes, and I particularly remember doing a mounted reconnaissance in the neighbourhood of Wellington Ridge, with, I think, Humble and one or two other officers. This, as things turned out, proved to be a most useful bit of work, as it gave us a knowledge of the ground over which we were subsequently to attack at night.

On 1st August, a new draft arrived under 2nd.-Lieut. J. S. Ralston, also some men back from hospital, another helpful contribution to our strength.

Ever since we had been ordered to return to Chabrias from Kantara, we had entertained shrewd suspicions that the Turks were moving against us. The 3rd and 4th August brought us definite intimation that this was so, in the shape of enemy aeroplanes which flew low over us and bombed us. It was then that the Turks, for the first time, used bombs with an iron spike which caused the burst to occur above the level of the sand; previously their effect had been lost, to a great extent, in the sand. It was very uncomfortable, but no damage was done to us, though some dumps at the railway were considerably knocked about. On the 4th the main attack on the Romani defences was launched by the Turk. I am indebted to Brigadier-General A. H. Leggett, C.M.G., D.S.O., then commanding the 1/5th R.S.F., which battalion was holding a number of the works round Katib Gannit, for a very lucid and interesting account of the action, as viewed and ascertained by him (Appendix No. III). As for my battalion's part in the action, I print the report made by me at the time.

NARRATIVE OF EVENTS LEADING UP TO THE CAPTURE OF WELLINGTON RIDGE ON NIGHT OF 4/5TH AUGUST, 1916

At about 1700 hours, on the evening of 4th August, 1916, I and the 7th Scottish Rifles received orders from Brigade to move up and occupy Wellington Ridge. The battalion moved out of camp at 1800 hours and rendezvoused with the 7th Scottish Rifles, who took up their position on our left behind Work 23. From there both battalions moved up towards the Ridge, each in four lines of platoons. My orders were to clear Wellington Ridge of the enemy and occupy it, digging ourselves in. The left of the 7th was to rest on Redoubt 22a, the 8th to prolong the line to the right, which flank was to be protected by the Anzac Mounted Brigade and the 42nd Divi-

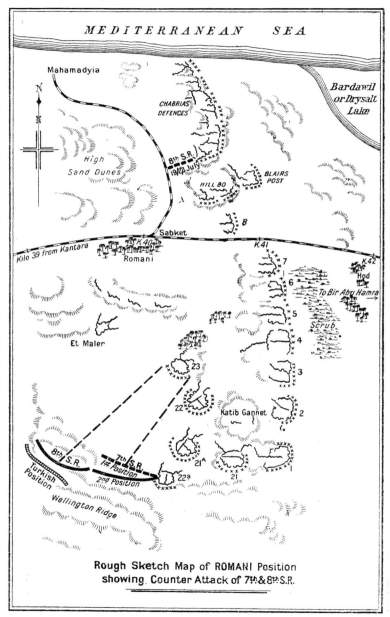

Rough Sketch Map of ROMANI Position showing Counter Attack of 7ᵗʰ & 8ᵗʰ S.R.

sion, who were coming up in this direction from Mount Royston. Both battalions had their Camel Train with ammunition in rear, plus a section each of four guns of the 156th Machine-Gun Company. At about 400 yards behind 22a, both battalions extended and advanced under a desultory sniping fire. On arriving at what they considered the position they were to occupy, which they did without opposition, the 7th Scottish Rifles commenced to dig-in. On their right, and on my front, however, was a nullah, and my battalion had to advance beyond this nullah because it was impossible to dig-in at its bottom, and also because the crest of the Ridge had not been reached, as ordered. After some difficulty with regard to direction, the battalion advanced to the crest and was suddenly heavily fired upon by the enemy who were entrenched on the top. The battalion displayed great coolness, lay down and replied, three Lewis guns being in the firing line and one in reserve. The Turks reinforced their line, and for a considerable time there was a heavy interchange of fire, all my companies, less three platoons, being eventually engaged. Time, 2300 hours.

Meantime the Transport-Officer sent word that the Egyptian Camel Drivers had fled, the guard having been inadequate to retain the camel drivers under fire. I was therefore much concerned about getting up ammunition, and I dispatched my Adjutant to see if he could collect the camels and bring up the reserve ammunition. I also communicated my position to the 7th Scottish Rifles, and asked them to move their right forward and join up with me. This was eventually done.

Whilst this was going on I had been receiving urgent messages asking for ammunition from the Company-Commanders, and was also informed that the Turks were trying to work round on my right flank. I reinforced it with one platoon, and sent up another to reinforce its own company, Z Company. At this time two Lewis guns came back for repairs, being jammed by the sand. They eventually returned to the firing line. Wounded began to be brought down, and as it was impossible to get through to Brigade by 'phone, I sent a message by mounted orderly and by 2nd-Lieut. Carslaw, who

ROMANI AND KATIB GANNET IN THE DISTANCE

Note the heaviness of the sand over which the infantry had to advance

8TH S.R. TRANSPORT

Featuring the Backbone of the British Army

had been wounded, to the Brigade, informing them that the Camel Train had broken away and asking for more ammunition and reinforcements.

About 0100 hours my Adjutant[1] succeeded in rounding up the camels with the reserve ammunition.

When the Camel Train came up two guns of the Machine-Gun Company came up along with it, and I sent one gun to my right flank and one to the centre of my position. Two guns still remained with the 7th Scottish Rifles where they should not have been, but eventually they came up, and were put in the firing line, just before dawn. The reserve ammunition was now taken up to the firing line from the camels.

I was still much concerned about my right flank, but my mind was relieved on being informed by Brigade that 7th Royal Scots who were holding redoubts on my right rear were to move an adequate number of companies forward to protect me there, also that one company of the 1/5th Royal Welsh Fusiliers was detailed to support me, and the latter eventually arrived and reinforced all along my line just before dawn. As the light grew stronger our fire became heavier until at about 0430 hours we ceased on the Turks putting up a flag of truce, and holding up their hands. Just at this time the Anzac Mounted Brigade moved out on our right and rounded up a further large number of Turks to our front and right flank. We took 364 prisoners and a considerable quantity of rifles, ammunition, and equipment, &c., including a German machine-gun company.

After sending off prisoners under escort, the battalion moved forward to the Turkish second line, which we occupied, reorganizing the companies and filling up with ammunition and water, the remainder of the camel train having been recovered by that time.

The 5th Royal Welsh Fusiliers (less one company already in the line) now came up on our right and undertook the job of collecting equipment, rifles, ammunition, shovels, &c., left on the ground. After a short rest and some food the battalion again moved forward, taking up a position on the right of the

---

[1] Lieut. W. D. Hannan was then acting Adjutant.

7th Scottish Rifles on the immediate left of Mount Meredith, facing south-east. Here we remained until the following morning, outposts being put out during the night by the 4th Royal Scots, when we returned to camp.

8/8/16   J. M. F.

NOTES

(1). During the whole night of 4th and 5th August, 1916, I never got into touch with the 158th Brigade or the Anzac Mounted Brigade, who should have been on my right.

(2). Sand caused both Lewis guns and rifles to jamb and at one time, in one platoon, there were only two rifles that were able to be fired.

(3). Telephone communication was inadequate. No line was pushed out to us from the Brigade, a line having to be laid by my Signalling Sergeant from the 7th S.R.

(4). Camel Guards must in future be stronger.

(5). All messages to be less of a jumpy nature.

(6). Platoon commanders must not reinforce without definite orders.

(7). Fire control must be more effective. On the appearance of an enemy surrendering, Platoon commanders must have their platoons absolutely in hand.

OUR CASUALTIES

KILLED	1 officer	13	other ranks
	(2nd-Lt. H. Lawson)		
DIED OF WOUNDS . .	—	3	,, ,,
WOUNDED	2 officers	15	,, ,,

The notes appended to the narrative were added for my own edification. I remember some few days after this action being called in question by the B.G.C. for sending him pessimistic messages during the night. I probably did paint the picture black, in the hope of expediting reinforcements. The position was as follows. My battalion, less than 300 rifles in strength, was up against the enemy, strength unknown, better entrenched and manifestly considerably stronger than myself; both my flanks were in the air. On the left, the 7th Scottish Rifles had dug-in considerably behind the line of our objective, Wellington Ridge, and were taking a long time to link up with us. On my right there was no sign of the expected 158th Brigade of the 42nd Division or of the Australian Light Horse. The enemies' front line was within 100 yards of ours, and there was a grave shortage of ammunition owing to the flight of the Egyptian camel drivers with their animals and our reserve ammunition. Messages giving these details having been sent to Brigade Head-quarters, I finally said I would assault at dawn if reinforced. As far as reinforcements were concerned, all that I got was a very tired and sleepy company of the R.W. Fusiliers. The O.C. 7th Royal Scots told me afterwards that he had never had any orders to reinforce me, though Brigade had informed me that he would do so. However, Providence was with us, and as dawn broke the Australian Light Horse, in considerable numbers, came up at last on my right. At the psychological moment when these reinforcements were getting up to my firing line, the Turks saw that they would be outflanked and surrendered.

I shall always bear the B.G.C. a grudge for the way in which he treated the battalion on this occasion. Not a word of thanks or of recognition beyond what was also accorded to the company of R.W. Fusiliers, who never were in action; no recognition of the fact that whatever may have been their Commanding Officer's enormities in the matter of gloomy messages, they, and they alone, took Wellington Ridge and 364 prisoners, including a Boche machine-gun company. If I had halted the battalion and linked up on the right of the 7th Scottish Rifles when they took up their original line as ordered, Wellington Ridge would never have been taken. On the contrary, next morning we should have been in a most unpleasant position, dominated by the enemy. But thanks to the lucky reconnaissance already referred to, I knew that we were not up to Wellington Ridge, our objective, and that we must push on. I recollect that during that night, Bilsland, who was temporarily attached to Brigade, came up to my H.Q. with a view to ascertaining my exact position. I gave it to him on the map, and morning proved that I had given him the correct co-ordinate.

We remained at Romani for some time after the battle, and took our turn as garrison in the Redoubt line. When not on outpost we carried out a musketry programme at a range constructed for the Brigade under Major Coulson's supervision. This range was adapted for long-range controlled fire, as well as shorter range individual firing. It was possible to shoot up to 1200 yards, and very useful practices were carried out. Doubts were cast upon its safety by those in authority, and I must say I was rather concerned one evening on riding over to the range to find Sir Charles Dobell, G.O.C. East Force, and a young aide abroad all unaware of it, although the Brigade had been duly asked to notify the location of the range to Division for promulgation to all units in the area. He came on with me to see the men shooting, and seemed pleased with what he saw.

During September the following immediate honours were awarded to the battalion for gallantry at the battle of Romani:

M.C.   2nd-Lieut. J. S. Ralston.
D.C.M.   C.S.M. J. Buchanan.
M.M.   Sergeant H. Ralston.
M.M.   Private W. Caskie (M.O.'s orderly).

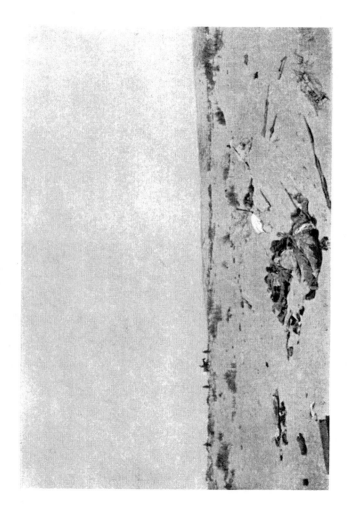

SINAI: WELLINGTON RIDGE AFTER THE BATTLE OF ROMANI

CHAPTER V

On Mobile Column

In October commenced the dreary trek through the Sinai Desert. I say dreary, because trekking over the sand was dreary and weary and monotonous. But we had intervals of pleasant enough little sojourns here and there en route.

On 11th October the Brigade moved to Er Raba, where we found traces of the Turkish occupation. This oasis had been the " jumping-off " ground for their attack on the defences of Romani. Er Raba was some 6 miles eastwards, and there we bivouacked for the night. On the night of the 12th we moved to Afein, a distance of 12 miles, halting at midday for about two hours at Negiliat; we bivouacked for the night at Afein.

On the 13th we moved to Bir-el-Abd, some 8 miles away. This was our railhead, and the 8th were on outpost on the left section covering railhead. At this time, in order to familiarize everybody with local features of the landscape, we named the various points held by companies on outpost duty. I well remember riding round my companies, of which W, X, and Y were on outpost, with Z in reserve. On reaching W company (Captain Humble in command), the local conditions and the Company Commander's reputation for culinary triumphs irresistibly suggested the title " Humble Pie " for the position they held, which name may still be found on the map. O.C. W company was unmercifully chaffed about the name of his stronghold.

On 17th, the Brigade went into Divisional Reserve at Abd. Abd was just like any other portion of the desert, though perhaps hotter and scrubbier than usual, and ten days afterwards we moved to Ganadil, covering on the right flank Sal-mana—the new railhead. The 8th were then in Brigade Reserve with Z Company at Hod Geem, covering gun positions on our right rear.

On 26th October, a draft of 18 other ranks arrived, including Sergeants Wilson and Duff, old members of the battalion. On the 11th November another draft arrived from home, Sergeant Blair and 28 other ranks. The battalion remained at Ganadil until the 1st December, and I think we all enjoyed our time there. We did a lot of good work, the weather was very pleasant, and the moon for a few nights very brilliant. During this time we built a very excellent rifle range, which was the admiration of the Australian patrols who passed it. I forget(?) where we got the wood from, but we made targets which pivoted up and down, and erected them in a deep trench, which was, of course, constantly falling in. On this range we carried out grouping, application, and rapid practices. Alongside of this we made a field-firing range, where we had snap-shooting at " Peeping Toms " and " Running Man ", and fire-control practices were carried out by N.C.Os. We also did some useful night-work, and Captain Carson, who had rejoined us at Bir-el-Abd, did great work with the Scouts.

Towards the end of the month, the Brigadier thought we might arrange a shooting meeting, and we proceeded to get things *en train*, but we moved off again before it was possible to hold it.

On 1st December the Brigade trekked forward to Tillul, about 10 miles eastwards, and the next day on to Mazar, where we arrived at 1300 hours. We remained at Mazar until the 20th, during which time we had two or three days' Divisional manœuvres, on a scheme which as nearly as possible represented the Turkish position at Masaid, covering El-Arish, which we expected to have to take before we got into Arish. Most of the time here, W and Y Companies, under Major Coulson, were at Gererat, about 3½ miles away, digging wells.

Six officers arrived during the month: 2nd-Lieutenants

A company football team at Ganadil

Chef Paddy Cassidy fanning the flame

One of the old and bold on guard

The brothers Thomson

"Tea up!"

SOME OF THE LADS

R. G. L. Gray (6th S.R.), Somerville (8th S.R.), A. F. Grierson (5th S.R.), S. M. Campbell (5th S.R.), J. Miller (6th S.R.), and G. H. Moir (8th S.R.). The last had left the battalion at Kantara for the Flying Corps. An intrepid lad, he unfortunately managed to wreck two aeroplanes. These disasters, after a considerable period in hospital, secured his return to his unit. Probationer pilots, after two smashes, were, according to regulations, debarred from further employment as Flying Officers. It was bad luck on Moir who was very keen to fly, and I do not think that when he returned to the battalion again he was really fit.

On the 20th we moved to Maadan, and then on 21st to Meshalfat, doing a night march to the latter place. Between Meshalfat and Arish was the Turkish position of Masaid, which was evacuated by the enemy in a hurry on 20th or 21st. It was a strong position, but in point of fact, their rearguard was not strong enough to put up a fight. On our march from Meshalfat to Arish on 22nd, we were most interested in the Turkish trench dispositions, as far as they could be seen by us. I remember all the trenches were revetted with scrub, which kept them together extraordinarily well, but from the point of view of aeroplane reconnaissance, made them very visible. I may mention here that the Turks had, with great labour and perseverance, constructed a road of brushwood laid along the sand, which, I think, reached nearly as far as Bir-el-Abd, so that their guns and transport-wagons could move along without the wheels being a foot deep in sand. It is not my purpose here to discuss the Turkish invasion of Sinai, culminating in their attack on Romani, but one must do them the justice of acknowledging their skill in organization, methods of transport, and systems of trenches. Lack of water was the strongest factor against them, because it restricted their numbers and hampered their movements.

We arrived at El-Arish at about 1300 hours on the 22nd, and were the first British Infantry Brigade to enter the town during the war, and the first British dismounted troops there since the days of the Crusades. The *Daily Telegraph* War Special relates it as follows:

THE CAPTURE OF EL-ARISH

A NIGHT MARCH THROUGH THE DESERT

(*Daily Telegraph* War Service, Copyright)

EL-ARISH,
21st December.

" With the evacuation of El-Arish ends the Turco-German pretensions to attack the Suez Canal and invade Egypt. The Turks have retired from the most important strategic point of eastern Egypt, and whatever else they and their German masters may attempt, the campaign against Egypt is a hopeless failure. The Desert Column which forms part of the eastern Egypt Force was already moving to attack El-Arish when the Turks cleared out of the town, declining to hold their strong natural position presenting many difficult points to the attackers. Part of the column was yesterday at railhead. Concentration began at day-break, and throughout the day the rolling desert presented a wonderful spectacle. As far as the eye could reach, lines of Australians and New Zealand horsemen and Yeomanry, with mounted Divisional companies, splendidly mounted Camel Corps and Territorial Infantry, wound over the high scrub-covered sand dunes, some hidden in the valleys, others cutting the sky-line like razor blades.

" The column was escorted by airmen, who were frequently 10,000 feet up, and who kept off the enemy machines, a precaution which the repeated though ineffectual bombing of the last few days made necessary. Our airmen from dawn to dusk not only patrolled to protect the column, but denied an opportunity to the enemy to reconnoitre. Heavily laden trains were always carrying forward stores. To the fighting forces were always attached thousands of transport camels, and as the whole moved on a comparatively narrow front, the desert presented a striking picture of movement, and long after nightfall the camel convoys continued to fill every track, moving with a silence almost uncanny.

" Early in the evening information was brought into railhead that the Turks were leaving El-Arish. It was decided to push forward the mounted Division and Camel Corps to secure the town. Notwithstanding a trying day's march, the mounted men were again on the move well before midnight, and this night march, over miles of extremely difficult country, was carried out with such precision that the Camel Corps and Cavalry had completely surrounded the town as the sun's first shafts of light were flung up behind the eastern dunes. El-Arish was deserted by the Turkish

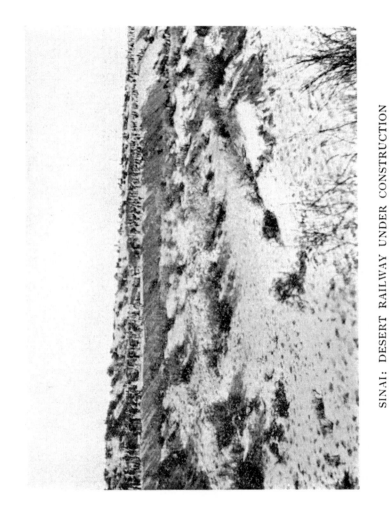

SINAI: DESERT RAILWAY UNDER CONSTRUCTION

troops. A few prisoners were taken outside, but the bulk of the population remained. They were hungry, but arrangements were soon made for feeding them.

" I rode from railhead to El-Arish with a mounted Brigade convoy. The country, seen by daylight, deeply impresses one with the character of the achievement of the mounted troops in the dark. For the first eight or nine miles there are rolling billows of sand, with the valleys gradually getting deeper, and plentiful scrub relieving the glare. Then commences a series of higher sandhills with no cover of vegetation, though here and there in the depression are small palm groves. These dunes have sharp crests, their sides in many places being as steep as cliffs, and the necessary windings are so frequent as materially to increase the crow-line distance. The hoof marks on these terrific gradients show that whole regiments often took the giddy path in very yielding sand, while seemingly impossible ascents make one regret that this night work could not be cinematographed to show the people at home how these intrepid horsemen got to their objectives.

" Towards the end of this waterless track the difficulties appear insurmountable. Perhaps the Turks so regarded them, for, though they were strongly entrenched at Masaid, five miles to the west, they had scarcely dug a trench at El-Arish. The trials of the horsemen were made vastly greater for the artillery, yet the guns were moved forward at the same time, though in places paths had to be beaten down on the sides of the hills. The whole movement affords high testimony to the magnificent efficiency of the force.

" El-Arish is a typical Oriental town of mud-brick dwellings, housing several thousand inhabitants. In peace time these people gain a livelihood from patches of cultivation in the Wadi-Arish and east thereof. The streets are wider and cleaner than is usual in such places, and there are fewer noisome smells than one is accustomed to in the native quarters of eastern towns. Except in one place, El-Arish showed few signs of warfare. The town had several times been bombarded from the sea. It is alike proof of the desire of the Navy to spare civilians and of its good gunnery that hardly a mud-brick house had been touched. The fort on the southern edge of the town, strongly built of stone, was demolished by the ships' gunfire at a range of several miles, and its thick walls were a mass of rubbish: yet the houses on three sides of the fort and close to it were undamaged.

" The population welcomed the arrival of the British Imperial troops. The first words from the poor people relieved from Turkish extortion and oppression were for ' Bakshish ' (present). They are getting this in the form of food, of which the Turks left them little."

This account deals chiefly with the achievements of the
mounted troops, and without doubt the chief onus of the
Magdaba-Nephl-Arish operations was borne by them, and to
them is due all credit. The slower infantry plodded doggedly
along in their wake enduring the well-accustomed hardships
of thirst, heat, and heavy going. They were an indispensable
backing for the Cavalry, and tradition has it that on one occasion
the Australians would only go forward on condition that the
52nd Division moved close upon their heels.

The night of the 22nd again saw us on outpost duty
covering the town to its east, with the 7th Royal Scots and the
7th Scottish Rifles on our right and left respectively, and we all
commenced at once to dig entrenchments. The last week of
December was cold and stormy; Christmas day itself was a
miserable day with heavy showers which flooded many a dug-
out, though we were much heartened by our home mail,
which, apart from private parcels, included the gifts from the
Regimental Comforts Fund, and " Jock's Box ".[1] One of the
great compensations of the campaign was the arrival of those
splendid packages from home, filled with every conceivable
thing calculated to conduce to the men's comfort. They owed
their being to the practical genius of Mrs. H. Monteith Hannan,
and to her untiring band of packers, backed up by the unfailing
Comforts Fund, which was ably administered by the Hon.
Colonel, Colonel Warden R. Maxwell, the late Captain J. W.
Arthur, and other generous-hearted friends of the battalion.
They would all have felt rewarded for their labours if they
could have seen the eagerness with which those large brown
sacking-covered parcels were hailed. Considering the difficulties of transport, both by sea and land, it was wonderful
how regularly our mails came in, though sometimes a fortnight elapsed between them.

January, 1917, was a quiet month, although we had some
visitations by day and by night from Taube aeroplanes, which
carried out some unpleasantly accurate bombing practices.
As a unit we were again lucky in escaping casualties. A facetious
message was sent from a company signaller, one Hunter, to

[1] Christmas gifts most generously sent out by the *Glasgow Evening News*.

his pal Connolly at Battalion Head-quarters, that " a Taube at night is the soldier's delight ", an unconcerned method of apprising us of the approach of the enemy aeroplane overhead, which, of course, everybody could hear. During the first week in January, the Wadi-Arish, which had been absolutely dry, in the course of a night suddenly became a fast-flowing river. One of the sentry posts of Y Company, placed somewhat low upon the river bank, was flooded out, and the occupants saved themselves with some difficulty from total immersion. Some native children, at the same time, who had essayed to cross the Wadi on a donkey's back, had a narrow escape from drowning. They were fortunately spotted by some of our men, who brought them back to terra firma. Bilsland, then with Z Company, on his return from the performance of some duty, came back to find his kit hanging out to dry upon a friendly fig tree, it having been rescued from drowning by his bâtman.

On the 9th we moved to a new outpost line on the east side of Wadi Arish, where we had to start afresh a new series of trenches. I remember I was rather pleased with our lot. We had three company areas with the 4th Company in reserve, beside Battalion Head-quarters. Each company lived just behind the trenches which it occupied at night. The trenches were well sited and at the same time well hidden. The formation of the ground, which was in small undulations with fig trees scattered here and there, lent itself successfully to this. But, of course, as usual, the trenches were never properly finished, because we moved forward just as they were beginning to look ship-shape. On the 22nd 2nd-Lieut. B. M. Walker and a further welcome addition of 26 other ranks arrived, and on 3rd February, Lieut. (Temp. Captain) R. S. Cree brought 22 other ranks.

During February we did some Brigade training from the 3rd to the 9th. We practised the formation of Brigade in attack, elementary night exercises, rear-guard action, and a night approach-march and attack, and then on the 21/22nd we carried out Divisional night-operations.

The Egyptian Labour Corps meantime had been working

hard at the Arish Defences, which were sited upon high sand dunes about one to one and a half miles east of the town, running from the shore for about two miles southwards and then south-westwards to the Wadi-Arish, and across it. The particular portion occupied and garrisoned by the battalion was Mount Murray, the most outstanding of these high sand dunes, which were in a way not unlike the Romani Defences, though the line was shorter and much steeper on the shore side. Mount Murray was so called after the Commander-in-Chief, Sir Archibald Murray, who came round and inspected the defences on the 28th February. With him were a few of his staff, including our old friend Major-General (now Sir) A. L. Lynden-Bell, his C.G.S. He had been the G.S.O. of 52nd Division before the war, when Major-General Spens commanded, and it was to him that the senior officers of the Division were indebted for a very great part of whatever we knew of tactical soldiering. It was good to see him again. Sir Archibald Murray was much interested in the defences, especially in a roomy Observation Post placed cunningly and well-hidden, which gave a wonderfully comprehensive view of the country to our front. The Arish Defences were constructed, as to the front-trenches at any rate, on a much more elaborate scale than those at Romani. Each trench, on account of the soft sand, had to be excavated to a greater depth and to more than double the breadth eventually required. That done, the double revetting, which was of wood and matting already prepared, was anchored in front and rear by means of wire stays, attached to deeply sunk stanchions. The revetting was given a certain amount of batter (i.e. made to lean outwards from the bottom upwards.) The sand was then again piled up outside in front and rear supporting the revetting to the height required for the parapets and parados. Finally elbow rests were constructed on the parapets, and to be more elaborate, dug-outs were here and there inserted, O.P.'s constructed, and recesses made for ammunition, water, &c. It was, of course, a costly business, thousands of Egyptian labourers being employed; but it was considered necessary, though, of course, we again moved forward before the de-

BATTALION HALTED ON THE MARCH FROM EL-ARISH

Showing wire netting laid on road to facilitate transport and marching on heavy sand

fences were nearly completed. As a matter of history, they were never used and soon became filled with sand. Constant occupation and attention is absolutely necessary to keep sand trenches serviceable. The amount of work the Labour Corps got through was gigantic—no trades-union " ca' canny " methods about them. Shirkers were summarily dealt with here. It was astonishing to notice almost incredible changes in the landscape whilst riding round, caused by the removal of whole sandhills. One of the officers in charge of this particular E.L.C. gang which worked upon Mount Murray was an ex-jockey who had been in the service of Kemal Pasha as such. At the outbreak of war he had been retained quietly for the first few months of the war, and then asked if he would give his " parole ". I do not know whether he gave it, but at any rate he escaped and came by a circuitous route to Egypt, and was taken on in the Labour Corps as he knew the " lingo ", and he certainly had a thorough grip of his gang. He informed me that if he were taken by the Turks he expected to be shot.

On 14th February Major R. N. Coulson was unfortunately again struck down with sciatica, and had to go off to hospital. I took on Carson as second-in-command, and A. F. Rogers was promoted Temporary Captain in command of Y Company.

About this time I recollect some sand shoes were issued out to us for trial. They were issued as an experiment and were somewhat similar to Canadian snow-shoes; they were alike also in that it was necessary to walk straight-footed, as the North American Indians do, or did. I know not if it was because there were many of us splay-footed or hen-toed, or because we were canny conservative Scots, but we found the new shoes more fatiguing to use than ordinary marching boots. It may be noted that the issue of these sand shoes, had it taken place, would have synchronized with our advent into Palestine, where the harder and rockier ground would have made them worse than useless.

Whilst at Mount Murray we again indulged each day in bathing parades, and also occasionally by night. In one unit (I forget which) one unfortunate while bathing got his false teeth dislocated in his mouth in such a way that he coughed them up and they became entombed in the depths of the Mediterranean. Thereafter was published a General Routine Order (G.R.O.) to the effect that men must remove their dentures while bathing.

On 6th March, Brigadier-General E. S. Girdwood was given the 74th Division, and promoted Major-General, and Lieut.-Colonel A. H. Leggett, D.S.O., from the 5th R.S.F. (155th Brigade) was posted to the 156th Brigade. We were sorry to lose General Girdwood, who had been for so long associated with the Brigade, but were pleased that he got a Division, and we knew that his successor was a first-rate soldier. The next day we moved forward to El Burg, and on the 8th again to Sheik Zowaid, where we went into bivouac. From here I had ten days' leave, Carson taking command. I think John Nicholl, my Transport-Officer, came on leave with me, and while he was away Bilsland acted as Transport-Officer. During the time he was in charge a camel broke loose, became " magnoon " and ran amuck, becoming positively dangerous. Male camels at the mating season often become unmanageable, and Bilsland dealt with this case in the only possible way— he put a bullet through the camel's head.

Arriving back on the 22nd from leave, I found myself in command of the Brigade, as the B.G.C. and Lieut.-Colonel Peebles had gone forward on a reconnaissance.

SINAI: SHEIK ZOWAID (ENTRANCE TO VILLAGE)

GAZA: SHEIK ABBAS—BATTALION HEAD-QUARTERS

On this, the most unpleasant, part of our line

CHAPTER VI

Gaza I, II, III

The Brigade crossed the frontier into Palestine on the 24th March, marching via Rafa, where a high straight rock is planted to mark the boundary, within a few miles of which across the border we found ourselves in gradually changing scenery. The everlasting sand gave place to somewhat barren and scrub-like undergrowth, then the country became more luxuriant, trees appeared miraculously, and flowers, somewhat sparsely, covered the sides of the road. It was really extraordinary how quickly, in the space of a few hours, the aspect of the country changed, and we began to experience some of the sensations which must have animated our old friend Joshua, who, if I remember aright, was the scout sent out by the Israelites to find a way to extricate them from the interminable sands of Sinai, when he found himself entering the Promised Land a few thousand years ago.

About 2100 we reached Khan Yunus, where we were met by the B.G.C. It had been a long march, but the pleasure of getting on to hard ground and of the new surroundings filled everyone with delight and anticipation.

On 28th March the first battle of Gaza was fought, and we could both hear and see something of it from Khan Yunus. On 30th the Brigade moved forward to Imseirat and rejoined the Division which was in general reserve there. We were never used during the battle. At Khan Yunus we had been on outpost duty guarding the right rear of the troops who took part in the attack, and also of our communications, because, if I remember aright, the railway line had reached that point just about this time. In fact, the Transport-Officer had the experience of taking the horses to water at Deir-el-Belah (the then railhead), along what appeared to be an ordinary track —on his return he found that the track had turned into a railway line. Modern magic as accomplished by desert engineers! We remained at Imseirat until the 16th April, during which time two officers, Lieut. E. R. Boyd and 2nd-Lieut. Bathgate, and 100 other ranks reported for duty. On the 15th the Turks, who occasionally harassed us with long-range H.E. shell fire, sent over a single well-directed shot into X Company's bivouac tents, killing one man, and severely wounding Lieut. J. K. Scotland and seven other ranks. I remember one day, we as a Brigade were required to do a march to the rear, to simulate a pretended retreat. Other troops did likewise, and still others moving backward used branches of trees to raise dust. During these convolutions the Turkish aeroplanes came over. History does not relate whether they were deceived, but at any rate it was some time before we got back to bivouac and a meal. On the 17th the battalion, less a nucleus of officers consisting of Lieut. (Temp. Captain) E. R. Boyd, Lieuts. M'Combie and R. S. Cree, 2nd-Lieut. Bathgate, and 87 other ranks, moved forward to a rendezvous on the other side of Wadi Guzzi—Y and Z Companies having to go off to form an escort under Major Carson to 261st and 262nd Batteries, R.F.A. On the 19th the second battle of Gaza took place, and I now print my orders for the approach-march, and narrative of events of the action as written by me at the time.

1/8TH SCOTTISH RIFLES
OPERATION ORDER No. 15
By Lieut.-Colonel J. M. Findlay, Commanding

16/4/17.
Reference map Gaza (X) 1. 40,000.
1. Information. As verbally explained to all Officers.
2. Intention.　　　,,　　　　　,,　　　　　,,
3. March.
　　(1). Battalion (less Y and Z Companies) will parade on battalion parade ground at 2130 to-night.

(2). *Dress and Equipment.* Equipment and rations as laid down in Battalion Order No. IV dated 13/4/17, to which should be added, 1 Haversack per man and 2 Haversacks per Bomber.

(3). *Ammunition.* No. of rounds to be carried by Specialists will be as under:

Lewis Gunners	.	50 Rounds.
Runners	.	100 ,,
Bombers	.	100 ,,
Signallers	.	50 ,,
Stretcher Bearers .	.	50 ,,
All other ranks carry	.	170 ,,

(4). *Stretcher Bearers* will carry Rifles.

(5). *Pipers* may carry their pipes.[1]

4. TRANSPORT.

(1). *Camels* will be drawn from lines at 2030 and will be loaded according to scale issued to Company Officers by Q.M. Companies will detail escort at rate of 1 man to three Camels.

Transport will be parked when loaded in front of 1/1 L.F.A.

(2). *Riders.* Following Riders only will be taken with battalion:

C.O. 1, 2nd in Command 1, Adjt. 1, Intelligence Officer 1, Liaison Officer 1.

(3). *1st-Line Transport* (S.A.A. Tools, Sig. and Med. Stores) will march immediately in rear of battalion. On arrival at crossings C17 it will take post in the Wadi Guzzi in a position which has been pointed out to all concerned and will come under the orders of the B.T.O.

(4). *2nd-Line Transport.* Rations and Transport will be brigaded under orders of Lieut. J. M. Nicholl to whom special instructions have been issued.

5. ESCORT TO R.A. Y and Z Companies under command of Major Carson will form an escort to Artillery. They will be accompanied by their Tool and S.A.A. Camels. Major Carson will issue special orders for the escort.

6. PICKS AND SHOVELS. As it is essential that every man should be dug-in by dawn on 17th, picks and shovels will be carried by the men to Brigade Rendezvous. These will be collected and returned to battalion Tool Camels in Wadi Guzzi by 0430 to-morrow.

7. LIGHTS, &c. No lights, fires, or talking will be permitted and special care is to be taken when digging-in, to prevent undue noise. Only after clear daylight may smoking be permitted.

8. WATER BOTTLES. Every officer and man will leave Camp with a full water bottle which must last until dark on 17th instant.

[1] Pipers ordinarily acted as stretcher bearers.

9. DUMP. All surplus kits, blankets, &c., will be dumped at Q.M.'s stores by 1900.

10. SPECIAL MESSAGE. The C.O. desires to express to all ranks that whatever may be the rôle attached to this battalion, he is confident that everyone will do his utmost to maintain the high reputation which it has earned during the war, and that all hardships and dangers will be borne unflinchingly during the next few days so that the battalion may have its share, and an honourable one, in the forthcoming defeat of the Turks.

11. REPORTS. To head of battalion.

Issued by Orderly at .... hour.

```
Copy No. 1 Brigade.
    „    2 C.O.
    „    3 Adjutant.
    „    4 O.C. W Company.
    „    5  „  X    „
    „    6  „  Y    „
    „    7  „  Z    „
    „    8 Transport-Officer.
    „    9 Q.M.
```

NARRATIVE OF OPERATIONS AND ACTION OF 1/8TH SCOTTISH RIFLES FROM 16TH TO 19TH APRIL, 1917 (INCLUSIVE)

16th April. With a view to taking part in operations against Gaza positions occupied by Turks, 156th Infantry Brigade, in Divisional Reserve, moved at 2130 to Wadi Guzzi, crossing by C17 and digging-in in neighbourhood of centre of T.1.2.7.8, the 8th Battalion Scottish Rifles (less two companies Y and Z) being about T.1.2.a.4.5.[1] The left half battalion (Y and Z companies) under Major Carson, detailed as escort to the 261st and 262nd Batteries, Royal Field Artillery, rendezvoused in neighbourhood of Sheikh Nebhan at 2200 yards west of Dorset House.

17th April. Brigade remained in same place all day while Sheikh Abbas and Mansura Ridges were being occupied by our troops. Gun escort received orders at 1748 to take up position in neighbourhood of Nukhabir Wadi and south-east

---

[1] Such hieroglyphics are map-coordinates.

BEFORE GAZA: Z COMPANY COOKHOUSE BEHIND KURD HILL

of double hills 230 R.29. Position actually taken up about R.30.C.3.

18th April. Brigade still in position of T.1.2.7.8. About 1800 battalion received orders to move to position under Mansura Ridge with a view to attack at dawn. Half battalion acting as gun escort rejoined battalion under Mansura Ridge between 2330 and 2400 midnight.

19th April. Our artillery began bombardment at 0530 and continued until 0730, at which hour the 52nd Division Infantry attack was timed to commence. 8th Scottish Rifles on the left of 156th Brigade was given a frontage of 400 yards, and was to advance with left directed on the centre of Green Hill, a pole on that hill marking quite definitely the left; immediate objective the capture of Green Hill and Ali-el-Muntar; advance to be by the left. 8th Scottish Rifles to link up with and conform to movements of the 1/4th Royal Scots Fusiliers, right battalion of 155th Brigade on our left—4th Royal Scots were on our right. Battalion went forward in 8 lines of half companies, at 200 yards distance, Z Company leading, followed by Y and W and X in that order. Major Carson followed on right rear of Y Company, with telephonic communication to Battalion Head-quarters, which was with X Company. Leading half company went over left corner Mansura Ridge, R.23 b.2.8. at 0735, the right of 155th Brigade not being sufficiently far advanced to admit of starting at appointed hour 0730. Our left linked up with the 155th Brigade at 0750. Advance continued slowly till about 0900, when it was held up till 155th Brigade captured Outpost Hill, which they did about 1000. Advance then continued until our leading line reached point about 400 yards south-west of track running out of enemy position between Middlesex Hill and Green Hill, i.e. between the arrow on and the M of Middlesex Hill, R.5.b.4.0. Orders were then received at 1140 from Brigade via 4th Royal Scots, not to advance farther till ordered, as 155th Brigade were checked. By this time the company of 1/4th Royal Scots Fusiliers on our left being comparatively screened from the enemy, had moved along to south-east slope of Middlesex Hill, and had got ahead of the remainder of their Brigade on the top of that hill, so that when the enemy counter-attacked, and the 155th Brigade was obliged to fall back from the north-west side of Middlesex Hill, this company got separated from the remainder of its Brigade, and along with our leading companies was in danger of being enfiladed and rolled up. The enemy, as far as could be seen, re-captured Outpost Hill about 1430. At this time enemy snipers began to move down the slopes of Middlesex Hill on the flank of 8th Scottish Rifles, and in rear of the company of 4th Royal Scots Fusiliers. To meet them, and any possible attack from that direction, 3 platoons of W Company were swung round on my orders to face Middlesex Hill. Orders were received from Brigade that positions were to be maintained till dark when our advanced line was to be withdrawn to point to be fixed, in rear. About 1730, however, enemy fire and pressure on the company of 155th Brigade on our left caused it to give way slightly, and this was followed by the unexpected retiral of the troops on our right, thus leaving my leading companies no option but to follow suit. The whole line then had to withdraw under heavy fire from enemy machine-guns, cross-rifle, and shell fire, and fell back about 800 yards and took up position near R.11d.3.8., where it was reinforced by the 7th Scottish Rifles and a section of the Machine-gun Company. With the exception of a few of the men who had been swung round to face Middlesex Hill, and who were caught up in the retiral of the company on our left, the battalion retired steadily and for the first half of the withdrawal the rear platoons constantly turned, lay down, and gave support to those retiring; this was facilitated and made possible by the fact that most of the enemy fire was from our left front and flank. Darkness had now set in, and steps were at once taken to consolidate and improve the new position against any possible counter-attack by the enemy. Connection was established and maintained with the 157th Brigade, who had replaced the 155th Brigade on our left; and before day-break, front line and a few support trenches had been dug and a certain amount of wiring had been done by the Royal Engineers. Our casualties during the day were between

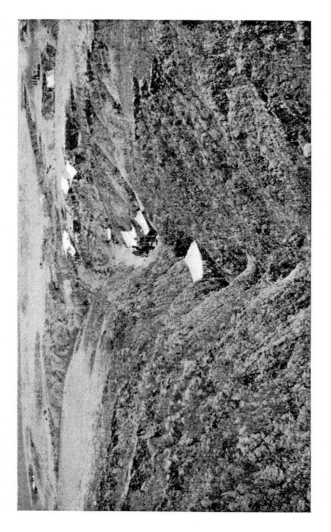

BEFORE GAZA: X COMPANY BIVOUACS

In a nullah typical of the many which intersected the entire front over which we had to advance on the first day of the Second Battle of Gaza

150–170 killed and wounded, including one officer killed and nine wounded,[1] and considering what had been accomplished they had been heavy. The great majority were amongst the two leading companies, and were the result chiefly of machine-gun and cross-rifle fire; the enemy shell fire, though at times heavy, did comparatively little damage. The loss of so many officers was more especially felt when those two companies had to withdraw from their advanced position. The weather all day was fine and the visibility good. As far as could be seen the enemy machine-gun positions at the base of the south-west end of Green Hill, from which fire was chiefly directed on our battalion, had been very little affected by our artillery bombardment.

28/4/17.   J. M. F.

NOTES

(1). More time should be given for food before men go into action.

(2). The entire success of the attack depended upon the taking of the enemy's strong points, and on carrying out of the turning movement by 54th Division. Neither of these came off, principally owing to the fact that the attack was more or less a repetition of the tactics employed on the previous attack (1st Gaza), and therefore the enemy were able to anticipate moves.

(3). The value of the artillery bombardment and the effect of the Tanks were much over-estimated.

(4). The trench mortars used by the enemy with H.E. did great damage.

(5). Turkish snipers were at first troublesome, but were soon got under.

(6). Enemy machine-gun emplacements were well hidden.

The attack of the Division over open country, by two Infantry Brigades (157th being in reserve), was a fine spectacle. For about 2 miles, both in breadth and depth, lines upon lines of men could be seen advancing, apparently impervious to the shells bursting among them. That was what we could see from a view point on the ground. From the air, the attack must have been a magnificent sight, with the 54th Division on our right, in similar formation, doing their big turning

---

[1] For exact casualties see Appendix II.

movement, and the 53rd on our left prolonging the attack up the coast.

As to the tactics of the battle, I am not in a position to say much. They were, as far as I can gather, much the same as the first Gaza show, which would have been entirely successful, according to general opinion, had more tenacity of purpose been shown. Anxiety then as to water for cavalry horses withdrew troops which, I have been told by Australians themselves, actually were in Gaza. I believe the 53rd Division did extremely well in the first Gaza battle, suffered severely, and were somewhat shaken. This naturally affected their performance in the second battle, their advance on the shore sector being held up early in the day.

I must say that I was very proud of the battalion, as they moved steadily forward, never flinching at the bursting shells and machine-gun fire. Z Company was most gallantly led by Captain C. E. Findlay, who with his officers carried out the movements as if on a peace parade, as did all the companies that followed. When the retiral took place, Captain Findlay brought up the rear of his company, carrying in, at the same time, a wounded man. His M.C. was well earned. One of his officers, 2nd-Lieut. V. C. A. M'Leod, a keen photographer, also earned the undying admiration of his company. Instead of lying as flat as he could, when shells burst near by, he jumped up on several occasions, ran as near to the explosion as he could get in the time, to photograph the shell burst, until ordered by his Company-Commander to cease his daft performances. However irregular, these are the sort of things which bind officers and men together in the understanding and affection which create *esprit de corps*. M'Leod was wounded, but returned in July only to be killed a couple of months after by an isolated shell, which got him in the front trenches one evening as he was going his rounds. He was a fine lad.

During the whole of this action I was in telephone communication with Brigade, and also, except for one or two intervals, on account of disturbance, with Major Carson, O.C. firing line. When the retiral took place, I expected a counter-attack by the Turks, but I think they were not

CAPTAIN DULIEU, ADJUTANT

In his Orderly Room at El-Sireh (before Gaza)

organized for it on any effective scale, and if they ever thought of it, which I now doubt, they were decided against it by the prompt action of General Leggett, who from his battle Head-quarters saw the retiral, and who turned all the available guns at his disposal on to the Turkish positions on Middlesex Hill.

That night was a much more anxious time for me than the day. I found that though it was reported to me that we were in touch with the 157th Brigade, we actually were not, and further, that my right flank was not linked up with the 7th Scottish Rifles, who, after reinforcing us, had moved off to our right, closing a gap between ourselves and the Royal Scots. The first was easy of adjustment, and touch with the 157th Brigade was established, but the second proved to be difficult. I went out myself with one or two Battalion Scouts, and having fixed up connection on my left with 157th Brigade I came along my front line and moved backwards and forwards on my right flank, but could not find the 7th Scottish Rifles. It was a pitch-black night, my battalion were digging and wiring hard, and if the line was not properly linked-up, it meant that a good deal of that work would go for nothing, and it was essential that our line should be intact by dawn. During the whole night I confidently expected a counter-attack from the Turks, and at one time, when well out in front in my search, they started a terrific blatter of fire, with shoutings and cursings, at us *sans doute*. The scouts didn't like it, but I remembered from Gallipoli experiences a little way the Turk had of firing in the air, with yells of defiance and adjurations to Allah. Moreover, we actually saw here and there the fire from rifle muzzles pointing heavenwards, and no movement forward was made by the enemy, for which I for one was devoutly thankful. The manifestations however showed me that we had come too far forward, and that my search could not continue farther in that direction, so we came back some distance and finally located the 7th Scottish Rifles. I then withdrew my right flank and linked up with them by putting out platoon and L.G. posts. We remained on this line for the next few days, thinning it out by day by two companies, which were ordered to slip back steadily in twos and threes, after " stand-down " each morning. They rendez-voused behind the Mansura Ridge, resting during the day, reinforcing the line again at night. On the evening of the 21st I received orders that the Brigade would retire to a line some 1200 yards in rear, and at midnight on 21/22nd we withdrew to the new line, bringing our sandbags and wire with us. The new line had been reconnoitred by the B.G.C. and traced with white tape, so that as soon as the withdrawal was completed (and it was carried out in excellent order), the usual unceasing digging and wiring could commence forthwith. By dawn on the 22nd the line was dug to a depth of 2 feet 6 inches, on a 1400 yards front, and wired throughout its whole length.

While those front trenches were being constructed a series of redoubt lines were also started, and on the 27th the battalion took its turn in their occupation and construction, moving back to El-Sireh on the 6th May, when the Brigade went into Divisional Reserve. Each company moved independently from a redoubt, leaving a party to hand over, X and Y Com-panies going direct to Slagheap, Z Company to the back of Kurdhill, and W Company, with Battalion Head-quarters and transport, to R.20.6.2.3, a position about 500 yards behind, or due west of Slagheap. Up till the end of May the battalion did a great deal of digging and wiring both in the front trenches and the redoubt line.

During May there were continuous movements of officers both coming from and going to the battalion. Major Carson and Dulieu went home on special leave, Captain Findlay, 2nd-Lieuts. R. G. L. Gray and A. Rodger went to hospital sick, while Lieut. H. Bowen, our old friend and valued Quarter-master, was killed while sitting in his bivouac reading his latest paper from home. The Turks had been shelling one of our aeroplanes, and it was a splinter from one of their shells that came right through the bivouac and killed him. He was an ideal Quartermaster, liked and admired by all, and he had the sunniest temperament ever gifted to man. We mourned his loss deeply, and when he was buried, despite our acquired

OUR MOST GALLANT AND UBIQUITOUS M.O.
CAPTAIN A. B. SLOAN

Through whose hands every man of us passed at some time or other

feeling of accustomedness to death, there was hardly a dry eye among us. Six officers arrived back to the battalion: Major R. N. Coulson from hospital, Captain Westland, Lieuts. Ferguson and MacLaren, and 2nd-Lieut. Carslaw, after recovery from wounds on 19th April, and 2nd-Lieut. J. T. Neilson from the armoured train to which he had been attached for some months. In June there were a lot of officer movements, some going on short leave to Cairo or to various places for Instructional Courses, and the usual quota to and from hospital. During this month also a draft of 28 other ranks arrived from home, most of whom had seen service on the same front already. The battalion strength at the beginning of the month was 20 officers and 652 other ranks, exclusive of those on detached duties, of whom there were usually about 4 officers and nearly 100 other ranks. Towards the end of the month 6 officers reported for duty from Garrison battalions, three from (The King's) Liverpool Regiment, Lieuts. G. P. Farran and G. P. Rowland and 2nd-Lieut. E. A. Settle, and three from 20th Battalion Rifle Brigade, Lieuts. D. J. P. Davies, J. Murray, and P. E. Frankau; Captain Humble (wounded 19/4/17) also returned from hospital on the 12th June, 1917.

On the 1st July, my Medical Officer, Captain A. B. Sloan, who had mobilized with the battalion, and who had rendered devoted service to all ranks at all times, had to go off to hospital, much to everyone's regret. He was a very conscientious and capable doctor, and he shone when the battalion was in action, never sparing himself—always cool and collected, he inspired his subordinates and was well served. He never came back to the battalion, being promoted Major, and eventually getting command of a Casualty-Clearing-Station at Belah. Captain J. Browne, R.A.M.C.(T.), replaced him. Shortly afterwards I lost two other useful officers, Lieut. A. S. Bilsland going to Brigade as Assistant Staff-Captain, and 2nd-Lieut. W. Somerville to the 156th Trench Mortar Battery.

We again went into the line on the 19th July, relieving the 16th Battalion Royal Devon Yeomanry Regiment at the Sheik Abbas Apex locality. While we were at the Apex we carried

8

out a considerable amount of patrolling in No Man's Land.
The Turks were also active in patrolling, and their numbers
on patrol were usually much stronger than ours. On the
night of the 25/26th July (I happened to be away on short
leave to Cairo), Captain Hannan was ordered to take out a
patrol consisting of 4 officers, 50 other ranks, and 2 Lewis
guns, with a view to taking on a strong Turkish patrol which
we had ascertained perambulated No Man's Land at its
pleasure. Captain Hannan had no difficulty in locating them,
but found them considerably stronger than his own patrol.
They must have numbered about 200, and they employed
the same tactics that we found later were practised by the
Germans. The patrol moved in fairly close formation, and as
soon as their advance-screen had located the enemy, detach-
ments were sent from behind to try to envelop each flank.
This is exactly what happened in this case; Hannan, as soon
as he found that he was up against the enemy, ordered his
men to lie down, got his guns on his flanks, and prepared to
take them on. No further movement on his front, but soon
he got hurried information that both flanks were being approached. He gave the order to retire so as to clear his
flanks, and immediately the retiral commenced the Turks
opened fire. He succeeded in getting clear, turned and proceeded to give the Turks rapid rifle and Lewis gun fire, which
effectually prevented them carrying out any further offensive
movement. He then brought his patrol in; his casualties were
four missing and eleven wounded. One of the missing was
Sergeant W. Leitch, a gallant and able N.C.O. who had a
few months previously been in charge of the Divisional Guard
supplied by our battalion, and who had been complimented
by the G.O.C. and the Corps Commander on its smartness
and efficiency.

Unexpected casualties by shell fire are recorded continuously in the War Diary for July. Poor M'Leod was killed
and his orderly wounded on the 18th. Four men of a wiring
party were killed on 24th, two men wounded on 28th, and
four on 29th, and on 30th four were killed and three
wounded, and another man was killed on 31st. In short,

the Apex locality was not a very healthy resort at that
time.

During the month Major Carson returned from home
leave, and Lieut. Ollerenshaw, who had been Bandmaster
with the battalion, turned up to fill the position of Quartermaster vice poor old Bowen.

The weather had, of course, become hotter and hotter
since the April battle, but there was no rest for the weary.
The Division was depleted in numbers, and this entailed all
the harder work upon those left. We were constantly employed
digging or wiring, or patrolling, or on ordinary trench duties.
Work had to be carried out at night, which from the temperature point of view was advantageous, but on the other hand
it was hardly possible to get any really sound sleep during the
day. We went into Divisional Reserve again on the 6th August,
being relieved at the Apex by the 6th Battalion Highland
Light Infantry — an expeditiously carried out relief — and
we marched back to a bivouac area on Wadi Simeon.
The next day Dulieu came back from home leave, and
young Souter left us for Divisional Staff where he was to
act as A.D.C. to Major - General Smith, the Divisional
Commander.

On the 11th, the Brigade took part in a raid by the Camel
Corps upon Sana, Hairpin, and Atawineh Redoubts, and the
Bagdad-Atawineh system, a series of Turkish defences, which
were about two miles away on our right front, east from
Mendur.[1] Our job was to protect the left flank of the Camel
Corps and to secure their withdrawal. The battalion was in
Brigade Reserve at Asafereiyeh, and was not called upon for
action until 2300, when X and Y Companies took up positions
covering Wadi Sihan and the approaches from Barley Ridge,
and blocking Vale of Dead Horse, where they remained until
the Brigade withdrew. Nothing was seen or heard of the
enemy by the battalion, and it was reported afterwards that
the Camel Corps had found the redoubts unoccupied. Battalion
Head-quarters and X and Y Companies were ordered to

---

[1] See map *Palestine: Gaza and Wadi Hesi* at end of book. Mendur is just off the map to
the south of Charing Cross.

withdraw at 0130 on the 12th August, and the rearguard W and Z Companies followed at 0200.

The same day the following officers arrived from the United Kingdom, along with a draft of 260 other ranks: 2nd-Lieuts. J. A. Anderson, H. G. Carswell, A. Macdougall, and G. D. Watson—a splendid reinforcement.

On the 23rd August we relieved the 5th Royal Scots Fusiliers in the Mendur locality, garrisoning the redoubts there as follows:

W Company.—Oxted, Milford, Woking, with a platoon in reserve.

X Company.—Ripley, Dorking, Reigate, with a platoon in reserve.

Y Company.—Croyden, Merrow, Farnham, Cobham (second-line redoubts).

Z Company.—In reserve.

The 13th Field Company, Royal Engineers (Major Jackson) was attached to us. The garrisoned second-line trenches were in rear and on the right of the redoubts. The Mendur locality is low-lying and very dusty. What little breeze came its way wafted the most penetrating and dirty sand into all the nooks and crannies of our dug-outs. There were a few broken-down houses which it was wise to avoid. The whole place seemed " germy " and filthy, and while there we were much troubled by outbreaks of sandfly fever. This was successfully disseminated by the clouds of dust raised by the continual traffic of horses, mules, and camels, interminable lines of which came to be watered at the pumping-station situated near by. One did not envy the job of the Sappers in charge.

Sandfly fever is a sort of mild dysentery. I fell a victim to it myself, and it is exceedingly unpleasant for a few days. It is more like influenza, I think, than anything else. The symptoms are lassitude, weariness, and headache, accompanied by high fever, during which time one may become delirious. After about five days the fever abates, leaving one faint, but rejoicing. 30 per cent or 40 per cent of the battalion

BEFORE GAZA: APSLEY HOUSE CAMP

Looking towards Wadi Nukhabir

were down with it from first to last, and practically all had to go off to hospital, returning after a compensating week or two of recuperation in Alexandria.

Major Carson commanded the battalion, in my absence on sick leave in Alexandria, from 31st August till 10th September, when Coulson returned from Zeitoun, where he had been attending a Senior Officers' Course. Then Carson went off to a Staff job, much to my regret and that of his company. He eventually was promoted to be Lieutenant-Colonel, and was awarded the O.B.E. During September we got through a lot of musketry on a local range, at which also the Lewis guns were tested. We had attached to us for a few days for instruction representatives of all ranks of the 123rd (Outram's) Rifles, Indian Army. The men were a fine-looking lot, clean and smart, and impressed me as reliable. Their Commanding Officer, Lieut.-Colonel Cassels, was a good soldier and a kindly man. The next time I came across him was at Neby Samwil, where his battalion had a very bad time, sustaining many casualties, but where they had done exceedingly well. A new Medical Officer arrived on the 13th for the battalion, Captain F. W. Clark, R.A.M.C., vice Browne, who went to a Casualty-Clearing-Station. Clark remained with the battalion until the beginning of 1919, and proved himself a keen and capable Medical Officer, popular with both officers and men, and always ready and willing for his job. His Military Cross was well earned later on in Flanders.

On the night of 13/14th, the battalion was relieved by the 1/4th Duke of Cornwall's Light Infantry, and went into bivouac at Apsley House, another dusty spot, being near a main road up to the Apex, and here I found them when I arrived back from hospital on 22nd.

It may be interesting to include here a strength return, giving the distribution of extra-regimentally employed men, to show the layman how with a nominal strength of 25 officers and 836 other ranks, a fighting strength of only about 500 is easily arrived at. Out of the total strength of the battalion a nucleus of about 3 officers and 150 other ranks had to be left behind, together with the transport personnel, &c.

	Officers.	Other Ranks.
Strength on 31st August, 1917	26	838
Left battalion	6	145
	20	693
Joined battalion	5	143
Strength on 30th September, 1917	25	836
With battalion	22	667
Transport	1	55
Battalion dump	—	3
S. 12a dump	—	2
A.S.C. dump	—	8
Divisional compound	—	4
" Change of air camp ", El-Arish	—	1
Divisional rest camp	—	6
Branch sch., El-Arish	—	4
Imperial sch., Zeitoun	—	3
Central sch., Tel-el-Kebir	—	1
Leave in Egypt	—	21
Divisional water course under W.S.O., 52nd Division	—	7
Pioneer company attached 412 field company, R.E.	—	33
New details camp, Belah	—	4
Attached 75th Division (Transport)	—	15
Duty	—	2
Attached 1/8 Scottish Rifles	2	—
	25	836

The latter half of September and month of October was spent in intensive training, with a move on 14th October to Regent's Park, rather a pleasant bivouac area near the sea where a fresh breeze usually tempered the mid-day heat.   A typical training programme (shown on p. 103) gives a good idea of our work.   It is a fairly comprehensive one, and it must be remembered that there were numberless other duties and supervisings required of officers and N.C.Os. not detailed in the programme.

While at Regent's Park, considerable administrative work was carried out.   Tin helmets were issued, tools were made up to mobile scale, and all kit, surplus to bare necessities, was collected and sent to a dump at Belah.

On the 30th September, Major-General J. Hill, D.S.O., inspected the Brigade.   General Hill had come to the Division vice Major-General W. E. B. Smith to France, at the

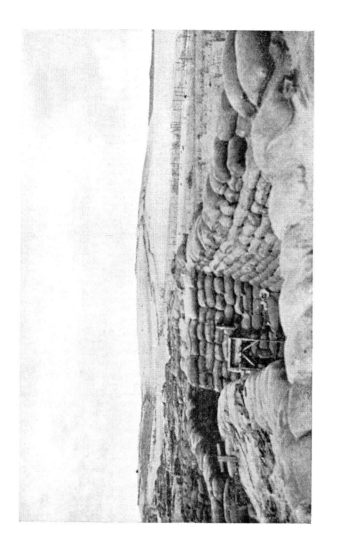

GAZA: SAMSON'S RIDGE

From part of our line on Hereford Ridge

1/8TH BATTALION SCOTTISH RIFLES

PROGRAMME OF TRAINING FOR WEEK ENDING 29TH SEPTEMBER, 1917

Hours of Parade.	Monday, 24/9/17.	Tuesday, 25/9/17.	Wednesday, 26/9/17.	Thursday, 27/9/17.	Friday, 28/9/17.	Saturday, 29/9/17.
0600 to 0700.	Bayonet Fighting. Rapid Loading and Firing.	Physical Drill. Dummy Bomb Throwing.	Bayonet Fighting. Rapid Loading and Firing.	Physical Drill. Dummy Bomb Throwing.	Bayonet Fighting. Rapid Loading and Firing.	Physical Drill. Dummy Bomb Throwing.
0800 to 0915.	Company Drill (Close Order) and Practice in Rapid Deployment.					
0930 to 1030.	LECTURE. (1) On *Esprit de Corps*, Regimental Achievements, Names, Ranks, and Appointments of Battalion Officers. (2) *Discipline*.	LECTURE. (1) On March Discipline. (2) *Gas Drill*. Standard Tests.	LECTURE. (1) On Short Reports and Messages. Sanitation and Cleanliness. (2) *Saluting Drill*.	LECTURE. (1) On the Normal Formation of the Attack. (2) *Gas Drill*. Standard Tests.	LECTURE. (1) On Place Names, Location of all Units in the vicinity. Points of the Compass. (2) *Saluting Drill*.	LECTURE. (1) On Battalion Organization and Points of Military Law. (2) *Gas Drill*. Standard Tests.
1515 to 1615.	*Normal Formation for the Attack by Companies*.	Route Marching by Companies. Details as to Route and Hour of Starting will be issued later. *Dress:* Fighting Order. No Packs.	HALF-HOLIDAY.	*Normal Formation for the Attack by Battalion*.	Route Marching by Companies. Details as to Route and Hour of Starting will be issued later. *Dress:* Fighting Order. No Packs.	HALF-HOLIDAY.
1615 to 1715.	Battalion Drill (ceremonial) and *Handling of Arms*.			Battalion Drill (ceremonial). The *March Past* to be practised.		

REMARKS.—(1) Except where otherwise ordered the DRESS for all TRAINING will be DRILL ORDER.   (2) C.O.'s Orderly Room will be held at 1130 Daily, at which all Officers will attend.   Orderly Room will be immediately followed by a LECTURE to all Officers given by the C.O. and Second in Command on alternate days.   (3) The ROLL showing exemptions from PARADE will be rigidly adhered to.   (4) Live Bomb Throwing for ALL RANKS who have not yet thrown a Live Bomb will be carried out on Thursday, commencing at 0600, and continuing at the rate of twenty men every one and a half hours till training is completed.   (5) Specialist Training will be carried out daily from 0930 to 1030.   (6) All Officers, Warrant Officers, Sergeants, and Lance-Sergeants will parade at 1700 on Wednesday for Instruction in Bayonet Fighting.   (7) Each Company will detail three N.C.Os. to report at Battalion Head-quarters at 0930 daily for Instruction in Machine Guns.

From 1030 to 1130 on Monday, 24 9 0 17, a demonstration of Rapid Wiring and Intensive Digging by Royal Engineers at Big Marquee will be given.   All available Officers and N.C.Os. will attend.

W. D. DULIEU, Lieutenant and Adjutant, 1 8 Scottish Rifles.

beginning of September, and, aware of our impending attack, the third on Gaza, he had instituted throughout the Division the intensive training we had spent the last few weeks in carrying out. I remember at the time we were having a platoon bivouac competition, which resulted in wonderful landscape gardening. Regent's Park, though so near the sea, was here and there clad in verdure; palms and junipers, and one or two trees which clustered round the well, gave the otherwise arid sandy waste its name. Rough hands were laid upon this vegetation, and many little platoon gardens were cleverly achieved, with name and address of occupants outlined in shells on the little sand-banks which did duty for the separating garden walls. General Hill was much pleased with the show. He was very keen on all units having tidy and smart camp areas, hence the competition. He also noticed a considerable improvement in the battalion's smartness as a result of our hard training. That same evening we left our " Garden City " and moved up to a position just behind the front line, called the Flintshire Defences, portion of a second line of redoubts, near Sheik Ajhlin. From here we used to go up regularly to the front-line O.P.'s, and scan the ground between us and the Turkish front-line trenches. Aeroplane photographs also helped our reconnaissances very much, so that when we came to do an attack we were able to recognize landmarks and profit by that knowledge. The actual time and date of our attack was dependent upon the success of our troops against Beersheba and its environments, situated some 30 miles on our right.

Beersheba was taken on 30th October, and 10 p.m. on 1st November was fixed as our " Zero hour ". For an attack of this sort orders in considerable detail have to be thought out and issued some time before the action; but it is only very shortly before the attack that one knows what moment " Zero hour " represents. The artillery bombardment was always intensified for an hour or two at nights, so that when our attack actually was launched the Turks, accustomed for some days to periodic intense bombardments, were not prepared (at least it was hoped not) for the ensuing infantry assault. The troops entrusted with the attack on the night of 1st

LIEUT.-COLONEL J. M. FINDLAY

At No. 1 Supply Dump (Third Battle of Gaza)

November were the 54th Division, to which was attached
the 156th Brigade. It is interesting to note that Major-General
S. W. Hare, G.O.C. of the 54th Division, had been our B.G.C.
in Falkirk at the beginning of the War, and if he was glad to
have us under his command (as he said he was), we were also
only too pleased to meet him, and to serve under him again.
To us, the 156th Brigade, were allotted two objectives, Umbrella Hill and El-Arish Redoubt, both of which positions it
was decided should be taken as preliminary operations to the
attack on the rest of the Turkish line to the sea, which the
54th were to undertake.

At this time on the ordinary roster for Brigade duties
it was our turn for the odd jobs, so to my chagrin it fell to our
lot to be split up, one company being attached to the 4th Royal
Scots, who were to attack El-Arish Redoubt, and one company
to the 7th Scottish Rifles, whose objective was Umbrella Hill.
Without doubt it was a necessary increase to these battalions,
especially the 4th Royal Scots, who not only required the
five companies they started with, but next day had to be reinforced by the 7th Royal Scots, who were Brigade Reserve.
My companies I detailed as follows: Y Company (Captain
R. S. Cree) to the 7th Scottish Rifles, and Z Company (Captain
J. J. M'Combie) to the 4th Royal Scots, whilst W Company
(Captain A. F. Rogers) and X Company (Captain W. D.
Hannan) were to act as carrying companies to these two
battalions respectively.

The usual nucleus of officers and other ranks having been
sent off to Belah, and having dispatched Y and Z to their
respective battalions, I proceeded with Battalion Head-
quarters and X Company to a huge dump of war material,
ammunition, bombs, sandbags, wire, picks, and shovels,
stakes, &c., which had been collected, and arranged by us for
immediate transfer to the enemy trenches, as soon as taken.
The dump, called No. 3 Dump, was situated just behind
our front line, and opposite to El-Arish Redoubt, which was
some 600 yards away across No Man's Land. My job was to
organize the continuous carrying of all this gear across No
Man's Land by X Company; Coulson, with W Company,

had a similar job at Nos. 1 and 2 Dumps, which were to feed the Umbrella Hill troops when they had taken it.

The attack on Umbrella Hill was timed for 2200 hours, and prompt to time the 7th Scottish Rifles got off the mark. Umbrella Hill was nearer our lines than El-Arish Redoubt, but still some 400 yards away. Our artillery still kept up their bombardment, intensifying it on Umbrella Hill, until just before the assault, when it was lifted on to the trenches behind. The assault was entirely successful, being, I have no doubt, something of a surprise to the Turk. O.C. 7th Scottish Rifles paid us a graceful compliment in allotting the leading position in the assault to Y Company, under Captain R. S. Cree, who led his men most gallantly and capably. As soon as his objectives were taken he was reinforced and then relieved by a company of 7th, and thereafter, as will be seen from Lieut.-Colonel Romanes' special order, along with W Company

SPECIAL ORDER BY LIEUT.-COLONEL ROMANES, D.S.O., COMMANDING 1/7TH SCOTTISH RIFLES, DATED 5TH NOVEMBER, 1917.

" Before W and Y Companies, 8th Scottish Rifles, return to their own unit, the Commanding Officer wishes to put on record the infinite debt of gratitude that this unit owes to these two Companies. After the assault on Umbrella Hill, itself a task which Y Company performed admirably, both these Companies, in a most gallant manner, went backward and forward through heavy enemy artillery barrage, whose intensity all ranks have appreciated, to carry the stores necessary for consolidation. For nearly thirty-six consecutive hours these Companies continued their work, to the nature of which their heavy casualty list is a melancholy tribute. Had such been previously lacking, the action of 1/2nd November, 1917 will be an unbreakable tie between the 7th and 8th Battalions.

HECTOR C. MacLEAN, Captain,
for Commanding Officer, 1/7th Scottish Rifles.

they carried across from our lines the stores necessary for consolidation to the captured position for the next 36 hours. The Turks did not sit down under the first successful assault, and the 7th had to prepare immediately for the enemy counter-attack, always a trying job. For trenches have to be reversed, parapets constructed, positions for Lewis guns made, wire put out, a hundred and one things are necessary, all to be done in the minimum of time. In this particular case both flanks of the 7th Scottish Rifles were unprotected: security on the left flank would be practically assured when El-Arish Redoubt had been taken and held, while for the right flank, a strong guard well dug-in was essential. Soon the Turkish artillery began to get busy on Umbrella Hill, and on to the ground between it and our lines. Their counter-attacks, however, all through the night were repulsed, but their artillery continued heavy harassing fire, upon both captured positions and the ground beyond them, until the main attack from El-Arish Redoubt (exclusive) to the sea was launched by the 54th Division at about 0300 on 2nd November, when it became appreciably less. Meantime, at 2300, the 4th Royal Scots launched their attack upon El-Arish Redoubt; they effected a good lodgment, captured the redoubt, but were held up for some time from attaining their final objective, the " Little Devil " Trench, a strong supporting point close to the right rear of El-Arish Redoubt. Possession of this point was determinedly resisted, but eventually they succeeded in capturing it, though not before the Turks had taken serious toll of their numbers.

By this time the work of the Carrying Companies was in full swing. From each dump across No Man's Land marched party after party of men carrying stores for consolidating the positions taken; back and forth they toiled, some of them making as many as thirteen journeys to El-Arish Redoubt, each time heavily laden. This was also kept up during the whole night, and for portions of the next day and night, to Umbrella Hill. At El-Arish Redoubt, however, early next morning, the O.C. 4th Royal Scots found that he had to utilize both of our companies in the defence of the captured trenches. It was fortunate that other means were at hand for transporting stores across. Brigade telephoned to me just at this time that my Transport-Officer was coming up with his mules to take across ammunition to El-Arish Redoubt. I was admittedly somewhat sceptical about the success of the proposed venture, and pointed out the difficulties; however, I was informed that it was an order, and when Nicholl came up with 28 mules and their drivers, we got them loaded up with two boxes of ammunition to each mule (56,000 rounds), and wishing them God speed, we dispatched them under Nicholl's leadership.

Though there was a very considerable barrage to the right of them and to the left of them, the mules went on quietly— no stampede. They delivered the goods, as quietly returned, and, strange to say, there were no casualties until they had got back and were within 100 yards of our lines, when a shell burst near the last mule, killing it and its man, and wounding another. It was miraculous that they got through with such slight casualties, but fortune favoured the brave, for it was a gallant and daring exploit, and proved how Nicholl knew his men and his mules. It was a wonderful testimony to the trust and affection which existed between the men and their animals. I put Nicholl in for an M.C., but to my disappointment it was turned down. Besides Nicholl's transport help materialized in the shape of two tanks which hove in sight by Dump 3, and which I commandeered to take across a load of stores. One of them got embedded in front of El-Arish Redoubt, but nevertheless its stores were distributed; the other returned later in the morning full of its success in the Turkish trenches, but bringing back the stores it had started with! The exuberant young officer in charge had his enthusiasm considerably damped by a few plain words from me when I caught sight of the stores still aboard.

A covered and strengthened portion of the communication trench was utilized by my Medical Officer as a Dressing Station. Captain Clark was kept busy there, and though it was well within the shelling area, it fortunately escaped, and evacuation from it was accomplished unscathed. Dump No. 3 itself seemed to be discovered; anyhow, we were constantly treated to a certain amount of Turkish attention, and the shelter in which Dulieu and I took refuge, when not supervising the carrying parties, was knocked about a bit on more than one occasion when we were inside.

On the morning of the 2nd, El-Arish Redoubt was counter-attacked in strength, and some companies of the 7th Royal Scots were rushed up to reinforce the 4th, who had had many casualties. This counter-attack was successfully repelled, as were other attacks launched by the Turks against some of the trenches taken by the 54th Division. The enemy still held

O.C. TRANSPORT, LIEUTENANT NICHOLL

Whose good work saved us on many an occasion

out for the next two or three days, though no more counter-attacks came, and on the 4th, W, X, and Y Companies came back to the battalion, as did Z on the 5th. On the night of 6/7th November, the Turks evacuated all the trenches defending Gaza, and next day we were able to walk in unopposed, though we were careful of " booby traps ". On this occasion the Ali-Muntar-Outpost-Hill-Labyrinth system on the south-east of Gaza, a very strong one, never had to be attacked, as at the first two battles of Gaza, and the Turks could have given us a good deal more trouble there. It should be explained that the enemy's retreat from Gaza was not occasioned entirely by the capture of the Gaza trenches mentioned above. Other and bigger factors contributed. On the 31st October, before we attacked Gaza, our troops on our extreme right had taken Beersheba, 26 miles away, and the next day pushed north-wards, and reached Ain Kuhleh and Dhaheriyeh. On the morning of the 6th, Kauwukah and the Hareira and Sheria Defences were captured, and this, combined with our cavalry flank movement, compelled the enemy to evacuate Gaza to avoid being cut off.

The whole action was planned in a masterly fashion, and carried out with determination to succeed. Enormous booty was captured, and some 7000 prisoners, including 300 officers.

I was particularly proud of the way in which the companies of the 8th did their jobs. It is a severe test of discipline for a battalion to be broken up in this way into companies to serve with other units. The corporate feeling in a battalion, which is such an enormous help in an engagement, is necessarily lost. On the other hand, each company felt on its mettle to show what the 8th could do, and very nobly they did it.

The following letter from the Commander of the 4th Royal Scots testifies to their performances in unstinted measure.

COPY OF LETTER FROM LIEUT.-COLONEL A. M. MITCHELL, COMMANDING 1/4TH BATTALION, THE ROYAL SCOTS, TO LIEUT.-COLONEL J. M. FINDLAY, COMMANDING 1/8TH SCOTTISH RIFLES, DATED 5TH NOVEMBER, 1917.

" Dear Colonel Findlay,
            " I desire to express to you personally my thanks for the good work done by the Companies of your Battalion assisting my

Battalion. The conduct and bearing of all ranks and the dash and determination with which the enemy works were carried, and the quiet steadiness
of all ranks during consolidation and counter attacks, adds yet another fine
record to the splendid record of British Infantry. I shall be glad if Captains
Hannan and M'Combie will furnish me with the names of N.C.Os. and
men whom they consider merit special recognition. I know there are several.
I regret, as you will, the loss of so many good comrades, but I know none of
us will forget the men who gave their lives so that success might be obtained.
Might I ask you to convey to Officers, N.C.Os. and Men who co-operated
with the 4th Royal Scots on the 2nd and 3rd November my great appreci-
ation of the work done by them.

I am,

Yours sincerely,

A. MACLAINE MITCHELL, Lieut.-Colonel,
Commanding 1/4th Battalion, The Royal Scots (Q.E.R.)

The B.G.C. himself very warmly congratulated me on their
conduct, and his cordial language and the many honours
awarded to my men were balm and bliss to me after my sore
feelings at the ruthless scattering of my flock.

To O/C 1/8th Scottish Rifles.

I want to thank you and every officer, N.C.O., and man in your battalion
for the gallant and invaluable services which you have one and all rendered.
Their conduct throughout has been magnificent, and contributed very largely
to the success achieved by the 156th Brigade.

No troops in the world could have done better work or displayed greater
bravery under exceptionally trying conditions, and I would like them to
know how intensely proud I am of you all.

I will at a later date, when we are together again, give myself the pleasure
of personally thanking all ranks for what they have done.

A. H. LEGGETT, Brigadier-General.

H.Q. 156th Brigade,
5/11/17.

General Hare of 54th Division sent the Brigade a letter of
thanks.[1]

Our casualties were 40 killed (or died of wounds), including
2nd-Lieuts. J. T. Neilson, P. E. Frankau, and S. J. Rowland,
who all did good and gallant work. It was, I think, the first
action in which each of them took part. Poor fellows, they gave
of their best. Three men were posted as " missing ", and there
were 112 wounded, of whom the officers were Lieut. W. S.
Scott, 2nd-Lieuts. J. E. Lyle, J. F. Grierson, and G. D. Watson,
the last of whom pluckily stuck to his job and did not go off
to hospital.

[1] See Appendix IV, p. 219.

.

CHAPTER VII

Operations up to the Capture of Jerusalem. Forcing the Auja River. Ballutah

On the 6th and 7th Nov. the battalion united again, re-armed, re-fitted, and rested. The nucleus returned from Belah, bringing with it 2nd-Lieut. H. Darsie, attached from Lanark-shire Yeomanry. On the 7th, the rest of the Division pushed forward along the shore, 157th Brigade leading, to find the heights above Wadi Hesi strongly held by a Turkish rearguard. Our Brigade moved up the following day, the 8th, to Wadi Hesi, and our arrival coincided with the Turkish retreat from there. It is not suggested that this was the cause and effect, though probably the Turks may have seen us coming along the shore. We took no part in the Wadi Hesi engagement, but on arrival were at once required to take up an outpost position covering the shore, at the mouth of the Wadi. I recollect on riding forward to reconnoitre the outpost line to allot it to companies, that the precipitate flight of the Turks was very noticeable; belts, rifles, ammunition, utensils, and headgear were strewn about. Their trenches, which had obviously been prepared some time previously, were now exceedingly useful to us. Though precipitate, their flight, as will be seen, was short-distanced. The 4th Royal Scots were on the right of the Brigade Outpost line, holding the sand dunes on the south of the Wadi through Herbiah to Sheraf, and the 7th Royal Scots on my left completed the circle to the sea, in a north-westerly direction, with the 7th Scottish Rifles in reserve.

Scarcely had we got into position at dusk, when the 157th Brigade moved through us to attack the Turks, who having retreated in an easterly direction were holding a position covering the railway from about Deir Sineid to Burbera. It was a bold move, this night attack over unreconnoitred country, but luck and daring made it successful. The 157th Brigade found themselves up against a tough proposition. The night approach-march had to be done on a compass-bearing with no surety that they would get there, over country in which it was very difficult to keep direction. Our old friends, the 5th Highland Light Infantry, in particular experienced one of the stiffest fights in which they ever took part. Their objective was a ridge (later called Sausage Ridge) about half way between Deir Seneid and Beit Jerga. They attacked once, twice, thrice, and each time were repulsed; but with grim determination they reorganized, and at last, at the fourth attempt, gained their objective, and turned the Turks out. My brother, Major J. A. Findlay, D.S.O., who was in charge of the firing line of the 5th Highland Light Infantry, fell mortally wounded just as his perseverance was rewarded. The 5th Highland Light Infantry lost over 200 killed and wounded in that action. This battalion's gallant fight gained the day for the 157th Brigade, and materially aided the action of the 155th Brigade on their left. The latter Brigade, after some preliminary gains, were counter-attacked, apparently in force, and had to fall back slightly on their left when that flank was seriously threatened; however, after the success of the 157th Brigade, their objectives were eventually gained.

As far as the 8th were concerned, the night passed quietly; we succoured a young Yeomanry officer who had lost his troop, and in the morning some of our scouts plucked our first oranges from a grove near Herbiah. These were sent by us as a present to Brigade. It was unkindly suggested that we did not keep them because they were still sour. Next day we moved to a bivouac area on the shore, and I remember the B.G.C. came into my bivouac and we talked over our recent actions. He was very proud of the Brigade, and, if possible, made me prouder than ever of my battalion. We moved off next morning towards Askalon and Mejdel, and that afternoon we were entertained to observe M'Clelland, who was Assistant Brigade-Major, returning from somewhere, at the head of a motley cavalcade of grooms and riders and cooks who were mounted on horses or mules, with or without saddles. It soon transpired that M'Clelland had been sent forward by the B.G.C. who had undertaken to find out what was the situation at Askalon and Mejdel. No other cavalry was available, so he sent M'Clelland with this heterogeneous but gallant band to clear up the situation. This they successfully did, found Askalon free of any enemy, and then pushed on to Mejdel. Here M'Clelland, as they made their way up the street, saw one or two Turks disappearing through a gateway. Boldly he took the risk of opposition, followed them, and found a considerable store of war material which he captured. Soon after there arrived on the scene a troop of Australian horsemen, who were annoyed and chagrined to find themselves forestalled by the Jocks. M'Clelland handed over the stores to the Australians, obtaining a receipt (in duplicate without doubt), and with his victorious army rejoined the Brigade—a delightful episode!

At Mejdel we lay overnight on a sparsely grassed field near the village. The B.G.C. being doubtful of the arrival of rations put us on half rations, and I think this was the only time that that occurred during all our operations in Palestine. The discovery of a granary by an Australian did not help us much, though the horses benefited. He, the said Australian, dashed up to me and delivered himself to the following effect: " Say, Jock, if there isn't a b——y guard put upon that b——y grain store, there won't be any b——y grain left in about two b——y minutes". This formal request resulted in his leading off an N.C.O. and six men of ours who put an end to the b——y looting of the b——y Arabs. Another incident at Mejdel afforded us malicious enjoyment. A batch of about 200 Turkish prisoners came in, under the escort of two or three Australians, who took occasion now and then to practise revolver shooting on horseback round about the column of prisoners—one appreciated their alarm.

From the stores captured by M'Clelland I recollect we secured some waterproof or bivouac sheets, and some pairs of

9

boots; the former were most useful, and the latter not of much value.

Next day we marched to Esdud, arriving at 1600. The Brigade moved out on the 12th and attacked a strong Turkish position at Burkah. In this attack the Brigade was well supported by three batteries of 18-pounders, one 60-pounder battery, and two 6-in. howitzers. I now print my report on the battle, which though short was severe, especially for the 4th Royal Scots who were up against stiff opposition in Brown Hill, which was most strongly held and determinedly denied them. The Burkah action would have been a more comprehensive success had a Brigade of Australian Light Horse executed their appointed rôle satisfactorily. They were under the command of our B.G.C., who had ordered them to make a big sweeping movement round the Turks' right flank and come round upon them from their right rear. They did not do so. Had they carried out orders we should have collared the whole lot. As it was, the Turks slipped away in the dark, leaving some 50 or 60 dead in our part of the line and a similar number of wounded.

REPORT ON ACTION AT BURKAH ON 12TH NOVEMBER, 1917, FROM THE POINT OF VIEW OF 1/8TH SCOTTISH RIFLES

Burkah is a small village situated at the south end of the salient which has its apex about 0.72 b 23. The rôles allotted to the units of the Brigade were:

1/4th Royal Scots to capture the hill H 25 to 28 and to cover the attack of the rest of the Brigade from the right flank.

1/7th Royal Scots to attack the main ridge about 1333d.

1/8th Scottish Rifles to attack echeloned to left rear of 7th Royal Scots; and to protect their left, and support them.

1/7th Scottish Rifles to be in reserve at about 13.33 A 68.

The 1/7th Royal Scots and 1/8th Scottish Rifles emerged from Esdud at about 1331 D. The advance commenced about 1130, both battalions moving forward in artillery formation. The 1/8th Scottish Rifles had only three companies, W Company having been detached as escort to guns. Y Company moved out first, followed by Z Company, with a sub-section of Machine-gun Company, X Company being in reserve, and moving with Battalion Head-quarters and the other sub-section of Machine-gun Company. The ground to be traversed was a flat plain about $1\frac{1}{2}$ to 2 miles from the Turkish position, two wadis being the only obstacles and at the same time the only cover to attacking troops. The Turks opened with shrapnel and high explosives, but the first wadi at B 33 B 20 was reached about mid-day with no casualties. From this wadi onwards the Turks kept up long-range machine-gun fire, but nevertheless the second wadi, running through B 21/22, was reached by this battalion at about 1300 with but few casualties. The battalion was, of course, now moving in extended order, and about this time I sent instructions for my O.C. firing line —Major Coulson— to push up his two machine-guns, escorted by a platoon, to the high ground about B 216 central, with the object of assisting the main attack from that flank. This was not carried out in time, as the runner could not find the Machine-gun Commander. The sub-section eventually joined up in the firing line.

At this point the 1/7th Royal Scots seemed inexplicably held up, and after communicating (by phone) with the O.C. I ordered Major Coulson to push forward his two companies and link up with the corresponding lines of the 7th Royal Scots, and prepare to advance with them. This was at 1400. At 1430 I got a message from Major Coulson saying that 7th Royal Scots were very short of ammunition, and he could not advance farther without them. I informed O.C. 7th Royal Scots. At 1500 I received a message that the crest of the ridge had been taken, and that the Royal Scots and my battalion were digging-in. Not being satisfied that they had got the main position, I sent to ask Major Coulson what ridge they actually were holding, pointing out that the enemy still seemed to occupy the main position. I similarly communicated with the O.C. 7th Royal Scots. I also sent up the other two machine-guns along with my reserve company to endeavour further to make a turning movement on the enemy's right. This company and these two guns I withdrew later into reserve again. I also sent up more ammunition to the firing line at Major Coulson's request.

At 1730 I received a message from him: " Am attacking with 7th Royal Scots ".

At 1810 Major Coulson reported that the final Turkish trenches had been taken, and that the whole line was consolidating.

There were no incidents during the night; some supplies came, and sand carts for evacuating wounded.

The artillery taking part in the action were three batteries of 18-pounders and two heavy guns. Their assistance was most efficacious, and during the action I was in touch with the 18-pounder F.O.O. all the time, and with the F.O.O. Heavies for two or three hours.

Communications were good by visual (i.e. helio.). When my Head-quarters was finally established in the forward wadi, there was some delay in communications because the Brigade telephone wire was too short to reach them; eventually, however, this was remedied.

Casualties	Officers	Other Ranks
Killed . . .	—	8
Died of Wounds .	1	4
Wounded . .	3	61
Missing . .	—	6
	4	79

17/11/17   (Sgd.) J. M. F.

Of the casualties, Captain R. S. Cree died of wounds. He was a sound and gallant officer, and a loss to the battalion. Lieut. J. A. MacLaren, 2nd-Lieuts. F. W. Mackinnon and G. D. Watson were wounded—Mackinnon had joined from Lanarkshire Yeomanry some time before, and Watson on this occasion did not succeed in keeping out of hospital.

In connection with the Australian Commander's indifference to orders, an amusing incident occurred in the afternoon of the attack. I had been watching X Company's assault through glasses, and I noticed about 100 or 200 yards in front of them what appeared to be Turkish snipers retiring in the long grass in face of the attack. I could see no attempt on the part of the company to capture them, or even shoot at them. I therefore sent up a message to Captain Hannan (O.C. X Company) informing him of what I saw, and ordering him to endeavour to capture them. He did so, and shortly after I saw a couple being escorted back from our front line. A few minutes afterwards I was telephoning Brigade, and in the course of conversation mentioned that there were two prisoners coming in. I know not whether Brigade saw the incident or suspected something, but a little later they rang up and said, " What about the prisoners?" I answered that I had just received a note from O.C. X Company, to the effect that they were not Turks, but Australians (unseemly mirth from Brigade!) who had thought that they would have a little dismounted action on their own, on that flank. I do not suppose that more than a troop or two were concerned, but they considerably embarrassed X Company's attack. Without any reference to anybody they initiated this manœuvre, moving across X Company's front from left to right. It was surprising that none of them had been shot. Hannan managed to round them up and send them back to their horses, which were waiting for them behind a knoll half a mile away on the left. In the long grass and wearing thin grey coats, they looked extraordinarily like Turks. It was an object lesson in the want of co-operation and co-ordination, as was their failure on a larger scale to co-operate with our Brigade in the attack on Burkah.

We bivouacked on the ground, and the next morning (the 13th) along with the 7th Scottish Rifles marched to Beshit. During this march we heard heavy firing to our front, and learned that the 155th Brigade was fiercely engaged at Katrah and Mughar. We reached Beshit at about 1700, and then came temporarily under the command of B.G.C. 157th Brigade, taking the place, along with 7th Scottish Rifles, of 5th and 6th Highland Light Infantry, who under Colonel Morrison, 5th Highland Light Infantry, were in occupation of Yebna, captured by them the day before. Our job next morning, the 14th, was to make good the high ground east of El-Mansura, so as to get command of the railway. The move on Mansura was a fine spectacular advance over the open country in artillery formation. The 157th Brigade debouched at 0800, through the line Katrah-Mughar (which had been taken by the 155th Brigade the previous evening), with 5th Argylls on the right and 7th Highland Light Infantry on the left, their front and depth extending to about 1200 yards and 600 yards respectively. Behind, in the same formation, came the 8th on the right, and the 7th Scottish Rifles on the left. It was a bloodless victory. The Turks having evacuated Katrah and Mughar were apparently in no mood to make another stand at Mansura. My scouts on the right searched Wadi Katrah and Wadi Meruba, and in the latter established touch with the cavalry of the 75th Division, of whom we had heard nothing for some days. We learnt later that, owing to some blundering, the cavalry had just arrived in time to see the last Turkish unit steaming northwards out of the railway station of El-Tire early that morning.

The 8th Scottish Rifles bivouacked for the night near Mansura, and next day marched to Ekron (Bir-El-Ghazlan), where we took up an outpost position facing north-east, covering Ekron. Y Company was in reserve, and Battalion Headquarters was in the school-house of the Jewish Colony there. Dulieu and Coulson spent a much disturbed night owing to the presence of the ubiquitous little insect common to most of these Palestine houses. I was fortunate enough to be in an iron bedstead which had no attraction for the pests, but Coulson and Dulieu had acquired mattresses on which they were sleeping on the floor—fatal move! They did not do it again. The next morning, the 16th, I received orders to collect all arms and munitions of war in the village. A curious creature whose name I forget, unclassifiable as to race, but probably a Levantine Jew, had proffered his services as interpreter. He was an unsavoury being, but he served the purpose. I sent for the burgomaster or head-man, and instructed him to inform the villagers that they would all assemble at the school-house at 0900 to hear a proclamation from me. In due course a huge crowd of people arrived, but kept their distance. Y Company formed a guard of honour, and somebody produced a Union

Jack, which was hoisted with due honour and solemnity. I then intimated to the assembled multitude that they were to produce all arms, munitions, and combatants, if hidden or disposed anywhere in the village, by 12 midday, after which hour a house-to-house visitation would be made by my troops to see if they had complied with my orders. Any failure to comply would be most severely dealt with. I went on to inform them that, if they obeyed my orders, they had nothing to fear. On the contrary, they could trade with my soldiers who wanted fruit, chickens, and eggs, &c., at prices to be fixed by me and their head-man. Anyone found selling raw spirits to my men would be severely punished.

A cheer greeted this harangue, and the head-man and his satellites bowed and scraped, while the guard of honour again presented arms. Then the head-man replied that they were very glad to welcome the brave British, that all orders would be carried out, and that as far as they could, they would trade with us, but he wished to explain how much they had been tyrannized over and thieved from by the Turks; not much was left. Then one of his minions whispered something in his ear; he duly explained to the interpreter, who then informed me that the school children wanted to sing a little hymn of praise in honour of the brave British, would I permit it? I graciously gave them permission; so they proceeded to form in pairs, and danced round us singing some ditty to the tune of " Little Bo-Peep has lost her Sheep ", with a seriousness of countenance befitting the solemn occasion.

By this time I could hardly keep my face straight, and after they had danced round twice, I simply could not stand the sniggers from Dulieu, Coulson, and Ferguson behind me, so I waved my hand for dispersal. The crowd, well-behaved and orderly, complied, the guard presented arms and marched off, and we escaped as fast as we could into the school. It was, I think, one of the most ludicrous incidents in which I ever took part. The seriousness of the crowd, the obsequiousness of the head-ones, the interpreter's long-winded speech and gesticulations, our suppressed mirth, and to crown all the children in white dancing round us—a scene, in truth, from a comic opera. The outcome was remarkable; that afternoon we sent off five limber-loads of war material, ancient and modern, to the Brigade collecting-dump. Possibly we acquired a souvenir or two, I did not inquire too closely.

Thinking that we might remain some time at Ekron, I dispatched Nicholl and his transport back to Esdud to fetch up the men's packs and the officers' extra baggage. He left at 0500 on the morning of 17th and arrived back at 0100 on the 18th. While the distance, as the crow flies, is only a journey of about 13 miles from Esdud to Ekron, the going was very bad, there being no road, and innumerable wadis had to be crossed. (Wadis are awkward places, often with precipitous sides down to a water-bed sometimes 20 and 30 feet below.) Moreover, nearly the whole of the trek back was performed in the dark; so it was a great feat, and I am sure no other unit in the Division recovered their packs so promptly. But we were not destined immediately to score by his work, for next morning (i.e. the morning of his arrival back) we moved at 0800 to Ramleh, arriving there at 1330. I had started earlier in the day with the B.G.C. and one or two other C.Os. for a reconnaissance into the hills beyond, and to the east of Ramleh and Ludd. It was a long tiring ride, and we got back to Ramleh at 1600 to find that we were to move forthwith to Ludd. The men had to pack up again, snatch a cold dinner, and we got on the move at 1800. The congestion on the road was most aggravating. All the Division seemed to be converging upon Ludd, and we did not arrive until 0300, a matter of six hours to do three miles—bad staff work. It began to rain, but having got up our transport, thanks to Nicholl's journey, we simply bivouacked in a couple of adjoining gardens for the night, and a very uncomfortable wet night it was. We were on the move next morning again at 0800, the destination of the whole Brigade being Beit Likia, via the old road, or rather track, through Jimzu and Berfiliya. The track was fairly easy going until about Jimzu, where we got into hilly and rocky ground, with boulders on each side, over parts of which we had to move in single file. The maps give no idea of the twists and turns and ups and downs of the road, making it most difficult to keep the battalion closed up. Eventually we arrived at Beit Likia, where W, Z, and Y Companies had to go on outpost covering the position to the south and east. It was a cold rainy night, with no cover except big boulders, and the men had no great-coats or blankets, and were still wearing khaki drill. We almost envied the 157th Brigade who moved through us that night; they at any rate were keeping warm.

Next day, the 20th, we changed bivouac, outpost companies being withdrawn (except day O.Ps.) to the low ground just below Beit Likia, a sheltered and comparatively good spot. Fires were permitted, so the men got some hot food, but during the night a very heavy deluge of rain poured upon us, soaking everyone and everything, and putting out the fires. It ceased about 0100, and by some miracle the cooks succeeded in lighting a fire again, though how they did it remains a mystery. Perhaps some stones kept the embers dry, or an odd corner of a wadi may have sheltered some dry wood; and, as soon as started, the fire grew with helpful good humour until it became big enough for the men, or a considerable number of them, to cluster around and try to dry themselves at its warmth. The harder you try the Lowland Scot the cheerier he becomes, and it was heartening to see in the dark the fire gradually assuming bigger dimensions and to hear the men, some going backwards and forwards tending it, others drying their garments, singing choruses around it, as if they were having the happiest time in their lives. I do not think that anyone who saw it will forget that scene. A padre the other day was bewailing from the pulpit what he called the demoralizing influence of the war. All I can say is, the realities of war also call forth the best in man. In some ways war *is* demoralizing, but among the fighting troops, qualities of un-selfishness, cheerfulness, and steadfastness, not to speak of bravery, were so constantly exhibited that they almost became a commonplace. Time and again I have come across unwitting examples of the innate goodness of man which emerges when he is up against realities, and which is so often obscured by the smothering and unreal complexities of modern life. In these days of intolerance of authority and social unrest, of strikes and class warfare and revolutionary ideas, it is difficult to believe that there is any underlying feeling towards truth, toleration, and unselfishness. It is there, nevertheless. The 21st November dawned a beautiful sunshiny day, and everybody got their things dried and had a day's rest. Next morning at 0530 off we started again along the old Roman stony track through Beit Anan, where we found the 157th Brigade making it into some semblance of a road; about mid-day we reached El-Kubeibeh. The ground here was very steep, deep ravines, high hills with great boulders jutting out here and there. Movement was extremely difficult, and single file only was possible along the tracks, such as they were. Lieut.-Colonel Romanes of 7th Scottish Rifles and I went forward with the B.G.C. to reconnoitre the country. From a vantage point at Biddu we had a most comprehensive view of the surrounding country, which was a forbidding-looking series of steep and rocky hills and valleys, with here and there desolate-looking clusters of houses perched upon the hills and in the hollows—no roads—no water—no vegetation, except hardy scrub amongst the rocks. General Leggett pointed out to us Neby Samwil, which was the most prominent feature of the landscape, some five miles north-west of Jerusalem, a steep stone-strewn hill rising abruptly from its surroundings, with the mosque (which then was still standing) towering majestically at its top; it was occupied by troops of the 234th Brigade of the 75th Division, who also held Beit Iksa, but who were being very hard pressed by the Turks. If I remember aright, on the left troops of the 155th Brigade were being pushed forward to occupy the ground between Biddu and El-Jib. Beyond them yeomanry of the Cavalry Division were holding posts at Beit Izza, Beit Dukka, and El-Tire.

The B.G.C. then gave me orders to move the 7th and 8th Battalions across country to reinforce the 234th Brigade at Neby Samwil, which they had captured the previous day. On our return to El-Kubeibeh I arranged with Romanes that we should move each battalion in single file as far as possible on different tracks, but keeping touch laterally (i.e. about 50 or 100 yards apart). Between Kubeibeh and Neby Samwil, which were each on high ground, there was a longish valley of about 2½ miles, apparently quite open to enemy observation, but we found that owing to a shoulder unobservable from Kubeibeh we were under cover from view until about half-way across. The 7th Scottish Rifles, being in front of my battalion, descended into the plain first, and the 8th followed closely upon them, about 100 yards on their right, until we arrived at the end of the said shoulder. At this point I found that the 7th Scottish Rifles had halted, and that Colonel Romanes was nowhere to be seen. Captain Mather, who was left in command, said that he (Colonel Romanes) had gone off with some Staff Officer of the 75th Division, and that he had told him to wait there with the battalion until his return. Realizing that it was imperative that we should reach Neby Samwil as soon as possible, I definitely ordered Mather both verbally and in writing to push on alongside of my battalion. His objective was to be the mosque, and mine a point 100 or 150 yards to its right. As soon as we moved we came under observation, but we were hardly shelled at all until we got close to Neby Samwil. The 7th, under Mather's able leadership, arrived unscathed at the psychological moment when the Turks, after hard fighting, had just got into the mosque. He immediately counter-attacked, and successfully ejected the Turks, and we were never near losing Neby Samwil again. The 8th I assembled in a gully about 200 yards behind Neby Samwil, there being at the time no room for them on the hill itself. It was a most unlucky spot. The Turks had got the range to a nicety, and gave us some nasty enfilading shells, killing 5 and wounding 30, including Lieut. J. H. Souter, who had come back from Division Head-quarters after Gaza. I made the battalion get down behind boulders and take what cover they could, and then proceeded up to 234th Brigade Head-quarters to ascertain the situation. There I found that they had been expecting the Turks to be on them each moment; bayonets were fixed, and they were prepared for anything. Our reinforcements had been in the nick of time. The B.G.C. was Charles MacLean, who had been with the 52nd Division as D.A.A. and Q.M.G., and had recently been given command of this Brigade; Lieut.-Colonel Cassels, commanding 123rd (Outram's) Rifles (mentioned supra), was there also. His battalion had had a bad doing, but behaved most gallantly, and he was terribly cut up about his losses; the B.M. was Graham, Royal Scots, whom I had met a few months previously when in hospital with sandfly fever. It will be understood that they were glad to see us. I also found Romanes here.

It is difficult to give an adequate description of Neby Samwil, which was going to prove one of the most uncomfortable corners we were ever in. It is about five miles north-west from Jerusalem, and the mosque, whose tower in the course of the next few days was shelled to smithereens by the Turks, is supposed to contain the remains of the Prophet Samuel. It is planted upon the top of a hill which rises precipitously on its east (the enemy) side, while on the north it slopes gradually towards the plain and El-Jib; on the south and west its right shoulder is continued in an undulating fashion towards Beit Iksa and Biddu. The Turks held the line El-Jib-Nebala north-west to Beit-ur-el-Tahta, and they had been reinforced in considerable numbers, while from east of Beit-ur-el-Tahta and in the region of Betunia and Ram Allah, the Turkish guns harried us with enfilade fire, as well as from their main position at Er Ram. From Neby Samwil towards Er Ram the rocky precipitous slopes descended in terraces, evidently man-made, which were very difficult to manœuvre troops across, but on the top, within 150 yards of the mosque, there was a plateau which could be, and was, occupied by the enemy, and which afforded them ample cover for sniping and machine-gun fire at close range. Behind the mosque (i.e. west) the ground sloped away gradually to a cliff, where about 20 feet below the summit there was a broad ledge upon which had been established the 234th Brigade Head-quarters, and where I also had mine. From this ledge the rocky ground steeply fell to a gully up to which the transport used to come at night with our rations, water, and munitions. Farther back, and to the south, was the other gully where the 8th had suffered from the enfilade shelling from Betunia.

It should be remembered that at this time the Division had moved so quickly forward, and over such rocky tracks, that our artillery could not follow us. We had therefore to suffer the enemy's shelling from both flanks and from the front in blasphemous silence. Wherever we turned we always offered the other cheek.

At 1700 the same day I received orders to relieve the 234th Brigade with the 7th and 8th Scottish Rifles, but still to remain under the orders of its B.G.C., who withdrew his Brigade about two miles back, immediately north of Biddu, and who was in touch with me by telephone. The dispositions taken up by the two battalions were as follows: the 8th with W and X Companies held the right side of the mosque to its centre; Z Company, on their right, garrisoned hastily constructed trenches clear of the mosque walls, facing east and south, with their right flank refused. Other troops of the 75th Division held Beit Iksa towards Z Company, but there was a considerable gap. Y Company was in reserve, crowded on a portion of the ledge afore-mentioned, beside my Head-quarters. The 7th continued the line from the centre of the mosque to the left, and occupied separated posts for about 300 yards from the mosque towards El-Jib. Except on Z Company's position, trenches were impossible on account of the rocky and terraced nature of the ground. Platoons lined the mosque walls, or had Lewis guns and rifles through loopholes, or did the best they could by constructing little sangars. At one place, in order to communicate with the next post, one had to skip, regardless of dignity, from behind a wall through a postern gate at its extremity, and then rush as best one could along a rocky path for about thirty yards in the open, until one again got under cover behind the corner of a derelict house, which sheltered a few of our bombers. It was bitterly cold that night, and the men had only their drill kits and no blankets. Rations also only consisted of the unexpired portion of some biscuits which had been issued after breakfast, so that everything considered conditions were cheerless, and we were all glad when dawn came, and the sun began gradually to thaw us.

During the 22nd we were wonderfully spared, having only

four killed and nine other ranks wounded. Late in the afternoon some 4.5-inch howitzers heralded their arrival by giving the Turks warm evening greetings. We were rejoiced to hear them, and realized that somebody must indeed have been working to good purpose on the track from Berfiliya to Beit Likia and Biddu. Their presence marked a feat of engineering skill and manual labour, and filled us with pride and confidence. More guns would probably arrive during the night, and what with counter-battery work and anxiety not to give away their gun positions, the Turks would not have much time or rounds to expend on the poor Scottish foot-sloggers. Nicholl and Boyd managed to bring up half rations that evening, but in the dark they had great difficulty with the camels on the rocky and precipitous ground, and finally the rations had to be carried up to our ledge from the gully beneath. A pleasant and truly welcome surprise was some whisky which the thoughtful fellows produced. It was another very cold night with again no blankets.

The next day a big Divisional effort was ordered with a view to getting command of the road north from Jerusalem, cutting off the Turkish retreat, and thus forcing the surrender of Jerusalem.

Here, perhaps, the attention of the reader should be directed to a more general view of the Division's movements. On the 18th the Division was concentrated on Ludd, having forced the Turks to evacuate one position after another from Gaza onwards. A similar process had been taking place on our right from Beersheba up to Jerusalem, or just short of it. Now the climax was to be the taking of Jerusalem. The Divisional movement from Ludd to Lifta, which point is, I think, the nearest to Jerusalem the Division succeeded in reaching, was, according to accepted tactical axioms, unsound. Such a march across our front, with only a weak cavalry screen covering us, was asking for trouble, as can be seen by a glance at the map. But knowing the world-wide political importance of the taking of Jerusalem, we relied upon our lucky star which seemed in the ascendant, and on the apparent demoralization of the enemy. It was, however, at this point that the

Turks received reinforcements and made a gallant stand. At one place after another they put up a desperate fight, and we now found ourselves held up. It was determined, however, to make a strong effort to force the capitulation of Jerusalem.

The 155th Brigade moving on our left was to take El-Jib, and push on and occupy Kulundia. The 156th Brigade was to clear the north-eastern slopes of Neby Samwil and seize Nebala; the 157th Brigade moving through us and on our right was to go straight for Er Ram.

In the Brigade my battalion was to hold Neby Samwil during the attack, taking over from 7th Scottish Rifles their portion of the line. The 7th were to move in conjunction with 155th Brigade and attack El-Jib on its right. The 7th Royal Scots were to debouch as best they could from both sides of the mosque, clear the ground and villages to north-east of Neby Samwil, and then co-operate, if necessary, against El-Jib. The 4th Royal Scots were to support the 7th Royal Scots and form a flank guard on the right. The attack was timed to start at 1205. It was foredoomed to failure. Impossibilities cannot be done; the difficulties of the ground and the facts that the Turks had been reinforced, that they were much stronger in guns than we were, and occupied strong positions, should have made clear the fact that success could not be achieved at this time. The 155th and the 157th Brigade, who never got near their objectives, suffered considerable casualties. In our Brigade the 7th Scottish Rifles, having formed an extended line on our left, practically never moved, the 7th Royal Scots, amidst enormous difficulties of terrain, succeeded in getting 200 yards forward, while the 4th Royal Scots could not move.

During the action, the 123rd (Outram's) Rifles and 4th Dorsets came up to relieve us (the 8th), but it was soon realized that the action would result in failure. " As you were " was ordered, and the 7th and 8th Scottish Rifles again took up their positions holding the mosque. The second relief was completed at 0130 on the night of the 24/25th after a long, trying and ineffectual day. Double rations, however,

came up.   Our casualties on the 24th November were:
2 officers wounded, 2nd-Lieuts. Carswell and Rodgers.
28 other ranks wounded.   8 other ranks killed.

I recollect that at dawn on that morning, before our attack,
the B.G.C. came up to my Head-quarters with a view to looking at the ground over which we would have to attack.   I
took him and Franklin[1] up to the front line, along with John
Miller, my Intelligence Officer.   Just as we got up we saw the
towers and minarets of Jerusalem silhouetted on the horizon,
with the sun from behind them striking a golden ray upon
their roofs.   It was my first view of Jerusalem, and it was a most
beautiful sight.   Contrasted with that, our next sight was a
dead body on our left front, which had caught fire from a shell
splinter, and was burning rapidly away.   We moved farther
on, and eventually found ourselves behind the wall and postern
gate afore-mentioned.   One by one we dashed across the open
and gained the shelter of the house.   A rifle section was under
cover there too, and noticing some Turkish snipers moving
to gain advantageous positions, the B.G.C. and I seized a
couple of rifles, and commenced to fire at them.   He put four
out of action, and I think that I gave two their quietus.   By
this time it was getting much lighter, and feeling that we had
drawn the enemy's attention to us by our shooting, we decided it was time to return.   Each of us again ran the gauntlet,
and by God's mercy all got across scatheless, though bullets
peppered our road.[2]

The morning of the 25th was quiet, but heavy shelling
descended upon us during the afternoon.   By this time I had
a F.O.O. with me from a battery stationed somewhere in the
rear.   I recollect spotting a working party of Turks digging

---

[1] Captain T. E. Franklin (Bedfords) had succeeded Tollemache as Brigade-Major a few
days before the change in the Brigade command.   Sad to say, he died of wounds received
from shell fire on my H.Q. ledge on the very morning of the visit to the mosque.

[2] The terrain around the mosque was not a pretty sight at this time.   Many Turks had
been killed, when the 234th Brigade took it, and that Brigade had had many casualties also
in the taking.   There were strewn everywhere around the dead bodies of English, Scottish,
Indian, Goorkha, and Turkish soldiers, which no one had the time to bury.   I remember
the body of one Turk, who though apparently dead, after three days came to life again.
Extraordinary vitality in one whose life, from all one heard and saw, seemed hardly worth
living!

what appeared to be a gun emplacement on a position about two miles west of Kulundia. Had we allowed them to proceed with their work, guns firing from there would have enfiladed the ledge and steep banks behind Neby Samwil in a more uncomfortable manner than ever before; however, the F.O.O. got his guns on the working party and scattered them, and they did not return, at any rate while we were there. Casualties during the day, 13 other ranks wounded.

That night, to our immense satisfaction, we were relieved by 2/17th and 2/19th battalions of the London Regiment, under the command of Lieut.-Colonel D. C. Sword of the Scottish Rifles, who took over from me, and I wished him the best of luck with a thankful heart. Companies of both battalions moved independently as soon as relieved to Beit Anan, where the last of us arrived at 0030 on the 26th, which day and the next were spent in sleeping, eating, cleaning, and resting generally. Our sojourn at Neby Samwil had been trying and fatiguing, and heavy toll had been taken of our numbers.

On the 28th the Brigade moved at 0900 back to the vicinity of Beit Likia, where we expected to have a rest, but about midday after arrival, I was ordered to take the 8th and report to 155th Brigade Head-quarters in the vicinity of Beit Sira. On arrival there Brigadier-General Pollock-M'Call told me that his Brigade had been hard put to it to maintain their position on a ridge running almost east and west, having Beit-ur-el-Tahta on its right, and El-Burg on its left rear. The Turks held Shilta, Suffa, and were very close to Tahta. Apparently this was a counter-attack to try to cut our communications, and the Turks were very aggressive. It was a natural result of our reverse on the 24th, and of further enemy reinforcements. We were now being " hoist with our own petard ". For a time, I believe, the Turkish counter-attack, directed to cut us off from Ludd and Ramleh, threatened serious things, but so far we had maintained our ground. The B.G.C. desired me to relieve the 4th K.O.S.B., who had driven the Turks off the hill now held, and had suffered considerably in accomplishing this. At the moment things were fairly quiet, and I went forward and had a look at the position

10

to be relieved. Brigade Head-quarters were beside Battalion Head-quarters, behind the front line, which was on the forward slope of a longish rocky ridge, facing a similar ridge held by the Turks, of corresponding height, to its north or northeast. A gully of considerable depth ran between the two. The 4th K.O.S.Bs. was the right battalion of the Brigade (the 155th), all battalions of which were, I think, in the line. The 7th Mounted Brigade held Tahta on the right, but there was a hiatus between of half a mile or so. The Turks had few guns, and apparently none opposite us, but they were strong in machine-guns, which were cleverly concealed. We had arrived at 1530, and the B.G.C. and I discussed the advisability of a daylight relief. I think he did not want to insist upon it, though he would like it, and he left it to me. Having seen the ground, and knowing that the companies would have only about 20 or 30 yards on the forward side of the ridge to traverse before they got behind the rocks held by the front line, I decided to try it. I therefore sent up each relieving O.C. Company to his corresponding number of the 4th K.O.S.B. to see the best line to approach, the extent of his frontage, and to get all other details required. The relief was accomplished quickly and easily, there being only nine casualties, two other ranks killed and seven wounded in Y Company. Soon thereafter my own B.G.C. came up to find us in position, and then the 156th Brigade took over entirely from the 155th Brigade, the 7th Royal Scots being on our left. From the K.O.S.Bs. we took over 4 Stokes guns and 4 machine-guns.

This was another awkward corner in which we found ourselves. My right again was in the air. Movement in the front line, except at certain times, was difficult, and the Turks were in considerable strength, we were told, and aggressive. The two ridges were rather similar as to height and conformation: they were covered with big boulders, and we had to make some sort of sangars as platoon posts, and similarly Lewis-gun and machine-gun positions were hidden by rocks. It became difficult to visit these platoon positions during the day, and the Turks had a couple of machine-guns cleverly posted so as to enfilade the gully between us. Late that afternoon some Australian gunners came up, and signalized their arrival by bombarding Brigade Head-quarters, which had been established about a quarter of a mile to our left rear. We all, of course, were wickedly delighted (there being no casualties), and the B.G.C. sent them some really choice words of thanks. Before this had happened he had come up to my Head-quarters and asked me if I could find out if a little mosque opposite my right was strongly garrisoned. I undertook to send some of my scouts (they were a good lot under 2nd-Lieut. J. Miller) across the gully to reconnoitre. I went out along on the right with Miller and pointed out what seemed to be as covered an approach as possible. Off they went, but not in wide enough order at first, some were spotted, one was killed, and Miller and another were wounded by a well-aimed shell. Scout-Sergt. Bond, however, carried on, and with three or four other trusty lads, got quite close to the mosque, unperceived. There they lay in wait, trying to find out numbers, and eventually withdrew after dark. This daylight patrol was a plucky bit of work, though not really fruitful of results— and earned Bond his D.C.M. During the night, however, I got one of the trench-mortars right up as close to the mosque on our side as possible, and at extreme range (700 yards then) we put in three or four good old noisy ones, which, I think, cleared the mosque of any occupants. Next day things were quieter, though periodically bursts of machine-gun fire skimmed round us. Major R. N. Coulson, much to my regret, was ordered off to take command of the 1/5th K.O.S.B. in the 155th Brigade. We were all very sorry, but it was promotion for him and a good thing, for he had had a long spell as second-in-command, after having commanded the battalion in my absence.

That night and next morning were comparatively quiet. 'Twas St. Andrew's Night, and by good luck we had a little of the wherewithal to celebrate, and Brigade sent us a present of some further " medical comforts ". Greetings came through from the Commander-in-Chief, Divisional-General, and the Brigade, and in the midst of death there was life. Here are those from the C.-in-C. and the B.G.C.

" To all units in 156th Brigade.

" On this St. Andrew's night, I drink to the health of every Officer, N.C.O. and man of the Brigade. All have fought gloriously, many have fallen gloriously, and all ranks of the Brigade have most gloriously up-held their high and noble traditions. No troops in the world can equal you for gallantry and devotion to duty. Next St. Andrew's Day will, please God, be spent in Bonnie Scotland. Good luck to you all.

A. LEGGETT, B.G.
Commanding 156th Brigade."

30/11/17.

" To all units 156th Brigade.

" Br. 88. 30-S.R.H.   Following from C.-in-C.   On St. Andrew's Day I take this opportunity of thanking you for the great spirit you have shown both on the battlefield and on the march during the past month. Inform all ranks.

From 156th Brigade."

30/11/17.

The 1st of December was also a quiet day for us, but the Turks launched persistent attacks against Tahta, and upon the ridge held by 1/5th K.O.S.B., between Burg and Suffa; they were, however, repelled at Tahta by the 5th H.L.I., and by the 1/5th K.O.S.B. in the latter locality. In the afternoon the O.C. and the Company-Commanders of the 5th Inniskilling Fusiliers (10th Division) came up to see our line. They eventually relieved us that evening, relief being completed at 2100. It was a very strong battalion compared to mine. My Y Company numbered only 23 rifles, and none of the others had more than 50. After the relief the Brigade concentrated about 1¼ miles west of Beit Likia, where we spent a restful night. Next morning we moved to Kubab, arriving there comfortably about 1600, and on the following day we reached a bivouac area, Surafend, three miles north-west of Ramleh. Here we remained for three days, resting and refitting with new clothing and boots, and thank heaven, our blankets and packs were brought back to us from Ludd.

On the afternoon of the 7th the Brigade moved, under my command, to a place called Selmeh, the B.G.C. and Lieut.-Colonel Peebles having preceded us on a reconnaissance. We left about 1600 and immediately it began to rain. We followed the Ramleh-Jaffa Road as far as Yasur, and then struck across country to the north. (I quote from my War Diary here.) "The track was feet deep in mud and the final two miles were very trying for the men who were carrying packs for the first time since trekking to Gaza. Neither camels nor transport could get across a deep wadi almost half-way from Yazur, and had to barrack there for the night. The infantry and pack mules managed to cross, but owing to the darkness, and to losing touch with the chain of scouts sent back by the advance party, the Brigade did not arrive at the bivouac area until 2330. The advance parties, who had arrived about 1930, had got fires and tea ready, but owing to the rain and long time of waiting the fires had gone out, and the tea was cold and diluted with rain. The men passed a miserably cold night, soaked to the skin. They had been moving with full packs and wet blankets, and no food, for 6½ hours, and, of course, there was no breakfast until the camels came up late next morning, when it had fortunately cleared." The camels become paralysed in the mud. They cannot keep their feet, and if they fall they cannot rise again. One poor beast split itself and had to be shot. If camels get their legs beyond a certain width apart, they cannot close them, and this animal's hind legs simply slipped apart wider and wider in the mud.

Next day, after a short march to Sarona, we found we were to be billeted there—under roofs! Sarona was a little village only two or three miles from where we were, and about 1½ miles from Jaffa. We arrived about 3 p.m., and every man in the battalion, for the first time for many months, slept under a roof. Battalion Head-quarters was in House 14, a good-sized one (for the place), in which we messed, slept, and carried through the usual Orderly-Room routine. Sarona is a picturesque little place, and the foliage and creepers about and upon the houses were charming to the eye. It was really a German-Jewish Colony, a similar sort of place to Ekron;

the men of military age had all been interned, and the remaining old men and women, after the terrible tales that had been served out to them, no doubt, as to the brutality of the British, went about their daily work in a very pianissimo fashion. Orange groves were scattered all round, and were evidently the principal occupation of the local populace. The whole of the district is, of course, devoted to this industry—Jaffa oranges.

We remained in Sarona until the 12th, when it became our turn to occupy the front-line position on the southern bank of the River Auja, which flows into the Mediterranean some 3000 yards north of Sarona. The 4th and 7th Royal Scots had held this from the time we left Selmeh, and we relieved the 4th Royal Scots in the left sector. The trenches were scattered; platoon posts in company areas were not always linked-up by trenches and movement between positions was easily observable from the Turkish position round Sheik Muannis, on the other side of the river. Such observations were also equally good on our side, and we made considerably more use of our opportunities for observation and reconnaissance than the enemy. Every day we were looking at their positions from all angles, until I, for one, had the whole of them photographed upon my memory; for it was proposed ere long to force the crossing of the Auja, and to clear the enemy out of their commanding position on the north side, whence they could observe movement and direct artillery fire right into Jaffa where Division had taken up their Head-quarters. It would never have done to allow D.H.Q. comfort to be disturbed by even occasional shells in their garden. As to how the crossing was to be effected was a very pretty little problem, and afforded us all considerable thought and interest. Eventually our B.G.C.'s (General Leggett's) scheme was adopted by Division, and its success proved its soundness. It was obvious that the crossing would have to be effected at night, and once on the other side further movement, even if not seriously opposed, would be difficult in the dark and over unknown country. Hence thorough reconnaissance by us was necessary.

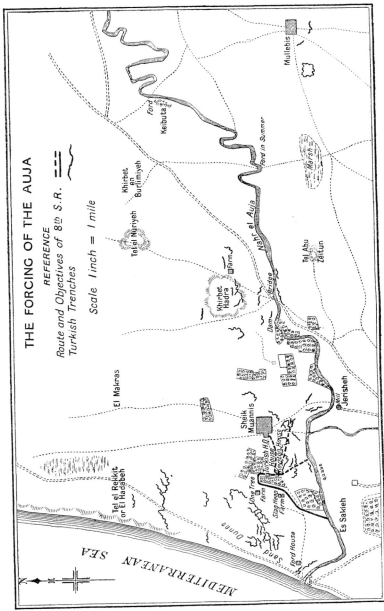

THE FORCING OF THE AUJA

REFERENCE

Route and Objectives of 8th S.R. ▬▬
Turkish Trenches ⟿

Scale 1 inch = 1 mile

MEDITERRANEAN SEA

Mullebis

Marsh

Ford
Keibuta

Khirbet
en
Burtimiyeh

Ford in Summer

Tel el Nuriyeh

Nahr el Auja

Tel Abu
Zeitun

Khirbet
Hadra

Farm

Dam

Bridge

El Makras

Mill
Jerisheh

Sheik
Muannis

Turkish HQ
House
Hospital House

Stone Tree
Farm

Slag Heap
Farm

Es Sakieh

Tel el Rekkit
or El Hadabeh

Sand Dunes

Ford House

The B.G.C.'s scheme was a bold one. There were to be three distinct objectives: the Khirbet Hadrah system opposite the bridge over the Auja, the Sheik Muannis trenches, and the series of trenches in the sand-dunes on the shore. The accompanying sketch gives no idea of the contours, but Khirbet Hadrah is a strongly entrenched hill about 500 feet high, rising formidably from the river. The Sheik Muannis trenches were similarly high, and were also strong and commanding. From positions in them the Turks sniped across to our bank. The sand-dune trenches were many, and had they been held in any strength would have been a serious obstacle to our project. They were moderately high, rising from the shore, and the number of trenches shown on the map (from our aeroplane photographs) were, I shrewdly suspect, dug more with the idea of deceiving us as to the numbers available to occupy them than for the serious occupation of them.

Each Brigade was allotted one of the three objectives: the 155th was to go for Khirbet Hadrah, 156th for Sheik Muannis, and 157th for the sand-dunes. The next problem was how these Brigades were to cross. The 155th had a bridge which was strongly guarded. (As a matter of history, it was here that the Turks put up the only serious resistance during the operation.) The H.L.I. Brigade were to cross the ford at the mouth of the river, and it was necessary to know the depth, breadth, and force of water at the ford. This was cleverly and gallantly accomplished by Lieut.-Colonel Anderson of the 6th H.L.I., who, with Lieut. Hill of his own battalion, swam one night from our side of the Ford right under the nose of a Turkish post at Ford House, gauged the depth and the breadth, and actually succeeded in driving sticks into the bed of the Ford to show the direction to be followed by the troops crossing. These sticks were not discovered by the Turks, and fortunately on the night of the crossing, a couple of days later, had not been submerged by the river swollen by the recent rains. Lieut.-Colonel Anderson brought back invaluable information, and his exploit won for him a bar to his D.S.O.

As for our Brigade, it was necessary to arrange for some sort of pontoon bridge; to have the pontoons carried down

IN THE JUDEAN HILLS: EMMAUS WITH NEBI SAMWIL BEYOND

during the night and hidden until required, and to choose
a spot to cross known to be unfrequented by Turkish patrols
and away from any posts. An excellent bit of reconnaissance
work was carried out by our Brigade I.O., Captain Stanley
Smith (5th Scottish Rifles, attached 7th Scottish Rifles), who
one evening was ferried across in a flat-bottomed boat, and
with a scout or two lay doggo on the enemy bank in order
to discover if they sent out river patrols during the night.
His report was in the negative, and indeed, at this time, the
Turks cannot be congratulated upon their vigilance or activity.
Lieut.-Colonel Anderson's exploit, Captain Smith's reconnaissance, and to crown all, the surprise crossing of the river
itself by the whole Division, prove that their morale was at a
low ebb, and that those opposed to us were " fed-up ".

There were two phases of the action. First, the crossing;
second, the taking of the Turkish positions. If I remember
aright, for some days before the crossing took place our guns
from 2000 hours to midnight kept up a continuous bombardment
upon the enemy trenches, so that when it came to the night
of the crossing the bombardment not only was nothing unusual
to the Turks, but prevented any noises occasioned by our
crossing being heard.

The spot chosen for the 156th Brigade to cross was approxi-
mately at Es Sakieh (see sketch map). The date decided upon
for our venture was the 20th December, and on the evening
of the 18th we were relieved in the front trenches by the Auck-
land Mounted Rifles. Now, when one unit relieves another in
trenches, it is usual for the relieving unit to take over all trench
stores (receipts in duplicate), and to ascertain important points,
to note company dispositions and what posts and patrols are
usually sent out, and always the relieved unit remains until the
relieving troops are in position. That is the methodical infantry
way, but the New Zealanders were not apparently accustomed
to such precise proceedings. Two Squadron-Commanders
arrived in advance of their units and proceeded to the front
line and met the Company-Commanders from whom they were
taking over. That done, they indicated that everything would
be all right; their boys would be along in a little while, and my

companies could now consider themselves relieved. Delightful, but hardly in accordance with our careful programme. We saw all arrive and take over before we left them to their own devices.

During the next two days we had practices in embarking and paddling in flat-bottomed punts, which proved exceedingly useful.

At about 1900 on the 20th the Brigade moved out from Sarona. It was pitch dark; had been raining considerably during the past two days, and the ground, as we approached the river, became softer and deeper and muddier the closer we came to it. However we reached the river about 2100, and were thankful that the bombardment was proceeding with great vehemence, that the rain, on the contrary, was ceasing, and that a grey lightness permitted one to see a few yards in front.

The first battalion to cross at our part was the 7th Battalion H.L.I., which had to move at once towards the river mouth where the rest of their Brigade was crossing, and assail the Ford House trenches from the flank. Then the 4th Royal Scots went over, their objective was the occupation of Slag-heap Farm; next across went the 7th Royal Scots, whose job it was to establish and hold a position round the northern slopes of Muannis to repel a possible enemy counter-attack. After them came the 8th Scottish Rifles, and we had to move through the 4th Royal Scots on our left, leave them in the region of One-Tree Farm, change direction to the right, and again to the right, and swoop down upon Turkish Head-quarters House from the orange grove in its rear. The 7th Scottish Rifles were to be in reserve at about the corner of the orange grove near the river.

After some natural hitches in crossing, owing to the darkness and to the fact that there were two sets of rafts about 100 yards apart, ferrying the troops across, we accomplished the crossing, and with the 7th Royal Scots on our left we progressed in fours, with small advance guards close to us, past Slag-Heap Farm. Then at the corner of the orange grove at One-Tree Farm we parted from the 7th Royal Scots and proceeded on our own objective. Up to this point our going had been fairly easy, though soft and marshy. We had not had a sign of any enemy, and as we moved up to the orange grove past Slag-Heap Farm without challenge, I felt that the gods were on our side, and that things would go well. But as soon as we struck east and then south through the lower orange grove we encountered difficulties. The groves were fairly thick, and the mud and drains which were dug between every second row of trees were so deep and sticky that going was exceedingly difficult. Men fell into the drains and stuck there; they could not move and had to be rescued as if from a morass, and it was difficult to keep in touch. With considerable efforts, however, we continued our stealthy movement, and then made our second change of direction. Our small advance guard soon came to Turkish Head-quarters House, which they surrounded, and after some bombing and vehement adjurations in Turkish learned for the occasion (Ablooka Olondonuz, or similar sounds, meaning " Surrender! you are surrounded "), succeeded in capturing the place, taking prisoner three officers, including a Battalion Commander and ten other ranks, besides an enormous amount of war material, machine-guns, and booty, including two arab stallions, one of which I annexed, and rode regularly for the next two or three months. Having closed up the battalion while this was going on, I moved on to Keyston House, pre-arranged to be my Battalion Head-quarters, time 0200, took one or two more prisoners, and then sent the companies about their business, which was that of mopping up the local system of trenches. Z Company cleared the trenches south of Keyston House (twelve prisoners), X Company the trenches adjoining to the east (six prisoners), and W Company the trenches near the town and the town itself, while Y Company, leaving a platoon at Battalion Head-quarters, employed three platoons to block the southern entrances to the town, and to act as a supporting company to W. Finally, having cleared the trenches, Z, W, and X Companies, leaving small garrisons in each, rendezvoused near Battalion Head-quarters. We had one casualty, one poor fellow killed by a bomb from a fleeing Turk, as we approached Turkish Head-quarters House.

The more one thinks of the action, the more one realizes how really lucky we were. Of course, the element of surprise was complete, except possibly at Khirbet Hadrah, to capture which the 155th Brigade had some stiff fighting, but the 157th Brigade had a bloodless victory, and gained all their objectives, the Turks retreating before them. Two other factors helped us, and these were the extraordinary laxity of vigilance displayed by the Turks, and also, I fancy, the fact that we over-estimated the numbers against us. It was altogether a most successful show, clearly and carefully planned, and the steadiness, silence, and perseverance of the men were beyond praise. I was especially pleased with my own battalion's work, and I know it could never have been accomplished without the many previous reconnaissances already referred to. During the whole night I was always at the end of a wire to Brigade. It says a good deal for our observation that the house captured by us, called Turkish Head-quarters House, actually turned out to be a Turkish Head-quarters. I shudder to think what would have been the result of the action had the Turks been alert and in greater numbers. There were times when a machine-gun could have mown us down like nine-pins, and, of course, had any of our crossings been located, some shells amongst us would have been highly uncomfortable, and might have frustrated the crossing of the Auja. Sir E. Allenby, in his dispatch dated 18th September, 1918, writes as follows:

" The successful crossing of the Nahr El Auja reflects great credit on the 52nd (Lowland) Division. It involved considerable preparation, the details of which were thought out with care and precision. The sodden state of the ground, and, on the night of the crossing, the swollen state of the river, added to the difficulties, yet by dawn the whole of the infantry had crossed. The fact that the enemy were taken by surprise, and that all resistance was overcome with the bayonet without a shot being fired, bears testimony to the discipline of this Division. Eleven officers, including two Battalion Commanders, and 305 other ranks, and ten machine guns were captured in this operation."

When morning dawned all Brigades had gained their objectives, and the Turks had retired in front of us, but not far;

for they could be seen some 2000 yards farther north, holding
a line of dug rifle-pits, evidently determined to put up some
rear-guard resistance.

We passed the day resting, the battalion having concentrated
in Muannis, and in the evening orders came for a further move
forwards on the 22nd. The whole Division advanced upon a
three-brigade front, the 155th and 157th on our right and left
respectively. The country, the southern part of the Plain of
Sharon, was generally undulating, with rolling downs and
gentle slopes, the surface of which sometimes was sandy and
sometimes muddy, and covered with turf and flowers, which
though sparse, gave a general spring-like look, but, after limbers
and guns had made a track, the going became heavy and difficult.
The 7th and 8th Scottish Rifles in artillery formation led the
Brigade, the 7th being on our right, and as we started off from
Muannis the spectacle of the Division advancing across country
was a very fine one, more like a peace parade effort than anything else. The Turks did not wait long for us; they were well
peppered by our gunners from our rear, and their hastily
flung-up rifle pits were not of much use as cover. But as we
got closer, here and there a machine-gun spoke out, and a
certain amount of rifle fire assailed our front lines. From where
I was riding I could see the Turks scuttling back from their
trenches, and as we continued on the move and did not use
any rifle fire, I rushed up my two machine-guns to the front,
and from a vantage ground got them on to the retreating Turks
at 700 or 1000 yards distance. It was an interesting show,
and not entirely bloodless, for Hannan was hit in the arm and
six other men wounded. Soon we reached our objectives,
and the Turks were turned out of Jellil, Tel-el-Nuriyeh,
Ballutah, Mukmar, and Arsuf. Nuriyeh and Ballutah were
the objectives allotted to 156th Brigade. A rough Divisional
line was selected, and we commenced to dig-in and consolidate
the line we had won.

The weather now, after a couple of fine days, again broke,
and that evening heavy rain and strong winds beat down
upon us, and our bivouacs were perilously near to being blown
over. Some *were* carried away. Boyd and Nicholl can testify

to a midnight flitting in mud and soaked clothes. Next day was Christmas Day, also cold and wet. It is recorded in my diary that packets of 10,000 " Three Castles " cigarettes were issued, also rum. That was the best we could do to cheer ourselves on the occasion, and I cannot recollect when the cigarettes arrived. Our mails were long overdue, as all the available transport was required for bringing ammunition and supplies up to the troops from railhead at Ludd.

On the 26th we moved forward about 1000 yards, and started to dig the agreed-upon final Divisional line, linked up with the other Brigades. We were now, together with the 7th Scottish Rifles and the 156th Brigade T.M. Battery, attached to the 155th Brigade, while the 4th and 7th Royal Scots on our left were attached to the 157th Brigade. Our own Brigade Head-quarters had moved back for a quiet sojourn at Sarona.

During this month the battalion strength had been increased by six officers and 200 other ranks, its effective strength now being 24 officers and 680 other ranks, of whom all the officers and 586 other ranks were with the battalion. The names of the officers joining or rejoining were: 2nd-Lieuts. G. M. Bathgate, A. Macdougall, A. F. Grierson, G. D. Watson, A. Paterson, and W. M. Winter.

The months of November and December, 1917, had been, in many ways, the most strenuous period of the battalion's experience in the war up till then, but it was a time which I am sure no one who went through it would have wished to have missed. Apart from the great experience of it (and that was, I imagine, one the like of which was unsurpassed in any of the theatres of war), it knitted the battalion together in a way which is only comparable to its state when we went to Gallipoli. At that time the battalion spirit was magnificent, men and officers loved and trusted each other; but it was then the trust of mutual liking and a common object, not one born of dangers, of deeds done together, and hardships endured. Now, the battalion, though much changed from Gallipoli days, through its experiences, had found itself, and, combined with the feeling of mutual trust, there was also the sense of self-reliance and knowledge of how to deal with situations which

was absent in our first adventure in Gallipoli, and which now
after these months of campaigning made itself realized throughout all ranks.

At the beginning of January, our belated Christmas gifts were
delivered, and they arrived in a pitiable state. The parcels had
been on the way out since October, and after arrival in Egypt
had been held up at various points. They had often been
dumped out in the open, drenched with rain, and actually
thrown out of the trains into mud and rain pools, as we heard
afterwards. They had, at one time, been returned to Kantara,
and eventually came up to Jaffa by sea. Practically all the
food was sodden, and the cigarettes soaked with rain; ad-
dresses were obliterated, and after all efforts were made to
find the owners, there still remained a considerable number
of derelict parcels unclaimed. Anything worth salvaging was
distributed round companies. We were as disappointed as
children. Here is General Hill's New Year Greeting to us:

" OFFICERS AND MEN OF THE
          52ND (LOWLAND) DIVISION!

        " At the end of the year it is generally the custom to look
back. The year 1917 is the 4th year of the Great War, and a great
year for the Allies in Europe, a greater year for the British in every
part of the world, and the greatest year for the 52nd (Lowland)
Division in Palestine.

        " In the attack on Gaza on the 1st November, the one Brigade,
the 156th, representing the Division, was the only Brigade who
took all its objectives. During the whole of our long advance through
Palestine you have never failed me; you went from trench warfare
to open warfare, and again to hill warfare, always cheerful, always
victorious; no matter how difficult was the operation I called upon
you to carry out, you carried it out with your usual dash and Scottish
determination. The whole of these operations ended in the forcing
of the passage of the River Auja, which was the hardest operation
I have called upon you to undertake. The difficulties were enormous
—first getting down to the river itself over waterlogged and boggy
country—then the crossing of the river—a river 35 yards in breadth
and varying between 12 and 14 feet in depth.

        " In order to make matters as difficult as possible for us, it rained
hard the three days previous to ' The Night '—the boggy country
got boggier—the river got broader and deeper. In order to make
the enterprise a surprise to the Turk, we all prayed for a wet night.

What did it matter if we were wetter than we had been for the past three days? But what happened? After raining all the night before and up to midday, it began to clear up, and when the time you were going to attempt your crossing and surprise arrived, there was hardly a cloud in the sky and a half moon. It looked almost impossible that the operation could be a success. However, I had every confidence in you, and I ordered the crossing to be carried out. The result now everyone knows, including the Turk, who had the greatest surprise of his life. By good discipline there was not a sound; eight battalions of stout-hearted Scots crossed, and an attack on an extremely strong fortified position covering a front of 7000 yards was commenced under the best barrage that Scottish Artillery have ever put up. Even then the attack was not bound to succeed—by no means. In order for that attack to succeed, it meant every Officer, every N.C.O., and every Man meant to win through: and that is why the Lowland Division that night won through, because everyone meant to win through. Scottish endurance, determination and pluck carried ' The Night '. By dawn I was able to report that we had taken every objective—a magnificent performance—a fitting ending to our triumphal progress through Palestine.

" This applies not only to the Infantry, who have borne the burden of the fight, but to the Artillery, without whom the Infantry could have done nothing, and to the R.E. (think of the River Auja!), the Divisional Train, without whom we should have starved, and our Lowland Ambulances, who have worked day and night in looking after our wounded. Our Signal Company, who have on every occasion been instrumental in keeping up communication which means everything in success.

" You can all be proud of what you have done. I can assure you that I am.

" I said that at the end of a year it is generally the custom to look back. Now I am going to look forward.

" A Company, a Battalion, a Brigade, and a Division wins a great name for itself by what it does in war; but it can lose it very easily by what it does while there is no fighting going on. Don't forget that all men, no matter whether they are Commanders-in-Chief or private soldiers, have very short memories. Everyone now is talking of the 52nd Division—what a splendid Division they are, &c., &c.

" I hate to have to look into the future, but I do so with a great purpose—a purpose over which I have no power—neither I as Divisional Commander, nor your Brigadiers, nor your Commanding Officers, nor your Company-Commanders—in short, no one—except yourselves.

A RUM ISSUE

C.S.M. Peter Campbell renewing the youth of his Sergeants.
His invariable practice was to serve out the rum up wind, thus
securing to himself a slight rebate

" By real hard fighting, determination, and Scottish pluck during two months you have won yourselves a great name. By drunkenness and insubordination you can lose that fine name in as many hours! You have clenched your teeth and fought. I ask you now to clench your teeth and observe discipline—if you will; I know you can.

" I thank you all and I wish you one and all a Happy New Year, and the very best of luck during 1918.

" Here's tae us—wha's like us!

(Signed) JOHN HILL,
Major-General,
Commanding 52nd (Lowland) Division."

1st January, 1918.

Up to the 4th January we remained under the wing of 155th Brigade, digging and wiring the front-line trenches. The weather was unsettled, but we were fairly comfortably dug-in, and experience of bad weather appalled us not at all.

On the 11th January, along with the rest of the Brigade Group, we moved back into billets in Sarona. And very pleasant it was again to be under a roof. I managed to get a large marquee, and we had a Battalion Mess, a thing which it had been impossible to arrange before, except during one short period at Romani, when we had a big hut in which we all messed together. The marquee was a great success, and Dulieu, who, had he not been cast for the Army, would have made his mark certainly as a landscape gardener, produced for our delectation flowers and shrubs, and arbours, and walks, which, in the dark, looked quite romantic until you saw farther round into the kitchen premises.

One night, when the B.G.C. and staff were dining with us, also my young cousin, Norman Crockatt, Royal Scots, then Major at Corps Head-quarters, the B.G.C. sprang upon us a practice alarm, the preliminary moves of which were carried through with his usual thoroughness. Just as we had finished dinner, an orderly arrived and a message was handed to Sayer, the B.M., who, after reading it, gravely handed it to the Brigadier. The latter then informed me that we should

have to move out at once to the second-line position, which
had been reconnoitred by us only two or three days before,
and which was about a mile in rear of our front line. Getting
up from the table with apologies for spoiling our dinner party,
he ordered me to report when we were ready to move. In a
moment we were off to our particular jobs, got into our fighting kit, and in a short time all companies reported ready to
move. Of course, it must be understood that all personal kit,
save what one could get into a haversack, or into saddlebags,
remained behind; all boxes of ammunition and bombs, Lewis
guns, signalling and medical apparatus were always carried
ready to be loaded up at a moment's notice; also, at the time
chosen, viz. 2200, all men were in billets, and we could turn
out for immediate action in considerably less than an hour.
If I remember aright, on this occasion, we were ready first of
the Brigade in about 35 minutes, and the other battalions
within 10 minutes after that. Only then were we informed
that parades could be dismissed. It was rather an anti-climax
to our guest-night, and though some gay spirits tried to revive
the atmosphere of conviviality, most fellows turned in.

When in billets in Sarona, we managed to get bathing for
the men in some locally arranged baths; we carried out a certain amount of refitting; disinfection and inoculation also
constantly reduced the numbers for parade, so that training
was carried on under the usual difficulties, but we did good
work with the signallers, Lewis gunners, and scouts.

At this time, as above mentioned, we reconnoitred a second-
line position in rear of our front line—first with the B.G.C.,
who allotted me an area, then with my Company-Commanders
to whom I in turn allotted areas. The Company-Commanders and Scouts reconnoitred their positions by day and
at night, so that there could be no mistake if they had to take
up a position at any time.

On the night 29/30th January, we relieved the 5th Royal
Scots Fusiliers, who were left-reserve battalion in the right
sector of the 52nd Divisional Sector, Sheik Ballutah area.
It was an easy relief, but Z Company had to go off about half
a mile away to be escort to Heavies near Burns' Cottage.

Another battalion of 156th Brigade likewise relieved their vis-à-vis of 155th Brigade on our right.

During February, inside the Brigade, we changed over twice with the 7th Royal Scots, always easily carried-out reliefs. Whether in the line or in reserve, we carried on the necessary work of digging and wiring and strengthening our positions.

While out of the line we were responsible for a certain amount of patrolling which had to be carried on in No Man's Land. This patrol work was exceedingly useful, and our experience here became of great value in France later on. At this time too, I carried on a good deal of scout and Lewis-gun training, and the scouts, under my I.O., 2nd-Lieut. J. Miller, became expert and self-reliant, and would go anywhere with him. They did some particularly useful night work with experiments in colour schemes. The weather during the month was cold and changeable, and cheerless generally. The following officers arrived from hospital: 2nd-Lieuts. R. G. L. Gray, and Lieut. G. D. Watson. From the United Kingdom came Lieuts. L. M. Watson and C. France, with drafts of 19 other ranks each. Captain W. R. Alexander-Keeble, 1st Loyal North Lancs., was posted to the battalion, and arrived on the 27th in a motor car, which came across country from the Auja. The car was filled with a wonderful amount of sports gear, which gave us an interesting side-light upon Keeble's idea of what he had come for. He was a keen officer, however, and soon assimilated ideas of trench work. The 155th Brigade at this time organized a little hunt in the low ground near Arsuf, where there were quite a number of foxes, or rather jackals, and once or twice we went over and had some good runs. Keeble on two occasions was first home, and on one occasion he got the brush and on another the pads. There were, of course, no hounds, so it was necessary to ride down the quarry until he or we could go no farther. Generally speaking, he succeeded in getting to ground somewhere in a hole in a wadi, so that though we often had goodish short runs, we seldom had a " kill ". Moreover the ground was treacherous. In some of the dura fields one would sink into soft parts up to one's horse's chest, and sometimes quite deep and rocky wadis would suddenly appear in an unexpected manner. On one occasion we followed Brer Fox through the wire into No Man's Land on to ground well-known to have been registered by the Turkish gunners. I suppose John Turk was interested in our amusement (if he was not asleep), and being a sportsman, he refrained from sending any shells among the field. Anyhow, he didn't fire a single shot, and having lost our quarry, we returned to other and safer hunting grounds. Reminds one of Wellington's officers and their hunt on the Peninsula a century ago. History is always repeating itself.

March also was a month of very changeable weather. On the 19th we were relieved by the 157th Brigade, the battalion changing over with the 6th Battalion H.L.I., whose billets in Sarona we took over and occupied. During our time in Sarona, we had sports and Brigade football tournaments, and other amusements, including a mess dinner presided over with great éclat by Keeble, in my absence on leave. I was informed afterwards that the dinner had been a most successful affair—they had succeeded in breaking the ankle of an unfortunate Flying Officer, who was rash enough to take part in a Rugby scrum amongst Scots forwards. A deal of time was passed (some young officers said wasted) in disinfectings and inoculations for T.A.B. A good deal of leave was permitted both to Cairo and Jerusalem, and at the same time there was a spate of courses which were attended by various officers, who I hope benefited therefrom. I left for short leave to Cairo myself, and I think the B.G.C., Bruce Allan, his Staff-Captain, and young Souter came along at the same time.

On the 28th the battalion moved back to Surafend near Ramleh, arriving there about 2330. By this time we were beginning to suspect that the 52nd Division was destined for another front. The March offensive of the Boches had put an end to vacillation about reinforcements to the Western Front. So we were all on tip-toe of expectation and hoping to have the opportunity of a " go " at the Huns. On this same date, Dulieu, who had been the Adjutant for nearly two years, left the battalion to take up the job of A.P.M., 52nd Division.

IN THE JUDEAN HILLS: CAMEL TRANSPORT RETURNING FROM THE HILLS

After bringing supplies to the Front Line

I was very sorry to lose him; he had been a most conscientious and capable Adjutant, liked by everybody, and excellent at instructing N.C.Os. Captain E. R. Boyd, who had been understudying Dulieu for some time past, assumed his mantle, and proved himself to be a thoroughly satisfactory successor. Lieut. F. S. V. Barr arrived from the United Kingdom on this date. On the 1st April I arrived back from leave to find the battalion preparing for entrainment to Kantara. On the 2nd Major W. R. Alexander-Keeble was transferred to another Division, and Major G. R. V. Hume-Gore, Gordon Highlanders, was posted as my second-in-command. Next morning, to our great grief, all our transport was taken from us. Those of us who were mounted, and all the transport personnel, had become during all those long months very much attached to our horses and mules, and it was a sad parting. Somebody took a photograph of my old " Squire ", who had carried me through many a day's trek in sand, in mud, in sun, in rain, never sick or sorry—an ideal officer's charger whose like I'll never see again. I never was the recipient of a copy of that photograph. I think that my faithful groom, Archie Ferguson, was sorrier even than I was to see the last of the good horse.

I cannot leave these chapters on our campaigns in Sinai and Palestine without some reference to the lighter side of our experiences. One of the compensations of a very strenuous period—and we had to be content with " sma' mercies "—was general good weather. I have mentioned our essays at hunting near Ballutah, and one or two dinners in Sarona, but these were officers' amusements. When opportunity came we had sports within the battalion, and football matches against other units in the Brigade. On one occasion I recollect we had rather good impromptu sports at Wadi Simeon, after being relieved at the Apex, in front of Gaza. We had an inter-company tug-of-war which created great rivalry, and a mule scurry, bare-backed across country, which was great fun. 2nd-Lieut. P. E. Frankau, who was a bit of a horseman, won it.

We also had many camp-fire concerts, which were appreciated according to the amount of sentimentality evoked by the singers. I expect the beauty and romance of these Eastern nights, coupled with a feeling of home-sickness, combined to make the men inclined—even more than usual—to senti-mental effusions. At any rate, " It's a long long trail ", and " Bonnie Scotland ", and the like, were the greatest favourites. Also we used to have a most popular song called " I'd love to be a sailor ", from Captain E. R. Boyd, which expressed in certain topical verses composed by himself some soldiers' views on the war and the services. Here they are:

Sometimes when we were fechtin' in that blinkin' Holy Land,
When we lived on iron rations and were chewing desert sand,
There was no tobacco issue, there was nothing strong to drink,
I lay in mud and shivered and would very often think

Chorus:

I wish I was a Sailor, a Sailor, a Sailor,
Sailing on the ocean deep and blue, yes I do;
I wish I was a Sailor, a Sailor, a Sailor,
Sailing on the good ship *Kangaroo*.

And when the shells were bursting and the battle raging hot
We aye were moving forward—though we'd really rather not,
And when the bullets flew around and whistled through our hair
We naturally fixed our swords and softly murmured there:

Now if we're ever called to fecht in any future war,
I won't forget the bombs and guns and bowler hats and gore,
And when the Boys go marching off with rifles, belts and packs
I'll go and join the Navy, and I'll hoist my bell-mouthed slacks.

Their effect depends entirely upon how they are sung, and Boyd certainly made a *succès fou* of the song.

The " turns " varied with the drafts we received and casualties incurred. In the summer of 1917 we had quite a plethora of talent. One Macinally, a pawky Scot, was a real humorist, and he used to regale us with tales of when he was a " caady "—I don't suppose he ever was one, but it was a good peg to hang his series of stories upon. I regret that the best of them are not suitable to these polite pages.

We also had a wonderful conjuror—Gilmour was his name—and his *chef-d'œuvre* was taking off a man's shirt, with his tunic still on him and buttoned up. He would get hold of some luckless wight of the latest draft and give him quite a rough time with his hands (*léger-de-main!*) and his tongue. The feat required a good deal of pulling and pushing and hauling and squeezing, took quite a considerable time, and invariably brought the house down, or made the heavens fall, or whatever suitable simile you may care to give to this moonlight episode.

CHAPTER VIII

France and Flanders

On the 3rd of April the battalion paraded at 1500 for the march to Ludd, where we were to entrain. Boyd and I had been lent a horse each to go to the station, and mine was a skittish young mare who had apparently never seen infantry. It was with some difficulty that I got her close enough to the battalion to give the necessary order to move. However, she calmed down on the march, though each motor lorry or other vehicle which passed us caused her an attack of St. Vitus's dance. But at our first halt, as I was dismounting, she plunged forward suddenly, throwing me on my head in the road. (She must have been badly treated at one time.) I was concussed for some hours, removed to a Field Hospital at Ludd, and next day forwarded on to Kantara en route for Alexandria. It is related—the reader can judge for himself with what accuracy —that as I lay at the side of the road, a somewhat sorry object, General Allenby passed in his car, and seeing me, remarked " Another of these drunken Scotsmen!" The battalion, now under the command of Hume-Gore, entrained and arrived at Kantara next morning for breakfast, where the following officers joined, having come from the United Kingdom: Lieut. C. C. Gordon, 2nd-Lieuts. J. Meikle, W. H. Reid, C. M. Russell, A. Brown, and Captain W. D. Hannan, M.C., from hospital. Next day, the 5th, the battalion arrived at Gabbari Dock, Alexandria, and embarked on board H.M.T. *Canberra*, which lay in the harbour until the 11th, when she sailed for Marseilles, in convoy with the remainder of 52nd Division, escorted by destroyers. Hume-Gore and Boyd during these days of leisure had found out my hospital in

Alexandria, and came to see me. I was quite all right as far
as my head was concerned, but my left knee had developed
a large and watery pad under and around the kneecap—somewhat painful, and a most infernal nuisance. I was most
thoroughly exasperated that I was to be left behind owing to
this silly cropper, but I just had to make the best of it.

The battalion arrived at Marseilles on the 17th, after a
peaceful voyage, and marched to Camp Fournier for the night,
where they were joined by 2nd-Lieuts. B. W. Palmer, T.
Gentleman, and J. C. Lucas, also the Rev. W. S. Wilson,
returned from home leave. After three nights in the train, with
occasional halts, the battalion reached Noyelles at 0630 on
the 20th, and proceeded to the town for breakfast, after which
they route-marched to Le Bout de Crocs via St. Firmin. Here
they were billeted in the village and neighbouring farms, and
remained until the 24th April, busily engaged in gas-drill,
close-order drill, musketry, and route marches. Soon they
moved on again, and after a night in the train they detrained
at Wizernes, in Belgium, and breakfasted in a field near the
station, after which they marched to Mametz where they found
most unsatisfactory billets; Battalion Head-quarters and Head-
quarters Company therefore moved to Glomenghen, a mile or
so away, thus giving more room for the remainder of the
battalion at Mametz. On the 29th the whole battalion attended
a lecture by Lieut.-Colonel R. B. Campbell, Gordon Highlanders, who was Army Instructor in bayonet fighting at the
time, and his blood-curdling and thrilling description of that
kind of hand-to-hand fighting did much, I have no doubt, to
inspire the battalion with the necessary " hate " prior to
meeting the Boche.

The battalion remained at Mametz until the 8th of May,
when they entrained at Aire for Acq, where they arrived at
1330, and after dinner they marched to a camp at Neuville
St. Vaast, near Arras, changing next day into Ottawa Camp
at Mont St. Eloi. Here I joined up again on the 13th May,
having managed to wangle my way out of hospital in Alexandria,
and my passage across. It is difficult enough to get out of
hospital when one is still considered unfit, but it is still more

difficult to get Transport authorities to do anything for an odd man whom they know nothing about, even though he be a battalion commander. It was necessary to be put on some nominal roll ordered to France, to have this authority, and that endorsement, and a discharge from hospital, and so on. Eventually I found a large draft of miscellaneous ones destined for the Lowland Division, bored to tears in a hot dusty camp near Alexandria. I arranged matters with Captain A. C. Stewart (6th attd. 8th Scottish Rifles) who commanded the draft, saw the Chief Embarkation Officer, produced my hardly-won hospital discharge, and on the 30th April, I think, we sailed for Marseilles on the *Kaiser-i-Hind*, in convoy with the 75th Division. On board were the Ayr and Lanark Yeomanry (now 12th Royal Scots Fusiliers), Lieut.-Colonel W. F. Houldsworth commanding; O.C. Troops was Lieut.-Colonel Beckett, D.S.O., commanding a pioneer battalion.

On arrival at Marseilles, I made myself pleasant to the railway people (fortunately the Chief R.T.O. was an old Cameronian), and was comfortably packed off by night in a wagon-lit, by the Sud Express for Paris, and so to the battalion. A goodly portion of the drafts for the Division on the *Kaiser-i-Hind* was destined for the 8th, but the men never materialized, many of them not even reaching the Division. On the day following my return to the battalion, by the kindly order of the B.G.C., I went off on fourteen days' home leave. After two years' absence, what was a fortnight? Well, at any rate, it was appreciated!

Two days later, on the 15th, the battalion relieved the 4th K.O.S.B. in the front line, opposite Arleux, and in front of Vimy. This at the time was a quiet front, and the work carried on was chiefly improvement of trenches and patrolling. On the 23rd the battalion relieved the 7th Royal Scots in the support line, and Battalion Head-quarters, X Company (less two platoons) and Y Company returned to Hills Camp, Neuville St. Vaast, the other companies being in bivouac just behind the reserve line, and it was in these positions that I found them when I arrived back from leave on the 1st June. Shortly before this, our C. of E. Padre, W. S. Wilson, who had been with the battalion since May, 1915, left us to our regret for some other sphere, and his place was filled by Padre Clairmonte, a man who had had a varied and interesting career. Having taken orders, he went to the South African War, then became a trader in North-West Canada, was appointed to a parish in South Africa, whence he came to serve in France. He was thoroughly approved of by all ranks. He used to go round the front-line trenches, and talk with the men, taking the same chances that they did—unfortunately he was retained with the 52nd Division when we left it.

June was an eventful month for us, though not from the fighting point of view. On the 2nd we went into Divisional Reserve, and on the 11th we again relieved the 4th K.O.S.B. in the front-line left sub-section of the Divisional sector, a daylight relief, completed at 1530. We remained there until the 20th, when we relieved the 7th Royal Scots again in the support line. During our period in the front line, we carried out valuable reconnaissances by night and by day, and we did a good deal of work in the way of wiring and digging.

On the 25th I received information that the infantry Brigades of our Division were to be reduced by one battalion, and the junior battalion was to be the one to go. This meant that we, the 5th K.O.S.B. and the 5th A. & S.H. would leave the 52nd Division. These three battalions were to constitute the 103rd Brigade of the 34th Division, which was being re-formed after very severe casualties incurred in March, 1918. This proposed change was a great shock, and a very real grief to us. To leave the old 156th Brigade with which we had fought and endured and suffered since the beginning, was a great wrench. We knew them, they knew us, and we had confidence in each other. A crumb of comfort was that the other units going with us and to be brigaded with us, were from the 52nd Division, but we knew nothing about any of our other new comrades; we felt as though we were being launched into the blue on a new venture. We had been such excellent friends in the 156th Brigade. We all adored and trusted our B.G.C., Brigadier-General Leggett. It was a hateful parting, but it had to be.

We were relieved by the 7th Royal Scots and 7th Scottish

Rifles in the support line on 27th June, and moved back to Mont St. Eloi, where the same evening we were inspected by Sir A. Hunter-Weston, Corps Commander, who was very complimentary. He asked that all men still in the battalion who had served in Gallipoli might fall out in the front of the battalion, and to my surprise nearly 130 did so. I would have put the number at not more than half that. He spoke to each of them individually.

Here are the letters of farewell which I received on our departure from Major-General Hill and Brigadier-General Leggett, commanding the Division and the Brigade respectively:

Head-quarters,
156th Infantry Brigade.

To
    Lieut.-Colonel J. M. Findlay, D.S.O., the Officers, Warrant Officers, Non-commissioned Officers, and men of the 1/8th The Cameronians (Scottish Rifles).

" It is with great regret that I have to write you this farewell order.

" Though I have only been associated with you as your Divisional Commander for the past ten months, I have had ample time to judge of your splendid behaviour both in billets and in the Field.

" From November 7th till December 23rd, 1917, you were called upon almost every day to take part in some offensive operation against the Turk and on every occasion you showed the magnificent fighting quality you possessed.

" You are now going to another Division and so are lost to the 52nd (Lowland) Division, but I can assure you that I, and all the Officers and men of the Lowland Division, will watch your further movements with the greatest confidence and interest.

" You and the other two Battalions leaving this Division will probably be formed into a Brigade. I want you never to forget that you once belonged to the 52nd (Lowland) Division.

" Good-bye and the very best of good luck is the wish of your very grateful Divisional Commander.

(Sgd.) John Hill,
Major-General,
Commanding 52nd (Lowland) Division."

26th June, 1918,
France.

HEAD-QUARTERS,
156th Infantry Brigade.

" My dear Findlay,

" The circumstances under which you and your battalion are leaving us prevent me, for obvious reasons, from issuing what I much wish to issue, namely a Special Brigade Order of the Day.

" I cannot let you leave, however, without letting you know how grieved and distressed I am that the requirements of the moment necessitate your leaving the 52nd Division, thereby depriving all of us of many a friend and this Brigade of a splendid fighting battalion.

" From Gallipoli days right through to the present time, under your gallant and fearless leadership, the Officers and men of the 1/8th Scottish Rifles have ever proved themselves second to none whenever great hardships had to be endured and whenever hard fighting had to be done. It is not too much to say that by the dauntless courage and dash displayed in every action in which your battalion has taken part, you its leader and all your gallant officers and men, have still further enhanced the great and glorious reputation of your Regiment, and done much to make the reputation which this Brigade enjoys to-day.

" Any words of mine are quite inadequate to convey to you and your lads the intense gratitude I have towards you all for your great services to me and this Brigade. I thank you with all my heart for what you have done. I shall be grateful if you will let it be clearly understood that the new Brigade of which you are to form a part has been formed from the Junior Battalion of each Brigade in this Division. The orders concerning this came from higher authority, were definite and final, and consequently could not be questioned.

" I know that the disappointment you all feel is necessarily bound to be great, but I can assure you it is equalled by the disappointment and regret we all have at losing you.

" Speaking for myself and on behalf of the whole Brigade I now wish you farewell and all possible good luck in the days to come.

" We shall, I trust, ever keep in touch with you and you with us. We shall follow your fortunes with the greatest interest and affection, and know that whatever you are called upon to do or face in the future, you will do as well and as gloriously as you have ever done in the past.

Always,
Yours very sincerely,
(Sgd.) A. H. Leggett, Brigadier-General,
Commanding 156th Brigade."

In the Field, 27/6/18.

Next day we embussed at 1030 at Château d'Acque for Belgium, and after being seen off in great style by the Division and Brigade we arrived at Bambecque at 2130. We billeted there for the night. On the 30th we marched to St. Janster-Beisin, a hutted camp about 12 miles away. It was a hot, airless, and dusty day; the men, unaccustomed to marching with packs, and being out of condition generally, found the march most trying, but we arrived. That morning our new B.G.C., Brigadier-General J. G. Chaplin, a Cameronian, visited us, along with Major-General C. L. Nicholson (now Sir Cecil), commanding the Division. They were both very charming and helpful, and one began to feel a little more at home with a Cameronian B.G.C. and a Divisional General both of whom inspired one with confidence, and who obviously had experience and capacity. The Divisional Staff also did all they could for us, and were good fellows.

St. Janster-Beisin was a poor place. The hutted camp we took over was dirty; its surroundings were drab and desolate, and the natives screwed the last penny they could out of any poor Jock who had a few centimes to spare. Belgium, in this respect, was, if possible, worse than France. One knows and deplores the enormous losses and hardships they endured owing to the invasion of the Boches, but one also knows of the very considerable personal gains they succeeded in acquiring from the British soldiery. I suppose it is natural, but one cannot but feel that they should have had a certain amount of gratitude to us as Britishers, which might have evinced itself in such small ways as dealing fairly with our soldiers when they bought vegetables, tabac, eggs, milk, &c. We thought that the Americans, being by now replete with British gold, might have been fairer game, especially as their pay was about five times that of our soldiers.

While in this delectable spot we were inspected by the Army Commander, General Sir H. Plumer, and the Corps Commander, Lieut.-General Sir C. Jacobs. Both, and especially the former, gave me the impression of extraordinary ability. I've no doubt that they will be duly flattered(?) if ever they see this, but I do not mean it in any other sense than to show that " Heid Yins " sometimes cannot hide their light. I believe they were satisfied with the battalion.

On the 5th July 2nd-Lieuts. N. C. Thomson, A. F. Mackay, and W. M. Crawford joined the battalion. Next day, all surplus baggage was collected and dispatched by transport by road to Cormette, whither the battalion, with the rest of the Brigade, entrained on the 7th. Cormette was a hutted musketry camp, and Brigade had made out a programme which all the battalions carried out for the next five days. Four hours or so of musketry was carried out every day, and the other training was close-order drill, gas drill, physical training, and bayonet fighting under a special instructor, C.S.M. Dixon, from the Bayonet-Fighting School. I also carried out a little battalion drill in close order. One morning, when engaged in battalion drill, I was endeavouring to instruct the battalion in the intricacies of the " wheel ", when my horse, bored to tears, lay down in the midst of my harangue. It says much for the discipline of the battalion that I observed never a smile, and that a groom, as if anticipating the event, approached with another horse and departed with the delinquent. I ought to have mentioned that on our arrival in France another complete transport was issued to us, including horses, mules, limbers, wagons, saddlery, and harness, which we had to make the best of. Some of the animals were not bad, but, generally speaking, the whole outfit was poor compared with what we had left in Palestine. Captain Nicholl, my Transport-Officer, however, after a time, succeeded in producing a most creditable-looking transport, but more of this anon.

On 13th July, at Cormette, I arranged a platoon attack competition, which was won by No. 16 Platoon of Z Company (Captain Findlay), but nobody could claim much credit for the show, as the weather was very bad and the shooting equally so.

On the 14th July we entrained for Proven, where we were for the time being in front of Ypres in reserve, and we carried out various reconnaissances with a view eventually to taking over a portion of the front line. However, suddenly after orders for the occupation of the reserve line had been issued, the B.G.C. came along and told me that we were " for " the south (destination unknown), and next morning, the 17th, we marched to Waayenburg and entrained for—somewhere unknown. We were detrained next day at 1200 at Survilliers, south of Chantilly. At 1630 we set out by route march for Balagny, some 3 or 4 miles east of Senlis, through which town we passed, arriving at Balagny footsore and weary at 2200. In the dark it was most difficult to spot billets, and owing to a mistake, 2nd-Lieut. Russell, who had been sent on in advance to arrange the billeting, had gone to Chantilly to meet us. However, he retrieved X Company, which had left Waayenburg by a later train than the remainder of the battalion, and eventually we all concentrated at Balagny. Next morning orders came at 0655 to embuss about a mile away at 0700. I was *au lit* when these arrived by the hand of a French Liaison Officer, who, voluble and polite, explained to me the position; he seemed to be accustomed to interviewing Commanding Officers in their beds. We actually embussed at 0815, which was a good effort considering that the men had breakfast during the interval, though various officers including the C.O. and Adjutant did not. The 34th Division, concentrated in the Senlis area, was now under the orders of General Penet, commanding the 30th Corps of the 10th French Army (General Mangin), who had on the 13th attacked the Boche north of Soissons and driven the enemy back some five miles, taking many prisoners and guns. We were to take part in the exploitation of this victory. The French arranged the embussing for us, and the busses were driven by Frenchmen. They provided a motor-car for myself and Adjutant, and as we went much faster than the busses we endeavoured to acquire some provender whilst passing through several villages en route. These, however, were absolutely devoid of anything in the way of food. I recollect that we at last secured one or two pomegranates or some such watery fruit. After we had covered some fifteen or twenty miles, we came to a little village called Russy, where we met the B.G.C., who told us we would bivouac there but that we must debuss some few miles farther on, and on a loop road, so as not to interfere with the traffic in the main road.

On we went to Vancièmes and marched back to Russy, only to find that we were not to billet in the village but to bivouac in an adjoining wood—the Bois-de-Tillet. This wood was delightful, cool and shady, and full of soft spots to sleep on, and the men were soon comfortably ensconced under the spreading branches, which tempted not the Boche aeroplanes which came over during the night. It had been a tiring hot day, with a scrappy meal to begin on, and an unnecessary march back from the aforesaid loop. On our journey to Vancièmes we passed a huge party of Hun prisoners, most of whom seemed done-in, ready to accept their lot, and grateful for a drink of water. It is significant to note that the battalion passed them without a word. I wonder if the same could be said of a Boche battalion under the same circumstances. It was late afternoon on the 19th when we arrived at the Bois-de-Tillet, and we had a complete day's rest there on the 20th which we all enjoyed thoroughly.

We may have thought that in our time we had got used to rain and mud, but the night of 20/21st and the morning of 21st July, were about as unhappy experiences in the wet we ever put in. We moved from the Bois-de-Tillet at 2000 hours, and leaving Hume-Gore with the nucleus and heavy baggage, joined the remainder of the Brigade at Feigneux. On our arrival at Brigade rendezvous at Feigneux, I received orders that our objective was Soucy, a little battered village near Villers-Cotterets, about 18 miles away, but we would not move until midnight, and with this cheering news came heavy drenching rain, accompanied by thunder and lightning, to add zest to our vigil, which was spent by all ranks trying to get shelter from the cold wet elements.

We at last got on the move thankfully about midnight, and, although held up by a Brigade of artillery at a cross roads, progressed fairly well. As dawn broke, we were traversing beautiful forests, which, of course, we appreciated thoroughly (?) The going was bad owing to the rain, and we were footsore, and tired and hungry, but it was astonishing how, when we eventually arrived at Soucy about 0930, the men chirped up, and cooked and cleaned and made themselves comfortable.

Soon after we had settled down, two home mails rolled up. How on earth it was managed, Heaven and the Postal Service alone know! One would have thought it impossible to get track of us so quickly; extraordinary! delightful happening! which changed all our ordinary views of the Army Postal Service.

A more devastated village than Soucy it would have been difficult to find. The whole place was dilapidation and dust. As I went round seeing if my companies were comfortable (comparatively speaking) I came across an old friend, Jack Spiers, who was there with some gunners, sitting down against a wall with one or two other fellows, trying to get some breakfast. I hadn't seen him for several years; he had come back from New Zealand, where he had been farming. I was glad to meet him again, and he was still with his beloved horses.

At Soucy, Brigade found me a bed in their Head-quarters' house, so, as we remained there overnight (21/22nd), I had a decent and much-needed sleep, and I don't think any of us failed to achieve this happy though temporary oblivion that night. Up with the lark next morning, I rode off with two Company-Commanders, Eric Findlay and M'Combie, for a reconnaissance of the French front on the Parcy-Tigny area. Our road lay through Longpoint, Villiers-Hellon, up to Bois-de-Maulay, where, in a cave, had been established a French Regimental (Brigade) Head-quarters. Ever since we had embussed from Balagny we had encountered all along the route, troops and more troops, some bivouacking in the woods, others on the move forwards or backwards, Dumps, Royal Engineers, Americans and French, the latter of whose guns were constantly barking and spitting, and whose ammunition columns spared not their horse-flesh. The country was very difficult from the point of view of observation. It was closely wooded, with numerous roads through the woods. Though undulating, there were few hills sufficiently high to give one much observation. Nothing could really be seen of either our own line or that of the Boche, unless one was actually on the positions held, but nevertheless both sides kept up vigilant observation upon the open spaces, and reconnoitring parties were apt to find themselves the object of an unexpected salvo of shrapnel if they exposed themselves for more than a minute or two. This was thoroughly impressed upon us by a young French Intelligence Officer attached to the Regimental Head-quarters aforesaid, who took us forward on foot to see what we could see. We did not see a great deal, and of warlike pre-parations none, but at any rate we located places and woods and got a general idea of the lie of the land, which was to prove useful later on. The French front ran nearly north and south from Soissons through Parcy-Tigny, Le Plessier-Huleu, Soucy-le-Château. It should be noted that though digging-in was still always carried out, we were now taking part in what may be called open warfare. We were trying to keep the Boches on the run. After our reconnaissance we returned to the Quartier-Général of the Regiment already referred to, and they gave us a very pleasant and welcome little lunch, finishing up with coffee and cognac. I found there our B.G.C., and after lunch again accompanied him on a further reconnaissance along with the same voluble young Intelligence-Officer, who was full of chat, and it was delicious to hear him instructing the Brigadier in all the arts and tactics of war. The latter's French was, perhaps, not his strong point; at any rate, he bore with the youth politely, answering his wonderful dicta with intelligent " *Oui oui's* " or " *Non non's* ".

After lunch I had sent off M'Combie and Findlay back to the battalion, which under the command of Captain W. W. Ferguson, M.C., had moved from Soucy that morning, and was bivouacking in the wood just west of Chavigny Farm, a mile or so from Longpoint. I now mounted and returned there myself, somewhat weary, as it had been a long and very hot day. On my way thither the B.G.C. came past me in a car, and explained that certain alterations in the scheme had been made. My battalion and the 5th Argylls were to be reserve to the 30th Army Corps, and were to concentrate in the neigh-bourhood of Blanzy, while the 5th K.O.S.B. and 4th Somersets (Pioneer Battalion) were to be Divisional Reserve. I think I arrived back to the battalion at about 2200, and we moved off an hour or so after that, our objective being Le-Bois-du Fond-de-Soissons, a wood within a couple of hundred yards from where I had been in the morning, so that though we came by another route, I found that my reconnaissance had been invaluable, as the French guides who had been sent to us did not know the wood. It was necessary also at the point where they met us to drop a connecting file to show the rear companies the track down to the wood, as we had to move with intervals of 100 yards between platoons to avoid casualties by shell fire. With Head-quarters Company, Boyd and I were leading, and just as we turned down the cart track we seemed to be in the middle of a blatter and din of shelling. The noise was partly from our own guns, but soon the Boche planted shrapnel round us. A splinter of this, unfortunately, hit Boyd in the arm, but he was able to go on forward. I sent for the Doctor, who was at the rear of the column some distance behind, and he arrived just as we got to the wood, and took Boyd, who was rather faint, over to a French Aid-Post. Meantime, I had gone back, as some of the rear companies had lost touch, collected and hustled them into the Bois, where, areas having been allotted, they dug-in and bedded down for the night (0200 on 23rd). On my return the Medical Officer reported that he had sent Boyd right off in an American ambulance, as his wound was more serious than he (Boyd) anticipated, and I was left to find another Adjutant. My choice fell upon Innes, who had had previous experience as Assistant Adjutant, while Russell, the pukka Assistant Adjutant, was with the nucleus. At that moment Innes was Signal Officer; under him, however, was Sergeant Kelly, a brave and reliable man, and a most excellent Signalling N.C.O., who could be left to carry on by himself with his well-trained signal section. Since Dulieu's departure, Boyd had been a most satisfactory Adjutant, painstaking, methodical, and a good organizer. He forgot nothing, and could issue excellent orders, clear and concise. With him one did not have to elaborate one's orders; I could indicate roughly my wishes, and in less than no time he'd have them down on paper and issued. He was, moreover, a favourite with officers and men, and his cheery disposition and determination to make the best of things helped everyone tremendously.

We remained doggo in the Bois-du-Fond-de-Soissons until the 27th, not immune from casualties, as we were subject to periodic shelling by the Boche, and three men were killed and twenty-one wounded, one shell landing in the middle of a platoon area. An officer of the Divisional Staff came up one day and his horse, which Prior, Boyd's servant, had been holding, was felled stone dead. Prior miraculously escaped scot-free, unfortunately to be killed later on. We were at this time in Corps Reserve.

During the 25th, I took Company-Commanders to reconnoitre the high ground about three-quarters of a mile south of the bois called Bois-de-la-Tuilerie; where positions were allotted to companies in case of a possible Boche counter-attack and break-through. That night we were heavily shelled all round the wood, but nothing more offensive occurred, and I think we escaped scatheless.

On the night of 27/28th we marched, via Blanzy, to Bois-de-Bœuf, where the whole Brigade was concentrated. On our way there we were again subjected to some heavy shelling, but most of it fell just short, and we were lucky in having no casualties. Next morning I took Miller, my I.O., with me and we reconnoitred an area past Germesine Farm, where we pushed through French posts. We found ourselves somewhere in the Bois-de-la-Bayette on top of some old trenches in a spot where a clearing had been made, by shelling, of the standing trees. Suddenly that self-same spot was nearly cleared also of the C.O. and the I.O. of the 8th Scottish Rifles, who rapidly disappeared into the trenches and returned to fight another day. All the same, if somewhat rash this was a most useful reconnaissance, as will shortly be seen. In the afternoon there was a conference at Brigade Head-quarters, at which General Nicholson explained the scheme of attack, which was to take place at 0400 next morning, the 29th July.

The general idea of the operations was that the 20th Corps on our left was to capture Tigny-Villemontoire and Taux, turn the wood north of Hartennes-et-Taux, while the right of the 30th Corps, advancing through Le Plessier-Huleu on the Orme du Grand Rozoy, was to turn the Bois du Plessier and Bois de St. Jean. The 34th Division and the French Divisions, 25th and 58th, on its immediate right and left, were to form the connection between the northern and southern turning movements, advancing due east to the high ground east of the Soissons-Château-Thierry road. A most important point in the scheme was that the 34th was not to move till the 20th Corps on its left had advanced across the Soissons-Château-Thierry road.

We paraded and left Bois-de-Bœuf at about 2200, and marched via Billy-sur-Ourcq and Oulchy-la-Ville to our position, which, thanks to the morning's reconnaissance, we had no difficulty in finding. It was necessary to take care that companies in rear kept in touch; it is the easiest thing in the world to lose touch and get lost in the dark, and in fact, owing to this, the 5th K.O.S.B. were only just in time for the kick-off, while we had a couple of hours' rest. The French 5th Division, who were holding the line, had sent guides who met us at Oulchy-la-Ville, but they were soon dismissed and, with their comrades who were holding the line, lost no time in clearing out as soon as we were in position. My dispositions were as follows:

Y and Z Companies in front line were to move in two lines at about 100 yards distance, X Company in similar formation in support; and W Company in reserve, with Battalion Head-quarters, were to move forward in artillery formation. Our right was more or less defined by the Rue-du-Chauday, on the other side of which we hoped in due course to see the French, and on our left were the 5th K.O.S.B.

We got off the mark promptly to time at 0400, but had got no farther than a couple of hundred yards when the Boche put down a shrapnel barrage. It was certainly somewhat erratic, but that possibly made it more annoying, and before we had moved through it many yards, we had casualties. It was very misty, but though difficult to keep direction, the railway line was reached without opposition. As day dawned we got our first experience of tear gas—which may have been clinging around the area through which we were marching, and been brought out by the evaporation of the damp atmosphere. It was most disagreeable for about half an hour, and here and there temporarily incapacitated men. Our attack was, of course, covered by an artillery barrage which was timed to lift at specific hours from one objective to a farther one. Accurate synchronizing of watches was therefore necessary.

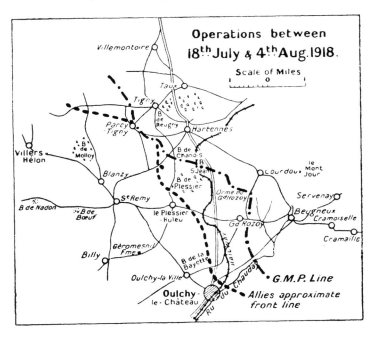

This had been done, but whether our advance had outstripped its timing at certain points, or whether the gunners did not keep to their times, it happened that several times I got messages that my front line was being shelled by our guns, and that on one occasion our barrage had come down between my front and support lines. We pushed on, however, and by 0600 had made considerable progress, though the leading companies suffered from heavy machine-gun fire. Referring to the sketch plan (p. 168), by 0700 Y Company had reached a point about 500 yards short of the station, where they were held up by machine-gun and rifle fire from Hill 158. Z Company sent in a dozen

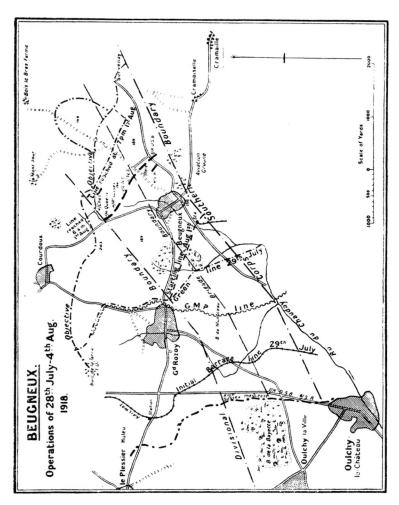

prisoners, and then found themselves also held up by heavy machine-gun fire from Beugneux itself. The advance had been made for the most part through standing corn and culti-

vated ground, and across the Gouvernement Militaire de Paris
trench line (which was originally to be the finally-held line for
the defence of Paris). The ground gradually sloped down to
the little burn crossing our front half-way to Beugneux, and
then rose again to that village, which was flanked on the south
by a wooded hill, Point 158, and on the north by Hill 189.
Therefore the advance was well under enemy observation as
soon as the G.M.P. line was left.

I now sent up X Company to reinforce the two front
companies, and intended to order Y Company to attack Point
158 from south while X held the front, if and when I could
get artillery to co-operate. All this time I was out of touch,
except by runner, with Brigade Head-quarters (who had had
orders to remain at Oulchy-la-Ville until Beugneux was taken),
and it took some considerable time to get there from my
Battalion Head-quarters, which were about a quarter of a mile
in front of G.M.P. line. I eventually managed to get some
artillery preparation as desired, but as soon as the companies
started moving I saw that no material harm had been inflicted
by the guns upon the Beugneux defences. I therefore stopped
the movement, and looked around for some other means of
accomplishing my object. My Head-quarters were, at this
time, rather awkwardly placed, being on the forward slope of
the hill. I moved forward a little into a slight hollow, but
that was of no advantage; if one got up one was peppered with
machine-gun bullets, if one remained doggo Minnenwerfer
searched us out. Now came catastrophe: one of the Minnenwerfer shells was lobbed right among us, killing one and
wounding two, I myself being the only officer untouched.

Johnnie Miller, who had been doing I.O. for me, was
killed on my right instantaneously; Innes, my Adjutant, was
badly wounded, and Lyle, who had just come from leave,
slightly. The last, fortunately, was able to carry on in a quiet
way, and he took on the duties of Adjutant pro tem. A few
more Minnenwerfer shells came over, and though they did
no harm, I moved Head-quarters some fifty yards and made
my gunners and signallers spread themselves a bit. Meantime
I found that the Argylls, who were battalion in reserve, were

coming forward past my Head-quarters and moving up in close support of my companies. This reinforcement was useless. What was wanted at that time was a diversion in the shape of a bigger movement to the north or south to turn Beugneux; not a reinforcing of the line already seriously held up. On my right, I was not really in touch with the French, though at one time, early in the morning, Y Company had reported connection. Now, however, they were nowhere to be seen. On my left the 101st Brigade had had it hot; elements of it had penetrated as far as the Courdoux-Beugneux Road, and I knew that a patrol of the 5th K.O.S.B. had come across them on Point 189, but they could maintain no position reached, the enemy machine-gun fire taking toll of them, and especially of their officers. The 102nd Brigade in Divisional Reserve (I know now) was ordered up to counter-attack with 2/4th Somersets and a company of the Machine-Gun Battalion, but before this could materialize the Germans themselves launched a heavy counter-attack, the weight of which fell upon the French, who were beyond the 101st Brigade on our left, and they were forced to retire. This was soon felt by the remnant of the 101st Brigade, and parties of men could be seen coming back, not only on my left, but through my lines. Not knowing of the retiral of the French, I ordered Major Agnew, then commanding the 5th A. & S. H. (as Lieut.-Colonel Barlow was then on leave), to extend and advance one of his companies with fixed bayonets to our left front; this company was to hustle the retiring men, to try to collect them and get them organized, and in any case to advance and make good the wood south of the Beugneux-Rozoy Road, refusing its left flank. A second company was to be in support just behind the woods. This seemed to stop the rot for a little, but the general retirement continued, and one can do little with small groups of scattered men. I now found myself in the air. The 5th K.O.S.B. had melted away, some had retired, many had been put out of action, and a few still maintained their positions. On my right, as I have said, the French had not materialized. The only thing to be done was to conform to the main retiral. This was properly organized and well carried out by my Company-Commanders. I further ordered each of them to collect his company and reorganize on the G.M.P. line. I also ordered Agnew to conform. The reorganization was completed as far as my unit was concerned by about 1500, and I allotted portions of the G.M.P. line to each unit.

The 34th Divisional History relates that " The enemy was prevented from taking any advantage of our withdrawal by the heavy barrage put down on his positions by the artillery of both nations ".

Very true; some of it also was put down upon both nations, and we on our position suffered. I know not whether it was British or French shelling, but just as some heavy stuff arrived, I was at last connected up by telephone to Brigade. Upon my information they must have acted promptly, as no more shells were planted upon our devoted heads.

About 1700 the B.G.C. came along. I was glad to see him and talk things over with him, in amplification of my series of messages throughout the day. Early that night I received orders to reoccupy in depth the position we had gained during the day, and by 2300 the most forward position we had achieved was again made good without opposition as follows: X Company across the road, with the station about 300 yards to their front; W Company some 300 yards in rear of X; Z Company some 300 yards in rear of W; Y Company some 300 yards in rear of Z; with Battalion Head-quarters on the G.M.P. line. The 5th Argylls were similarly organized on our right, between the French and my battalion and the 7th Cheshires on my left. All companies dug themselves in, and, in addition, X Company carried out active patrolling to get in touch with units on their left and right.

That night we at Battalion Head-quarters were subjected to a bout of gas shelling. These mustard shells are insidious in that they hardly make any explosion, and so do not waken up tired men unless they burst alongside them. I was awakened about 0200 by the explosion of one just above my head (I was sleeping below a little bank) which sprinkled my hair, face, and clothes with its beastly mixture. I did not realize thoroughly that it was gas at the time, but I had some suspicion of it as I now heard other soft explosions around. I awoke the Gas N.C.O., who got up, sniffed, looked around and heard some slight explosions a little way off. He assured me that it was not of any consequence. In the morning about 0800 some of us felt pretty seedy, and by midday there were 19, including Lyle and myself, Sergeant-Major W. Gray and Sergeant Wylie,[1] all cases for hospital, suffering from severe mustard-gas poisoning. Poor Gray died of it. He was an excellent sergeant-major, a good disciplinarian, instructor, and capable in the Orderly Room. Mustard gas is most penetrative. It finds its way through the thickest of clothes, and its fumes affect people coming near the patient. Inwardly it affects one's throat and lungs, and outwardly makes festering sores and blisters; one's eyes are painfully blinded, and take a long time to recover after the other sores are healed.

We were all taken in ambulances to a French C.C.S. and then to Rouen, where Lyle and I were very comfortably bedded in No. 2 Red Cross Hospital.

[1] Sergeant Wylie was Gas N.C.O.

CHAPTER IX

The Advance to Victory

By Captain W. WHIGHAM FERGUSON, M.C.

The morning after a battle, be it successful or not, is often peaceful, and despite the personal losses sustained one must confess to a sense of thankfulness amounting sometimes to a joyful relief that the gods have been kind. I was just in this mood and was trying on a Boche burberry in the early hours of 30th July. Shelling had begun in my company area; the men, cheerful after the effort of yesterday, were treating it all lightly and shouting corrections to the enemy artillery, together with pithy criticisms of their gunnery skill; my subalterns and I had breakfasted—dry—and were just enjoying a pipe when an orderly darted in and thrust the following message into my hands:

" Colonel Findlay's compliments. You will please report at once to Battalion Head-quarters. You will hand over command of your company to Lieut. Cairns." This, over the signature of Lyle, a former subaltern, and a real good chap, seemed to portend serious things.

So, quickly collecting my straps and note-book, and not forgetting the 24-hours emergency ration, I nimbly scuttled in true rabbit fashion down to the ill-fated hollow where Battalion Head-quarters lay. Things here seemed somewhat confused. The various groups composing Battalion Head-quarters were congregated together, and there was a touch of melancholy in all their faces. Picking out a small bunch, I approached and found in their midst Colonel Findlay. He could not see and was lying on a stretcher, his face and head positively parboiled with mustard gas. As he heard my voice he

called me to his side, and told me to take over command against
Major Hume-Gore's arrival, and to find an Adjutant in lieu
of Lyle, who also had been very badly gassed. The Colonel
was surprisingly chirpy, though I felt that he had grave doubts
as to whether he was to have eyes to see with again. He breathed
anathemas upon mustard gas, and I knew that he was thoroughly
angry at having to go to hospital. I managed to draw a laugh
from him once or twice, and by good luck and previous masterly
self-control, I was in a position to give him a " deoch-an-doris ".
But it was all too sad.

The first message I, as C.O., received just a quarter of an
hour later reported the deaths of Lieut. Cairns and C.S.M.
Ralston of my company, whom I had just left in answer to
the Colonel's message. The Boche unfortunately had found
the range. I felt the loss of both of them more than I can
say.

That afternoon a Brigade conference was held at which a
second attack on Beugneux was outlined to Battalion Commanders, timed to commence at 0500 on 31st July—the following morning. Orders for this were given out to Company-Commanders, but these were subsequently cancelled. Major Hume-
Gore and Captain Hannan arrived at 2200 that night, the former
taking over command from me, and the Boche contrived to
disturb our slumbers with intermittent shelling.

The following morning stands out in bold relief in my
recollection, since advantage was taken of a temporarily increased water ration to have a really good shave! And so I
returned to the maudlin duties of a Company-Commander
under sentence to be called on again should occasion arise.
On the afternoon of 31st July, orders were issued for the second
attack, and by 0200 on 1st August we were again at the jumping-
off place. Y Company (under my command) led off, closely
followed by Z, but we were this time in close support to the
5th K.O.S.B. W and X Companies were in a similar position
with the 5th Argylls.

The advance commenced at 0415, and was conducted in
a dense fog of mist, shell-smoke and mustard gas. Confusion
was inevitable, but the right of the line reached Hill 158,

cleared it, and continued on to the southern outskirts of Beugneux. By this time I had gathered a mixed command of our own men, K.O.S.Bs, and Argylls, and found the new mixed unit most successful. We got a goodly bag of Boche, including machine-guns, though the enemy put up a stiff fight.

When, the night before, I resumed command of Y Company I found that I had lost all my officers, and had only three N.C.Os. remaining. In the darkness two hours prior to zero hour, two new officers were sent up, Captain Johnstone and Lieut. Hardie. This was the latter's first experience of being under fire. I explained the position to them by the failing light of an "orilux" electric lamp, with the aid of a map and sketches. Four hours later, when the objective was reached, it was my sad experience to find that both these officers were casualties, Captain Johnstone having paid the full sacrifice, and Lieut. Hardie being wounded.

The ground south of Beugneux is high lying, and admirably suited to cover any attack on the village. The C.O. 5th K.O.S.B., a respected Cameronian (Lieut.-Colonel R. N. Coulson) in temporary guise, ordered the two companies of the 8th Scottish Rifles in close support to him to strengthen his front line. We therefore pushed on and dug-in. Desultory artillery and machine-gun fire was dropping around us the while, but despite persistent rumours of a likely counter-attack by the Boche, it was fairly obvious that he was merely covering his retreat. That night all was quiet, and we established a very well-placed front line, and pushed out reconnoitring posts with Lewis guns lest anything untoward might occur.

Dawn on 2nd August assured us that the enemy were in full retreat; and the reflection that after a deal of travail our task was accomplished made buoyant souls of us all, and dispelled all thoughts of the weariness which was in our bones. A single high-velocity gun troubled us now and then, but more disconcerting was the heavy rain which soaked us all to the skin. Orders to be prepared for a further advance were not received with great enthusiasm, and when these were countermanded by a message that the Brigade would rest the night in Beugneux, there was acclamation amongst all ranks. We cheerfully shouted words of encouragement to the French cavalry, infantry, and artillery, who passed through us in a continuous stream. Not a little humour was enjoyed in watching the " Christmas Tree " appearance of the Poilus, and especially of their transport, which had all the appearance of a " moonlight flittin' ", but we were all agreed that the stolidity, cheerfulness, and fine physique of our Allies who passed through us to the attack were remarkable.

The French have a happy way of recognizing gallantry by a system of " immediate awards ",[1] and on the following day a number of our officers and men were presented by Major-General Nicholson in presence of a representative of the French Army Commander, General Mangin, with various grades of the Croix de Guerre. We were all particularly glad to learn that Colonel Findlay had also received the Legion of Honour, and wherever he was we hoped that the news to him in his state of suffering would indeed be heartening.

The village of Beugneux was in a sorry state when we took it, and there was not one house, outhouse or shed, which did not bear trace of the ravages of shell fire. Some of us might have suspected, like inimitable " Old Bill ", that the rats and moths had been active in Beugneux, but from one who has had the tiring experience you may take it that it is no easy task to find a corner in a shell-ridden house which might be reckoned to be snugly isolated from all draughts. A deal of heavy patch-work was required before we settled down for the night.

Sunday, 4th August, and four years from the date when war was declared! Yes, even in the thick of it, one paused to reflect. This was the war which was to last only a few months, and we were still wallowing away in it. Immediate prospects of success, it seemed to us, were not in any way bright. Personally, I mused on the fact that the farther we pushed, the longer became our lines of communication, and the nearer

---

[1] *Note by Colonel Findlay.* We also, as an army, followed the French example, but our so-called " immediate awards " never seemed to have the spontaneity of the French ones.

did the Boche get to his own well-established frontier. While victory was assured us in the end, the toll of the victors must be very heavy. The Boche had already had wonderful lessons from us in the science of well-conducted retreats, and he had profited, as he always will, by the experience of others.

The Brigade celebrated the occasion by going for a charming bus-ride in real live London 'busses through deeply wooded forests. Starting off from Oulchy-le-Château, on the Château-Thierry-Soissons Road, we reached Rouvres near Paris at 6 p.m., where we halted for the night. Being some distance from regular billeting areas, we were eminently comfortable, both officers and men. To pass the night in a bedroom with a polished floor, fully and tastefully furnished, and to have the additional luxury of a dressing-room, complete with bath— this was joy all astounding! The rest of the war for us might not insupportably have been waged in Rouvres, but fate only fêted us for two days, and on 6th August we entrained at St. Maro Station for an unknown destination. Finally we detrained the following day at Wormhoudht, comfortably settled ourselves there, and pursued general training until 13th August. We overhauled our kits, and received new drafts, which brought us up to goodly numbers again. We had the privilege of a glimpse of His Majesty the King, and held continual séances with the staffs of Brigade, Division, Army Corps and Army. They were all very pleasant, all confident we were winning, and all delighted to listen to the usual obvious bluff as to what we were doing in the way of training the men. Though the new drafts were well knocked about and a deal of hard work was done in reorganization of companies, this continual visitation from staffs became most demoralizing! We marched off from Wormhoudht on 13th August, and reached the School Camp of St. Janster-Beisin (of ancient memory) at 2 p.m. the same day. Here we remained three days only, to move on again to " Dirty Bucket Area ". These marches were carried out by order of the B.G.C. (Brigadier-General Chaplin, an old Cameronian), with the strictest possible march discipline. Many of our men were new, and the quick succession of changing camp made any organized scheme of training quite out of the question.

It is a strange fact that we might have been dubbed a travelling pioneer battalion or Brigade, since it was our invariable experience to take over a dirty camp and leave it clean to those who followed after. Was this part of the great scheme of things?

19th August, 1918.

" Message from G.O.C. 52nd Division to 103rd Brigade.

" Your old comrades and brothers in arms of 52nd Division send you greetings. They regret that they were not with you fighting side by side with you as in the past, during the battle which has acquired for you the admiration of both the French and British Armies. They deplore with you your losses, feeling that your losses are their own, and they wish you God speed in the future.

52nd DIVISION."

Our next spell in the line was just in front and in full view of Kemmel Hill, where we took over an area where the trenches were but a series of manholes. During our spell here the line was advanced a distance of 100 yards, as a demonstration covering an attack on Kemmel from the right flank. We suffered casualties mainly from shell fire, and had the great misfortune to lose a number of valuable Head-quarters Signallers, into whose dug-out a shell landed with disastrous effect. We had no better type of men in the battalion. Otherwise the war, as far as we were concerned at the time, was comparatively quiet, though nasty rumbling noises were heard day and night over the whole Ypres salient. It required only a cursory look at the map and at the progress of the troops around us, to foretell that our opportunity was daily approaching nearer and nearer.

On 5th September, we were relieved and moved into Sherpenburg Redoubt, Major R. D. Hunter (1st Cameronians) having taken over command of the battalion vice Lieut.-Colonel Hume-Gore gone to hospital. The quarters here were merely rabbit-warren dug-outs, with no over-head protection, and all were flooded out with the rain which fell unceasingly. Being placed on the guarded side of hills and

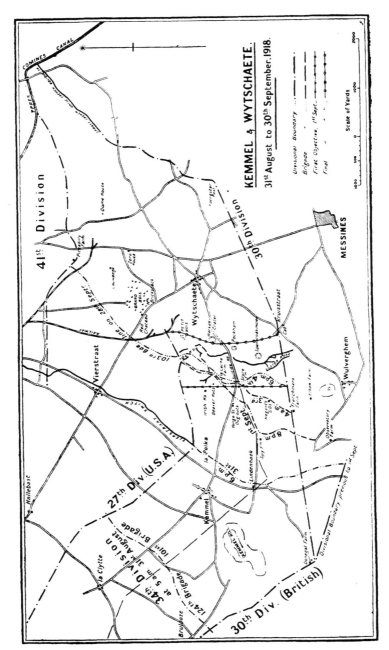

KEMMEL & WYTSCHAETE.
31st August to 30th September, 1918.

Divisional Boundary
Brigade
First Objective, 1st Sept.
Final

Scale of Yards

MESSINES

41st Division

30th Division

Vierstraat

Wytschaete

Wulverghem

27th Div. (U.S.A.)

Hallebast

la Polka

Kemmel

la Clytte

34th Division
at 5 a.m. 31st August

124th Brigade

101st Brigade

30th Div. (British)

hummocks, they afforded a little protection from shell fire, which reached its maximum as darkness fell. We were nevertheless quite glad to move in a few days into billets at Eperlecques, journeying thither by march to Steenvoorde, and light-railway to near St. Omer, where we detrained, and marched by devious paths to individual camping billets, mostly in farmhouses. Here we remained only one night, passing on to Abeele, and thence to Hallebasse " Cross Roads ". Here, as battalion in Brigade Reserve, we furnished working parties for five days. On 28th September the 34th Division attacked on a two-Brigade front, extending from Kemmel to Wytschaete. The 8th Scottish Rifles were in reserve to the 103rd Brigade, which occupied the right of the Divisional line. The Brigade advanced at 1530 on 28th September, in thick mist and heavy rain. Their first objective, roughly the Wytschaete-St. Eloi Road, running due north and south, was secured, very little shell fire being encountered. At 1430 the battalion was ordered forward, following the general advance of the line, and at 1815 moved in support of the two front-line battalions, a further general advance being imminent. This was delayed till 29th September, and at dawn, the 8th passing through the other battalions in the line, advanced with no opposition, except from occasional machine-gun fire, finally reaching the line of Comines Canal at 1130, a total advance of two and a half miles in six hours. On this line we remained till the evening of 29th September, withdrawing to Dammstrasse to pass a most miserable pitch-black night in no shelter, and with rain pitilessly drenching everyone and everything.

The following day was spent in endeavouring to be cheerful, an extremely difficult task since the country was of an unrelieved dreariness, and rain continued pouring down on us all day long. For four days thereafter the battalion took over a sector of line from the 30th Division, and came out to rest in Kruiseck for two or three days. Ninth October saw us in the line again near to Gheluwe, on the Ypres-Menin Road, our neighbours being the 5th K.O.S.Bs. on the left, and 7th Cheshires on our right.

As was to be expected, another scheme of attack reached

us by the first available post. The village of Gheluwe was doomed, and was due to disappear on 14th October. Two considerations seemed to weigh lightly with our staff. First that the troops with whom they were playing had just got comfortably settled in pill-boxes of latest Boche model; and secondly, that Gheluwe was a nice little village, and might have been made quite comfortable. The writer recalls some very charming night excursions along with the late Lieut. Martin, in and out of the houses and outhouses of this village. Much information was gleaned, apart from the fun of it all, and the poor old Boche did not at all enjoy Martin's deadly aim with a bomb. We went out on grounds of pure personal spite, and the details of these trips were included in the morning intelligence report: " All was quiet on this front ". Martin was one of the stoutest-hearted officers we ever had, but, alas, he was killed on the eve of final victory. At this stage the battalion was holding the line in depth with Y, the only front-line company.

The " special idea " for the attack on Gheluwe was out-lined by Lieut.-Colonel Hunter with unerring clarity. The scheme was that the 8th Scottish Rifles and 5th K.O.S.B. should advance on the flanks of the village, the innermost leading company in each case being distanced not more than 100 yards from Gheluwe. Mopping-up was left to the rear company of each battalion, and once east of Gheluwe, by a converging movement on the part of the front companies of both battalions, the line was to be re-formed with the right flank resting on the Menin Road, when the advance would continue. Gheluwe was to be treated to an intense bombard-ment of shell, smoke-shells and thermite by our friends the gunners and Royal Engineers, and the barrage was to advance at the rate of 100 yards every two minutes.

True to time, the battalion at 1430 (Y Company leading) was on the jumping-off position, which had been taped out to help to maintain direction. The Boche, sensing what was in store for him, was pushing over shrapnel and gas in an angry manner. A heavy mist hung around, and a dense smoke cloud added to the murkiness. Occasional flares pierced the darkness, followed by the rat-tat-tat of machine-guns, and the dull thud of a bomb. The men were in great form. The leading company's small advance groups were keeping up a steady nagging. Shortly before zero, hell arose around us. Thermite shells burst over Gheluwe and sent tongues of flame leaping into the air. The advance began, and despite many difficulties direction was maintained. East of Gheluwe touch was established with the K.O.S.B., and some 100 prisoners fell into our hands, together with machine-guns and stores. The poor old Boches were terror-stricken, and clamoured piteously for mercy. Y Company reached the Green line, which was marked by a mill, and had good sport at pill-boxes by the wayside. The battalion frontage was here enlarged to two companies, X coming up on the left, and a farther advance began.

It is really surprising to what good use even a German officer can be put. I had the opportunity personally of securing one—a major—all to myself. We met in dense fog and smoke, with no one near at hand. Having disarmed him—his revolver is still in my possession—I secured his services for purposes of direction, appropriated his field glasses as we became more chummy, and, once the final objective was reached, made a hearty meal along with some of my Company Head-quarters of the food in his haversack!

On continuing the advance from the first objective we encountered most deadly machine-gun fire issuing from a pill-box which covered a flat area of ground immediately in the line of our advance. Many fell victims to its deadly accuracy, including Captain W. D. Hannan, O.C. X Company, a good man and true. Messages issued direct along the firing line and through Battalion Head-quarters resulted in out-flanking this stronghold, and, with a farther advance, a half-battery of field guns fell into our hands.

Menin was reached (unofficially), and word was passed back that all was clear. The 5th A. & S.H. relieved us that night, but the battalion was held in readiness for a farther advance across the river Lys, which separates Menin from Halluin. This crossing was effected by Lieut. Martin, Y Company, that evening, and the battalion commenced crossing

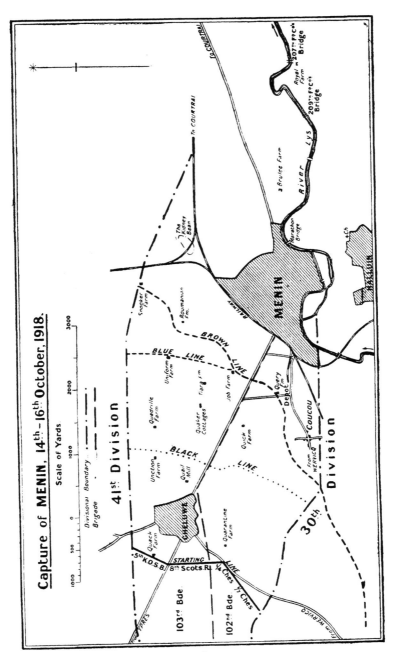

Capture of **MENIN**, 14th.–16th. October, 1918.

before dawn on the following day, 16th October. Z Company
had just got over by a pontoon bridge, and had no sooner
reached the farther side than a heavy machine-gun fire opened
on them. Their exposure was murderous, on dead level ground
in full view of the enemy, and the Boches made things more
uncomfortable by bringing a trench mortar into play against
them. Lieut.-Colonel Hunter himself went over by the
rickety bridge and succeeded in guiding the majority of the
men back to the far bank of the canal where some appreciable

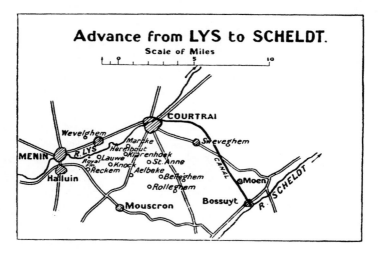

Advance from LYS to SCHELDT.

cover was obtainable. This action was only one of the many
inspiring examples which this officer gave to those under his
command.

Farther advance was delayed pending a concerted bombardment on Halluin, and the companies which were ready
to effect the crossing were delayed. Though the position of
affairs was reported, and the futility of endeavouring further to
conduct troops over a bridge in full view of the enemy seemed
so obvious, the conditions remained unchanged all day. Word
was received that a fresh attempt was to be made to carry the
line forward, but there were no guns at hand apparently to
cover such an attempt. Happily the enemy evacuated Halluin

that night, and the battalion was withdrawn into support west of Menin.

The whole Brigade was then concentrated on 17th October north-east of Menin, and remained there in rest for three days, moving then to Lauwe, where training was carried out for four days. It was now well-known by the successful progress which the Allies had made, that the enemy were well on the run, and that the pursuit must be relentless. Training and refitting during these short periods of rest were very difficult. Casualties had made deep inroads into all companies, and very few senior N.C.Os. or men were remaining. Promotion had to be quick, and the material offered was by no means experienced. It was perhaps fortunate that there were men willing to take responsibility in emergency, even against all their preconceived resolutions and prejudices. But it should be recorded that during these latter days of the war the commissioned ranks were worked to the utmost of their capacity both in and out of the line. The battalion was most fortunate in its new blood.

Making due east from Lauwe, the Brigade marched via Aelbeke, Rolleghem to the neighbourhood of Moen, where a night was spent. The line here was reconnoitred by Headquarters and Company-Commanders, but the projected relief did not materialize, and the Brigade moved on the following day to Marcke, thence to Desselghem, via Courtrai and Harlebeke.

Here the Brigade settled, while Battalion Commanders rode forward and reconnoitred the line. The same evening, 27th October, the battalion took over the line as part of the Brigade relief. The 5th K.O.S.B. were on the left flank, the 5th A. & S.H. in reserve at Vichte, and the battalion frontage extended roughly north and south in front of Anseghem from the railway triangle along the branch line to Waereghem northward to midway between the villages of Heirweg and Kruisweg. Z Company was kept in battalion reserve, the other companies running from left to right in the line being Y, X, W.

Details of an attack on the village of Anseghem on 31st October were received. The French were co-operating on the left flank of the battalion and the 5th K.O.S.B. on the right.

On the night of 30th October W and Y Companies extended their line inwards, thus relieving X Company which concentrated behind the line. At zero hour the following day an attack against the village was to be launched with the aid of two sections of French tanks which, with the support of X Company, were to mop-up Anseghem, that company acting as a screen to their advance. Unfortunately the tanks started off from their bivouac area too late and, finding difficulty in crossing the stream Dommelbeek, were not at the jumping-off line till well after zero hour. The scheme of attack purposed that W and Y Companies should advance under cover of these tanks. Their absence, therefore, made the advance a much more difficult operation, and Y Company also unfortunately had their flank unprotected by the failure of the French to secure Kruisweg, and suffered heavily. W Company happily succeeded in getting forward and established a line on the south of the village. Once the French tanks *did* arrive they cleared the village from south to north, having followed the line of W Company's advance, but they failed to mop-up the machine-guns which kept Y Company in check. The village was occupied finally at night, but not until we had suffered over sixty casualties, including three of our best officers, Lieuts. MacDougall, Martin, and Braidwood, while Captain W. J. Westland (Y Company), an old and trusted servant of the battalion and a very gallant gentleman, was badly wounded and died later on in hospital.

The sad news of Braidwood's death recalled to me an incident when the 7th and 8th Scottish Rifles were a combined battalion in Gallipoli. On the night of 8th January, 1916, at five minutes before the zero hour which was to mark our farewell to the Turk, I made a tour of the line to see that all was in readiness for the last march down to the beach. In the company sector were one or two bombing saps, and one which was pushed out to within fifteen yards of the Turkish trenches was held by a small garrison under Sergeant Braidwood. There was a great stillness, only broken now and again by the ping-ping of desultory sniping. The men in the sap lay huddled together except for the sentry on duty. Inquiry found that

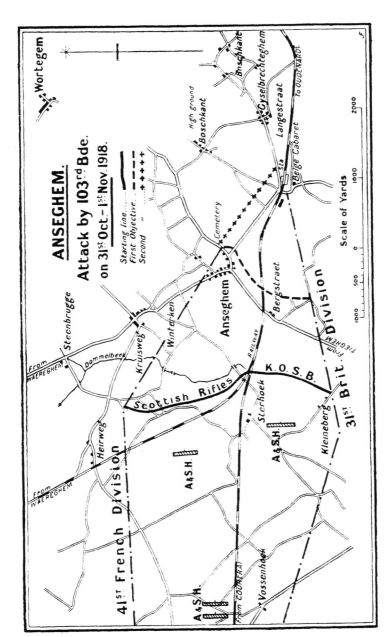

no one knew where Sergeant Braidwood was, but a marked reticence, as of some unexpressed knowledge, could be sensed amongst the men. Suddenly the dull thud of the explosion of several bombs out in front pierced the air, followed by a burst of machine-gun fire. Then a silence, and another lot of bombs let loose. A veritable strafe now arose in front, and just after the usual weird blue-green Turkish Very light had risen into the darkness and come to earth behind us, a dark figure crept stealthily back into the sap. It was Sergeant Braidwood of the 7th Scottish Rifles, returning from taking a last farewell of his old enemy.

Anseghem was the last action in which the battalion took part. It was evacuated by the enemy in the evening of 31st October, and the following day the 5th K.O.S.B. and 5th Argylls encountered no opposition in their advance to the River Scheldt in front of Audenarde.

On 3rd November the Brigade went into reserve at Bissenghem, and remained there in training till 7th November. From Bissenghem we marched back to Halluin, where we were in billets when the Armistice was declared on 11th November, 1918.

CHAPTER X

Germany

Very soon we learnt that the Division was to be one of those to march into Germany, and that the 8th was to be one of the first units to move, but our moves for some time did not bring us any nearer. On the 14th November we moved to Dottignies, next day to Molemlaix, and then to Quesnoy, and on the 18th to Scaubecq, where on 4th December Lieut.-Colonel G. W. Bennet-Clark of the Royal Scots took over command from Lieut.-Colonel R. D. Hunter. On the 12th December they started by route-march for the promised land—Germany. The first stage was completed on reaching Auvelais on the 22nd, via Thoricourt, Nautefolie, Tazeguies, Charleroi, Le Roux, and Wepion. Christmas and New Year were spent in Auvelais, and special New Year's dinners were produced for all ranks, after great difficulties were overcome in connection with getting them up from the base.

Up till the 20th January the battalion remained at Auvelais, and on the 21st entrained for Slighburgh-Muldorf, in the area round Cologne, which was the bridgehead occupied by the British Army of Occupation. The billets provided by the Maire of the town were excellent, and all the men had beds. There did not seem to be any rancour or malice amongst the Germans, or at any rate, if there was, it was well concealed. The weather now became cold and frosty, with a little snow every day.

On the 30th January Major C. O. Underhill (Worcesters) arrived and took over the duties of Second-in-Command, and on the 1st February the battalion proceeded by route-march to Wahn Barracks, where the accommodation was good, but rooms extremely dirty. But in a few days it was made thoroughly clean, and the battalion which took over from the 8th on the 23rd were thoroughly pleased with the smartness and cleanliness of their new quarters. The 8th proceeded to Seigburg by train, thence by route-march to Neunkirchen, where they took over the centre section of the outpost line from the 2nd Loyal North Lancs. The line was a very long one, and the battalion found ten posts, so that every available man was employed. These posts were in houses, which were put into a state of defence, or were prepared for sandbagged loopholes in the case of a possible attack. Along the whole line the men were in comfortable billets when not actually on duty.

On the 4th February, Captain E. R. Saltonstall, M.C., Yorkshire Regiment, reported for duty, and was appointed Adjutant. Since the Armistice, demobilization had been proceeding slowly upon orders which had been carefully prepared beforehand. Those units, however, which formed part of the Army of Occupation, could not be reduced beyond reasonable working numbers, unlike those remaining in France and Belgium, and a minimum of 500 of all ranks was fixed for infantry battalions.

On the 14th March, the 6th Royal West Kents relieved the battalion in the outpost line. They marched to Hemel and entrained for Wahn again, arriving at the barracks about 1700, when they came under the orders of the G.O.C. 101st Brigade. They found 10 officers (including Major F. Eaves, D.S.O., commanding) and 145 other ranks of the 18th Scottish Rifles awaiting them as reinforcements. Next day the battalion entrained for Hilden, and marched to billets at Benrath, some three miles away. On the 14th further reinforcements arrived from 2nd H.L.I., 15 officers and 180 other ranks. These were posted right away to companies which were now reorganized, and training again started. The outpost line (right sub-section of Brigade front) now had to be wired, and working parties of 10 officers and 140–200 other ranks were detailed for this duty daily. Z Company, however, was sent to Rhenania Petroleum Works for guard duties. Rhenania Petroleum Works were about two miles out of Benrath, and as the petrol was largely used for public services, it was essential that these works should be protected, in the interest of the British Army of Occupation, especially as the country was at the time in a somewhat disturbed state from labour disputes, as will be seen later.

It should be explained here that the occupied and defended areas, taken over by the British, American, and French, were the Bridgeheads of Cologne, Bonn, and Coblentz respectively. The perimeters around these areas were on a circumference with a radius of about twenty-five miles or so from these towns: beyond that, there was an unoccupied area (i.e. unoccupied by fighting troops) with a depth of about ten miles, into which Allied or German troops were forbidden to enter. There were, however, constantly occurring questions about the land and railways and inhabitants, which required mutual agreement to arrange, and with a view to solve these, certain authorized Allied officers met weekly (or as required) German officers in No Man's Land to discuss and settle them. At all railway stations on the perimeters, there were special R.T. officers, whose duty it was to control and superintend the traffic, and to investigate cases of suspected contraband and espionage. These officers were, generally speaking, willingly assisted by the German railway authorities, in whose best interests the work and investigations were carried out. At this time, there was a great deal of smuggling from the occupied area into the unoccupied territory beyond, and their work was chiefly directed to prevent and detect this. At big stations there were quite large contingents of officers, N.C.Os. and men constantly employed. At main thoroughfares through the outpost lines also barricades were erected and guards posted, and all ingress and egress closely watched.

On the 3rd April, the battalion moved to Hilden, and took over the billets vacated by the London Scottish. These were good billets, with beds for all men, and rooms in private houses for the officers. The men's messing arrangements were also excellent. About this time there was a re-allocation of troops to Divisions, and Scottish units of the 9th and 34th Divisions, and of other formations found themselves in the Lowland Division. The 8th now formed part of the 3rd

Lowland Brigade, along with the 9th Scottish Rifles and the 4th Royal Scots Fusiliers, which were commanded respectively by Lieut.-Colonel W. V. Lumsden, D.S.O., and Lieut.-Colonel E. Gibb. The other infantry in the Division were, as far as I can recollect, the 15th, 16th, and 17th H.L.I., and 10th and 11th Royal Scots, and 4th K.O.S.B.

On the 13th April, after considerable difficulties, I arrived back to the battalion and again took over command. It is a small world, and who should I find in command of the Brigade but my old Brigadier in Egypt, E. S. Girdwood, looking as young and as debonair as ever. Thanks to the drafts, the battalion was not too weak, and there were only two officers and 56 other ranks due for demobilization. I found things going well, training and wiring being carried out daily; battalion workshops running smoothly; every man in possession of two suits of clothing; men's messing arrangements good; and finally, sports arrangements in full swing. The battalion ration strength at the end of the month was 26 officers and 538 other ranks. After a survey of things on my arrival, I wrote to the Honorary Colonel, Colonel W. R. Maxwell, who had been throughout the war the generous custodian and administrator of our private funds, and explained the position to him. Now was the time to spend money, to impress the Hun, and, like a sportsman, he sent out funds, which I think were spent to good effect. Black Scottish Rifles buttons were purchased, and smart saddle cloths; the Officers' Mess was subsidized and improved, and a grant given to the Sergeants' Mess, which I restarted; we had sports and concerts to which the other Divisional troops were invited, and cinema performances; the officers gave dances and dinners; football kits and balls were purchased; and in many other ways, not forgetting prizes, we spent the money to our great advantage, and in furtherance (let it be hoped) of our prestige among the Boches.

I must say that, at this period, the rank and file were fed like fighting-cocks. The Company cook-houses were excellently run, being mostly in Boche restaurants, the proprietors of which helped now and again to vary the diet. All companies had roasts and stews, and fried and boiled things, baked tarts and bread, and all kinds of savoury and appetizing food. When we took over from the London Scottish we found that they had had some arrangement with the various restaurants by which they (the latter) would do the cooking and supply the dishes for a consideration. The Boches were only too glad to do this at first, but became greedy later on, and when I arrived I found that there were constant difficulties at the various billets on this account, so that having strong views on the subject, I was glad to be furnished with an additional reason for ordering that no German cooks were to be employed at all.

Hilden is, I suppose, a typical little town in the Cologne district. It is clean, and has a tram line which runs to Benrath, a bigger and more commercial town three miles away. The local populace are very like Scots folk, one cannot help remarking, and they appeared to be devout and good church goers, and the children were well-clothed and went regularly to school. They were, when I got there, apparently quite reconciled to our occupation, and gave no trouble; my officers, who were billeted in private houses, were kindly and hospitably treated, and in fact, they really took a great interest in us. Now and then a complaint from the Burgomaster would come into my office, but mostly these were trivial affairs, easily settled. On one occasion, however, a special messenger came post-haste from the Burgomaster to say that a portion of the great forest which is near the outskirts of the town on two sides, had caught fire, and was burning rapidly, with the wind in the direction of the town. Their Motor Fire Engine had broken down, would I lend them a couple of horses to take the engine to the scene of the fire? " I guess I saved that town from destruction ", as the Americans would say. These forest fires are apparently common enough in the district, and their method of extinguishing them is to confine the fire to an area by means of damp sacks and to spray with water the trees on the edge of these areas. This is the more easily accomplished, by reason of the many roads and tracks intersecting the woods. I recollect a few days later on, when riding through the woods, noticing the distinct line gutted by the fire, which on the occasion in question was most destructive. Of course the Boches turn out in their hundreds to fight the fire; I believe there are special forest wardens for this, and other duties.

In this occupied area there was little or no sign of poverty. The people looked prosperous, the children well cared for, and there was a general air of well-being. There were indications of industrial trouble, but slums as we know them were not to be seen. I am told that, thanks to our occupation, this district was the most prosperous in the whole of Germany, but the Occupation, in any numbers, was for a comparatively short time, and when one knows that the taxation per head in Germany is about one-seventh of that of Britain, one is apt to be sceptical about incapacity to pay the indemnities.

The people there are very musical. The concerts in Cologne were fine, and even local bands played extraordinarily well. We employed one on one or two occasions when we gave a dance or dinner. The young German men and girls go about in large walking parties of ten to twenty, marching along to the tune of a mandoline or some such string instrument, and singing choruses as they go. Extraordinary that such people could be the brutes we found them to be! Of course these Rhenishers are not like the Prussians, whom they do not like; they are easily led and influenced, and without doubt they were sincerely glad that the war had come to an end.

On 3rd May I left the battalion to take command of the Brigade and of the area. Brigade Head-quarters was in a big comfortable house near Benrath. While on this job I got an interesting sidelight into industrial conditions in the Cologne district. On the 10th May there was a general and concerted strike by all the workers in the Benrath-Hilden district. It was, of course, essential that all the local public services should be kept going for the benefit of the Army of Occupation, i.e. lighting, both electrical and petrol, the tramways, and water power. Beyond that, and the maintaining of order and peace, it did not matter to us in the least whether the workmen turned out one bar of steel or fifty (or whatever commodity may have been in question), provided they went to their works and did not mass in the streets. I had various interviews with both the workmen and their masters, and I must confess that my sympathies were with the workmen. These men actually had agreed not to demand any increase of pay while the war was going on.[1] They had been given two rises in pay, but these were not asked for. One can understand that the masters were not actuated by philanthropic motives or even generous ones in granting these increases, and it appeared that as a matter of fair dealing the men were entitled to some further increase, especially in view of the greater cost of living. They, however, put themselves in the wrong by striking *en masse* instead of having their case brought before an Arbitration Court set up for the purpose of adjusting such differences. Trade Unions did not then appear to be so far advanced or so well organized in the Rhineland as they are in Britain, and it seemed to me that these men were only just beginning to know and realize their power, and really were rather lost as to *modus operandi*. At the various meetings I had with the masters and men, I explained the position as far as we were concerned, and ordered the men to go back to their works and the masters to put no obstacle in the way of their return. (Some of them proposed to lock the men out.) Meantime I sent a couple of platoons to guard the Electric Power Station at Holthausen (a continuation of Benrath, a couple of miles northwards), and reinforced the Rhenania Petrol Works guard. It was on a Friday that I had the interviews with both sides. Nothing happened on Saturday, except that all Benrath saw Head-quarters and two companies of the 8th Scottish Rifles marching in full panoply of war into the town. Not only so, but on Sunday I asked for a couple of companies of Royal Scots from the Brigade at Duren to further reinforce my garrison. These two companies, as luck would have it, were strong ones and physically fine fellows, and they marched into Benrath on Sunday evening with pipes playing, limbers rattling, and with a fine martial air, just at the hour when the whole populace were taking their evening stroll. Next morning I divided the town into areas, and ordered the troops to parade through the streets, halting outside all

[1] Compare this with our Trade Union patriotism.

the various works, and while the officers inquired whether the workmen had returned to their places the troops outside practised fixing bayonets. I also asked the Commanding Officer of a Brigade of gunners stationed near by to have a route-march through the town that morning.

With practically no exception all the men were back at their works. This, however, did not finally solve the problem, and I recollect another interesting interview between the men's representatives and Lieut.-General Sir Richard Butler, Divisional, and I think at the time, also Acting Corps Commander. I do not think that anything new cropped up; the General was insistent upon their pursuing the legal and regular methods of arbitration. Their first arbitration court was German; if they were still unsatisfied their case would be referred to a British court as a last resort, and that court's decision would be final. My chief recollection of this interview was the sort of astonished gratification which these Boche workmen evinced that actually a British high General should condescend to hear (apparently sympathetically) their view of a squabble, which they probably considered not only outside his purview, but almost beneath his consideration. They could not understand it, and I think myself that it may have given them an inflated idea of their position and of its justice. At any rate, at the end of the month, after Girdwood's return to the Brigade, another and possibly more formidable strike broke out in the district. I remember his telling me that some of the troops in Benrath had to charge and disperse an unauthorized crowd.

The Brigade Staff at Benrath consisted of Captain and Bt. Major E. C. Morgan, M.C., South Wales Borderers, Captain W. J. Willis, M.C., Staff Captain, a Staff Captain for Civil affairs (Lawson), whose job was most onerous, and Captain W. S. Stavers, Royal Scots Fusiliers, who was a universal provider. He it was who ran all our Brigade fêtes, dances, garden parties, sports, and tennis grounds. Owing to his initiative we soon had five tennis courts going at Benrath, ash ones, all done by Boche labour, plus British direction and capital. Where he got the latter from to make the courts and to run the most elaborate dances and fêtes is beyond me.

During the months at Hilden we had many lecturers, distinguished in their own line, who came and talked to the men: Sir Harry Johnston, the African explorer; Dr. Wallace Williamson, the Moderator of the Church of Scotland; Mr. J. J. M'Cabe, who lectured on life in the past ages; Brigadier-General Stone, and several others. All these lectures were part and parcel of a scheme of education which was pursued with varying success for the benefit of the British soldiers of the Rhine. In battalions which had no duties on the perimeter or in connection with smuggling, this scheme of education may have been successful. As far as we were concerned it was not, in my opinion, of much value. I had two Education Officers, and they held forth upon geography, history, arithmetic, languages, &c., but owing to our situation on the perimeter, which entailed protective duties, it was not possible to do much in that way. What were of greater value, however, were the battalion workshops and institutes which we had. Apart from the Orderly Room, which gave a certain amount of education in clerking, letter-writing, and filing, we had a carpenter's shop run by the Pioneer Sergeant, who also was a useful plumber, a barber's shop, a tailor's shop, a bootmaker's shop, the last two of which were constantly employed, a post office, a garden, and pigs and a goat to be looked after. Company cooks were learning things every day from well-disposed Boches, signallers were at the end of telephones, transport men were becoming grooms, and mess waiters were learning their jobs as such, and, in fact, all these battalion requirements, which were fulfilled in varying degrees of efficiency, were, to my mind, of infinitely greater value from an educational and practical point of view than bits of book-learning. I had almost forgotten to say that we had an excellent battalion library of all kinds of literature, which was exceedingly well conducted by 2nd-Lieut. Telfer, who as well as being one of my Education Officers, was demobilization officer and a good organizer of concerts, fêtes, and sports.

Quite a lot of home leave was being granted at this time, and all kinds of arrangements were being made to keep the men employed and happy. Daily steamer trips were arranged up and down the Rhine. Inter-Brigade and Divisional football matches were arranged. Concert parties came along and entertained us, a moonlight Divisional torchlight tattoo was successfully carried through. Sports, including mule and horse races, with a totalizator, were of almost weekly occurrence; and yet there was, here and there, a certain amount of discontent in the Division, though not in the 8th. Men expected to be demobilized without any consideration for the necessities of the Army of Occupation; and once the strain of strenuous campaigning was over, a reaction set in which was difficult in some units to counteract. It was essential to keep all ranks employed, and we were fortunate in being responsible on the outpost line for the prevention of smuggling across into the unoccupied area. This was very prevalent, and very profitable, because goods could be bought in our territory which, if successfully smuggled across the frontier, would fetch ten or twenty times the amount paid. Cigarettes, chocolates, hams, coffee-beans, tea, paper, all kinds of things, including machinery, were the most frequently attempted. Sometimes the method was clever, but in the majority of cases it was very clumsy. Many tales were told of the attempts to get things through at the railway stations on the frontier and at the barriers on the main thoroughfares. At night the whole front was patrolled along the wire, which, by the end of May, extended practically right round the perimeter, and many were the captures made. Units were allowed to retain the captured pelf, and I can recollect how we kept ourselves in cigarettes and coffee for quite a long period. On one occasion, Dalrymple, my Company-Commander at Holthausen, asked me if I would care to go out with him one night to lie in wait for some smugglers, who were reported to be going to try and get through a gap in the wire. We proceeded, he and I, and ensconced ourselves in a hayfield near the gap. We waited a good long time and I went to sleep, to be awakened by a " Come on, Sir ". We rounded up five of the most pitiful creatures you ever saw, each of them carrying two large bags of coffee-beans. It was painfully easy and unexciting. It occurred to me that their capture might be a bit of bluff, that some other and much more important smuggling might be proceeding elsewhere, while this, which seemed a simpleton's work, was merely a blind to take our attention off another move. However, nothing more eventuated, even though, having escorted our captures into safe custody, we came out again, and also sent special patrols to other known favourite spots for getting through the wire.

One could not help pitying some of these smugglers. They used to be hauled up before a court presided over by battalion C.Os. in turn, and one could fine them from five Marks up to 50,000 Marks, and alternatively, or additionally, imprison them. One had to differentiate if possible, between the smuggling that was done for the purpose of trading, and smuggling for the purpose merely of helping a hungry family. Sometimes one found that the smuggler, case-hardened, and expecting to be found guilty, had the fine all in readiness: at other times, with weeping and protestations, the culprit had not a Mark to produce. In the first case, the fine was naturally as severe as one thought just; in the second case, if other circumstances proved poverty and a family, the fine was light. The Proceedings of all these cases were sent to Cologne, where the Military Governor, Lieut.-General Sir Charles Ferguson, personally reviewed them. His point of view always was: " We are Britishers, we stand for justice, we must not lend ourselves to petty retribution. We are here to show the Boche the dignity of fairplay, humanity, and consideration for others." One could not but admire this standard, however much one might be tempted to think that the Boche did not understand it. So long had the Boche been accustomed to military supremacy that any kindly consideration for custom, institutions, or civilians' feelings seemed to him but a sign of weakness, confirming him in his then national opinion that they were not the vanquished, but the honoured opponent. The neglect to exact from Boche officials an extension to our army of their habit of saluting officers: the omission to secure priority for British officers in railway trains: the order that no buildings were to be requisitioned without reference to the Burgomaster: and other similar magnanimities contributed to this idea, and from being servile the Boche soon became somewhat presumptuous, and even a little contemptuous. In my humble opinion, I think that the policy was wrong, considering the state of the Boche mind, and its effect was humiliating to the British regimental officer. The Boche seems unable to understand a high-minded and generous attitude: he thinks it weakness; his mind seeks ulterior motives in what is straightforward.

There were many who shared Sir Charles' view, and it was noticeable in men who had had no actual field experiences with the Boche. It was the bigger and more detached point of view, but amongst regimental officers it was conspicuous by its absence. A little incident which was related to me at the time throws an illuminating side-light upon this question. The last thing which would occur to a Boche in a tramcar would be to give up his seat to a woman. On one occasion two young British officers were in a tramcar—it was full. Two fat Boches sat near them, and at a halt a couple of women got in. The Britishers felt uncomfortable, and didn't see why they should give up their seats and let the Boche men remain seated. Consultation ensued, and they made the Boches give up their seats, and motioned to the women to seat themselves, and (believe me) the women refused. Why? They thought that the British officers had done this because they had designs upon them! This gives one to think, does it not?

On looking over the War Diary for June, I am struck with the number of holidays we seem to have had served out to us. Third June, the King's Birthday, was of course one. We had a short parade of the troops at Hilden, saluted the Flag and gave three cheers for the King, and thereafter we all went to Benrath, where in the Schloss Gardens there were sports and races and amusements of all kinds. On the 14th again, we had a great garden fête at the Schloss, Benrath, organized by our great Brigade Pooh-Bah, Captain Stavers, who had a genius for this kind of thing. (His top-boots were always a joy to behold!) It really was a race meeting with etceteras. The battalion had its own marquee erected, and we did our guests proud. There were horse races, mule races, foot races, tugs-of-war, the totalizator, two bands, one of the 17th Lancers and one American Jazz Band. The Lena Ashwell Concert Party also gave a jolly good open-air show. Tea, food and beer were served upon the ground, and in fact it was a most successful affair.

All these riotous proceedings calmed down when, ere long, news came through that the Boche was recalcitrant as to signing the Peace Treaty, and preparations were made for a move forward into the unoccupied area should he prove obdurate. In that event the Brigade was to move forward some ten or twelve miles and occupy an already reconnoitred line. On the 18th the 6th Black Watch, which was to relieve us when we moved forward, arrived in Hilden, and was with some difficulty doubled up with us. The battalion, though still responsible for finding posts at Holthausen, Himmelgeist, and Rhenania, was to concentrate at Hilden, and on " J Day " to move forward as part of the Advance Guard (which I was to command) to the remainder of the Brigade Group in the direction of Dusseldorf, which itself was destined for occupation by the French. A section of Machine-gun Corps, under Lieut. Burke, D.S.O., was allotted to the battalion, and I think that we were actually looking forward to a resumption of the offensive. However, as all the world knows, the Peace Treaty was signed on the 28th June, 1919, and we remained where we were.

On the 26th June, Captain E. R. S. Saltonstall, the West Yorks, who had been acting as Adjutant for me, went to Brigade, and I appointed Captain G. Menary, M.C. (10th Scottish Rifles, attached 8th Scottish Rifles), as Adjutant in his place, and a very good Adjutant he was.

We had our battalion sports on the 29th, and the following is a report of them printed in the *Cologne Gazette*.[1]

[1] A weekly newspaper printed for the benefit of the British Army of Occupation.

BATTALION SPORTS

of

8TH BATTALION THE CAMERONIANS (SCOTTISH RIFLES)

The Sports of the 8th Battalion The Cameronians (Scottish Rifles) took place at Hilden on Sunday, 29th June, before a large concourse of spectators.

The tastily printed programme showed a galaxy of events, there being no fewer than twenty-one.

The flat races attracted large entries and the two open events, the mile and the 440 yards, drew good fields and furnished some excellent running.

A feature of the short distance races was the attractive sprinting of Captain E. R. Saltonstall, late Adjutant of the battalion, who produced splendid form, worthy of one who has run at Olympic Games.

The miscellaneous races were a source of much amusement, the boat race, three-legged and palliasse races especially appealing to the large German spectatorate round the ropes.

Much credit redounded on the Transport section of the unit for the great show they made, both in the number of events they provided and in the excellence of their efforts. In the Alarm Race one did not know what to admire the more, the dexterity of the drivers in harnessing the animals or the fleetness of the horses when they got off their mark.

The mounted men also did well in the keenly contested Tug-of-War, as after an intense struggle they vanquished Z Company, who had already laid low a team of which much was expected.

Much hilarity and merriment was caused by the appearance on the field of certain " ladies ", garbed in what certainly could be called " the latest fashion ". Several disported themselves on mule back in such a way as would have caused the " unco guid " to have raised their hands to heaven in pious horror, but which elicited shrieks of laughter from the assembled crowd.

At intervals during the afternoon the pipers of the 11th Royal Scots played selections and the wild skirling of the pipes obviously awed the Huns, who to all appearances were less interested in a local Instrumental Band which also played tasteful airs.

Tea and refreshments were served on the ground, and at the conclusion of the Sports the prizes were presented by Brigadier-General E. S. Girdwood, C.B., C.M.G., 3rd Lowland Infantry Brigade, who afterwards on the proposal of Lieut.-Colonel Findlay, D.S.O., Commanding the 8th Cameronians, was heartily cheered. Among other spectators were Lieut.-Colonel M'Kenzie, Lowland

Division, Lieut.-Colonel Green, 6th Royal Highlanders, and numerous officers and men from both Lowland and Highland Divisions.

A proposed Camp-Fire Concert had to be abandoned owing to the heavy shower of rain, but this was no loss, for a great audience gathered in the well-equipped Recreation Hall of the battalion and listened with rapt attention to a splendid recital of song and story. C.S.M. Searles as a comedian made a great hit, and the singing of Pte. Ward was much appreciated, while Pte. Thomson in the "Yukon Trail" impressed everyone by a wonderful dramatic display. After a speech by the Colonel the proceedings terminated with the singing of the National Anthem and "Auld Lang Syne".

Much of the success of the Sports was due to the splendid organization of the Sports Committee and to the energetic fashion in which they did their work.

RESULT OF THE EVENTS

Mules Scurry—1, Wilson; 2, Aitken; 3, Agnew.

100 Yards—1, Nichol; 2, M'Kelvie; 3, Lowie.

Wheelbarrow Race—1, Kay & Anderson; 2, M'Millan & Ramsay; 3, Whitehill & Campbell.

1 Mile (open)—1, Thirwall (R.E.); 2, Grabham (M.G.C.); 3, Plummer (M.G.C.).

Best Turn Out—1, Clark; 2 & 3, divided Marshall & Smith.

Boat Race—Y Company.

Tug-of-War—1, Transport; 2, Z Company.

V.C. Race—1, Ross; 2, Renwick; 3, Aitken.

Three-Legged Race—1, Anderson & Kay; 2, Thomson & Neville.

100 Yards Old Soldiers' Race—1, Matthews; 2, Searles; 3, Ryan.

440 Yards (Open)—1, Plummer (M.G.C.); 2, Salvona; 3, Cassels.

Slow Cycle Race—1, Taylor.

Best Comic Turn Out—1, (divided) Searles & Coffield; 2, Carmichael.

Wrestling on Mules—1, Cruickshanks; 2, Wilson.

220 Yards—1, Warburton; 2, Salvona; 3, Badger.

"Wooden Spoon"—(Officers' mule race)—Captain Brook.

Palliasse Race—1, Darlison; 2, Anderson.

Alarm Race—1, Ross; 2, Agnew; 3, Devaney.

Singing Competition—1, Thomson; 2, Ward.

Driving Competition—1, Gibson.

Best Company Aggregate—Y Company.

Total Prize Money—Value 3000 Marks.

On 1st July we had our Officers' Peace dinner and dance. The difficulty always was to get ladies, but we had several charming W.A.A.C. Officers, Nursing Sisters, two delightful French nurses, and, of course, Miss Mathieson, Miss Halliday, and Miss Paul from the Scottish Churches' Hut at Benrath. Then Brigade must also have a dance at the Schloss, and as well as the above-mentioned ladies, they produced some of the staff from the Leave Club at Cologne, by permission of Miss Decima Moore. We all enjoyed these shows immensely. For the men an open-air concert was held in the Bier Garten, and on the 4th July a very successful whist drive at Hilden. Telfer, assisted by Lamb, ran the show admirably, and the men seemed to enjoy it thoroughly. A proportion of officers and men from the Control Posts at Holthausen, Himmelgeist, and Rhenania were given permission to attend.

I seem to have been recording a continuous series of gaiety of some sort or other. And so it was. Thanks to the money from Colonel Maxwell the battalion did itself well, and all sorts of people from Divisional Staffs, other Brigades, and all over the area used to come to our shows, and I hope enjoyed our hospitality.

In the transport at this time were a pair of beautiful white mules; I had a word with Nicholl, my Transport-Officer, and in no time I was equipped with a fine turn-out. A graceful four-wheeled dog-cart with red wheels was forthcoming from some Boche stable, together with harness for a pair. It was much admired by other units, and a little display impresses the Boches.

About the beginning of July General Girdwood told me that it was the intention to move the Brigade back into the Bedburg-Königshoven area, near the French, and on the 8th we entrained at Hilden, arrived the same day at Bedburg, and marched to Königshoven. This was a little village perched upon a hill, picturesque enough, but dull and dirty, good drainage not being considered a necessity. The country around was typically and solely an agricultural one, but, unlike our farming counties, there were no steadings scattered about in the midst of their own land. All the farmers concentrated in the village, and every day they and their labourers proceeded out of the village to their farms—sometimes three or four miles away. This system had some advantages socially, perhaps, but the concentration into a village of thirty or forty steadings, each with its own dung-heap, &c., and with faulty drainage arrangements, does not conduce to healthy sanitation. The men had to be billeted in some of these farm steadings, and so the first thing which had to be done after our arrival there was to seek out the most sanitary for them, and dispatch an order to the Burgomaster as to the drains. Apart from the village the country all around was beautiful, fertile, and full of game. It was most intensively cultivated, and not an inch was wasted. It was a revelation to see how every yard was utilized, compared with our hedged and fenced and dyked countryside, where fields, whether alongside a road or not, usually spare a yard or so on both sides of the fence. The farmers and their men were most industrious; they never seemed to tire; no half-days off on Saturdays—but that is typical of the whole country. Work? Britishers do not know what work is compared with the Boches.

The Great Victory March took place in Paris on the 8th July, a march, I think, in which all units of all the Allies took part. I sent Lieut. F. S. V. Barr, M.C., Croix de Guerre, C.Q.M.S. F. Partington, M.M., Croix de Guerre, Sergeant C. Ramage, D.C.M., M.M., Private J. Irvine, M.M., Private J. Walker, M.M., to represent the battalion in the pageant, which they reported was a very fine and inspiring affair. They were fêted and dined and wined during two days, and I gathered unofficially that it was more by good fortune than strict discipline that they all came back to time.

At Königshoven, after the drains were improved, we were very comfortable and healthy. We carried out all our ordinary training, and at Morken, where there was a fairly well-equipped rifle range, we put all companies through a useful and comprehensive musketry course, including Lewis-gun shooting. It was, of course, a quieter neighbourhood than Hilden, but nevertheless we managed some sports meetings, and football matches, and concerts, &c., and Division gave a dance. We had several happy encounters, convivial and sportive, with Colonel Brunet and his 159th Régiment d'Infanterie Alpine (Régiment is equivalent to our Brigade). They were quartered at Oetzenrath, some five miles away, and the following letter shows their magnificent hospitality.

Corps d'Armée.
77ᵉ Division.

No.........
Objet:

Aux Armées, le 12 Juillet, 1919.

....
....

" Le Lt.-Colonel BRUNET,
    Commandant le 159ᵉ Régt. d'Infie.

M. Le Lt.-Colonel J. M. FINDLAY, 1/8 Scottish Rifles.

"Le 159ᵉ R.I.A. célébrera la Fête Nationale française lundi 14 Juillet. J'ai l'honneur de vous demander de bien vouloir assister avec vos Officiers, vos sous-officiers et vos hommes, aux jeux qui auront lieu ce jour-là, à 15 heures à Otzenrath où est cantonné le 3ᵉ Bataillon du Régiment.

"Afin de permettre à quelques-uns de vos Officiers, de vos sous-officiers et de vos hommes d'assister au concert qui aura lieu le soir à 20 h. 30, je vous demanderais de bien vouloir accepter à dîner à ma table avec 3 de vos Officiers. Trois autres Officiers seront reçus à la table du Chef de Bataillon Cdt le 3ᵉ Btn. Enfin je vous demanderais de désigner 5 groupes de 5 sous-officiers chacun, et 5 groupes de 10 soldats chacun. Ces sous-officiers et ces hommes seront invités pour le repas du soir aux tables des sous-officiers et des soldats de chacune des unités suivantes: C.H.R., 9ᵉ Cie, 10ᵉ Cie, 11ᵉ Cie, C.M. 3.

"Les jeux auront lieu au terrain de Sports du Btn. sur la route de la gare d'Otzenrath.

"En cas de pluie, les jeux seraient remis à une date ultérieure, mais le concert aura toujours lieu.

"Dans l'espoir d'une réponse favorable, veuillez agréer, Mon Colonel, l'expression de mes sentiments les plus distingués.

G. BRUNET."

TRANSLATION

Army Corps.
  77th Division
    159th Infantry Brigade.

In the field 12th July, 1919.

Number........
Object:
....
....

" *From* Lieut.-Colonel G. BRUNET,
    Commanding 159th Infantry Brigade.

To Lieut.-Colonel J. M. FINDLAY, 1/8 Scottish Rifles.

  " The 159th Infantry Brigade will celebrate the French National Fête on the 14th July, and I have the honour to ask you and your Officers and men to come to our Sports which will take place that day at 15 o'clock at Oetzenrath where the 3rd Battalion of the Regiment is billeted.

  " In order to have some of your Officers, N.C.Os. and men at the concert which will take place in the evening at 2030 o'clock, I will be very glad if you will come and dine with me along with three of your officers. The Mess of the 3rd Battalion will be glad to receive other three of your officers. Moreover, would you kindly detail five groups of 5 N.C.Os. each, and 5 groups of 10 men each, who are invited to the evening meal at the Messes of the N.C.Os. and men of each of the following units: H.Q. Coy, 9th Coy., 10th Coy., 11th Coy., 3rd Battalion M.G. Coy.

  " The sports will take place at the Field of the 3rd Battalion on the Station Road at Oetzenrath.

  " In case of rain, the Sports will be put off until a later date, but the concert will take place.

  " Hoping that you will give a favourable answer, please accept, Colonel, my kind regards.

G. BRUNET."

We also in our turn entertained them to sports and dinner and concert, and I now print the programme of this " Meeting Sportif Inter-Allié ".

MEETING SPORTIF INTER-ALLIÉ

du 159ᵉ Régiment d'Infanterie Alpine

et du 8ᵉ Bataillon The Cameronians
(Scottish Rifles)

À

KÖNIGSHOVEN

Samedi, le 26 juillet 1919, à 14 heures

Les Prix seront présentés par le
Général Tudor, C.B., C.M.G., Commandant Lowland Division

PROGRAMME

1. Match de Football: Les Fleurs de Lys v. Les Chardons. (Médailles.)
2. Eliminatoires de Course de 100 mètres.
3. Course de Mulets (pour les sous-officiers et les hommes). Prix 50, 30, 20 Marks.
4. Le Saut en longueur. Prix 50, 30, 20 Marks.
5. Lutte de traction à la corde. (Eliminatoires, 1 équipe de dix hommes par bataillon.)
6. Course de 1500 mètres. Prix 300, 100, 50 Marks.
7. Semi-finale des 100 mètres.
8. Course d'obstacle. Prix 80, 40, 20 Marks.
9. Eliminatoires de Course de 200 mètres.
10. Le Saut en hauteur. Prix 50, 30, 20 Marks.
11. Course en sac. Prix 50, 30, 20 Marks.
12. Finale des 100 mètres. Prix 100, 50, 30 Marks.
13. Lutte de traction à la corde. (Eliminatoires.)
14. Course de 400 mètres. Prix 100, 50, 30 Marks.
15. Finale des 200 mètres. Prix 80, 40, 20 Marks.
16. Exhibition de Boxe. (Médailles Inscrites.)
17. Finale de lutte de traction à la corde.
18. Course de Mulets pour les officiers.

VIVE L'ENTENTE CORDIALE

Pendant l'après-midi la Musique du 159ᵉ Régiment d'Infanterie Alpine jouera ainsi que les cornemuses du 11ᵉ Bataillon The Royal Scots.
Rafraîchissements sur le terrain.
Le soir un grand concert inter-allié sur le terrain.

INTER-ALLIED SPORTS MEETING

of 159ᵉ Rég. d'Infanterie Alpine

and 8th Batt. The Cameronians

(Scottish Rifles)

at

KÖNIGSHOVEN

on Saturday, 26th July, 1919, commencing at 14 hours

The Prizes will be presented by
Major-General Tudor, C.B., C.M.G., Commanding Lowland Division

PROGRAMME

1. Inter - Battalion Soccer Match: Fleurs de Lys v. Les Chardons. 15 minutes each way. (Medals.)
2. Heats of 100 metres race.
3. Mules' Scurry for N.C.Os. and Men. (Open.) Prizes value 50, 30, 20 Marks.
4. Long Jump. Prizes value 50, 30, 20 Marks.
5. Tug-of-War. (1st Round.)
6. 1500 Metres Race. (Open.) Prizes value 300, 100, 50 Marks.
7. Semi-Final of 100 metres.
8. Obstacle Race. Prizes value 80, 40, 20 Marks.
9. Heats of 200 metres Race.
10. High Jump. Prizes value 50, 30, 20 Marks.
11. Paillasse Race. Prizes value 50, 30, 20 Marks.
12. Final of 100 metres. Prizes value 100, 50, 30 Marks.
13. Tug-of-War. (2nd Round.)
14. 400 Metres Race. (Open.) Prizes value 100, 50, 30 Marks.
15. Final of 200 metres. Prizes value 80, 40, 20 Marks.
16. Boxing Exhibition. (Medals.)
17. Final of Tug-of-War. Prizes value 300, 200 Marks.
18. Musical Chairs for Mounted Officers.

VIVE L'ENTENTE CORDIALE

During the afternoon selections will be played by the Band of the 159ᵉ Rég. Inf. Alp. and by the Pipers of the 11th Battalion The Royal Scots.

Refreshments can be obtained on the field.

In the evening there will be an Inter-Allied Camp-Fire Concert on the Sports Field.

15

On the 27th July I went off for a month's home leave, but the battalion kept up its cordial liaison with our French friends in a hearty manner, which was equally heartily reciprocated. On the 11th August we played their 1st Battalion at football and won 4–1, and Major F. Eaves, D.S.O., my Second-in-Command, and six officers were entertained to dinner by Major Tremblay, their C.O. Then a couple of days afterwards we had a mounted paper chase and another on the 17th, to each of which a good field turned out, including some French officers and a contingent of our transport mounted on mules. History relates that they had a good day's sport.

On the 14th a billeting party of B Battery, 51st Brigade, R.F.A., arrived to spy out the land, and this was the first inkling we got that we were destined ere long for home. Home leave was stopped, and, with the gradual daily return of men from leave, the battalion became stronger.

On the 26th the last paper chase was held, B Battery supplying the hares this time. The course was nine miles long, but despite the drenching rain the chase was very successful. The last few days of the month were spent in packing up and getting off heavy baggage and stores. On the 31st the battalion paraded to receive Brigadier-General Girdwood, who bade us farewell, and recalling his long association with us, he thanked all ranks for their loyal support and good work, and exhorted them to maintain the great traditions they and those who had gone before them had established.

Next day, the 1st September, the battalion entrained at Horff for Calais. The whole of the Brigade Staff and many of the Division came to see the battalion off, and an excellent train ration was served out as a free gift from the Brigade Canteen.

Calais was reached at 2000 hours on the 2nd, and next day the battalion embarked (strength: 23 officers and 511 other ranks) on the *Maid of Orleans* and arrived at Dover at 1300, having been on active service for four years one hundred and nine days. Its home destination, however, was the Curragh, County Kildare, Ireland, and it arrived there on the 5th September. Next day I arrived back from leave and took over command again for the last lap.

ON THE RHINE—THE BATTALION GUARD STANDING EASY

After saluting the Flag before marching off to entrain for home

CHAPTER XI

Demobilization

I found the battalion comfortably installed in hutments in Rath Camp, Curragh, whence it was intended to demobilize the battalion. But demobilization cannot be done in a day; all sorts of papers have to be prepared, and it is not feasible when demobilization is proceeding all over the kingdom to push off more than a limited number from each unit at a time. My recollection is that few men went off during September. On the 17th of that month I took over to Glasgow Captain J. M. Nicholl, Lieuts. A. F. Rogers, F. S. V. Barr, and a contingent of a hundred other ranks of the men of the battalion who had been longest with it, to be entertained by the Corporation at a luncheon in the City Chambers. The Lord Provost, Sir John Stewart, presided, and we were royally entertained. Rogers and I and C.S.M. Coffield were the only remaining members of the battalion who originally went overseas with it in 1915. We embarked that same night for the return journey to the Curragh, and I recollect well the number of friends and old members of the battalion who saw us off. Shortly after this I was ordered to send all men not due for demobilization to the 1st Cameronians at Gough Barracks. These were sent off to the number of about 200 under Captain Dalrymple, and then commenced a regular series of departures—sometimes in batches of 70 to 100, sometimes of 10 to 20. We Scots have an inborn dislike to any display of emotion. Despite this, there were some poignant moments when it came to the final farewells. The batches were paraded for me before they departed, and I must say I found these goodbye parades as trying as anything I experienced during the War—and the men did also. Sometimes they broke down, as I shook hands with them. We had gone through a good deal together: we were dispersing to all parts of the globe: we had been comrades, and the parting showed how closely we had been knit together.[1] Gradually the battalion diminished, and by the end of October there were only some three officers and seven men left. On 1st November I brought over to Glasgow this last remnant together with the battalion books and records destined for the depot at Hamilton Barracks, and there, on 7th November, 1919, the 8th Scottish Rifles finished its career in the Great War.

[1] Some of us were, however, destined to meet again, when, upon the reconstruction of the Territorial Force early in 1920, the 8th was reformed under the command of Lieut.-Colonel R. N. Coulson, D.S.O., and formed part of the Cameronians and H.L.I. Brigade, which I had the good fortune to be appointed to command. In 1922, in consequence of fresh amalgamations of units throughout the army, the 8th was joined up with the 5th battalion, and the combined unit is now known as 5/8 Cameronians (Scottish Rifles).

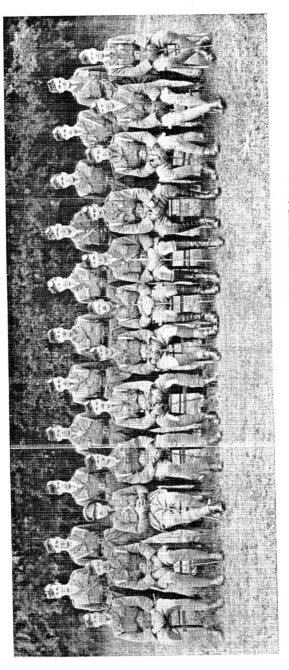

OFFICERS OF 1/8TH BATTALION SCOTTISH RIFLES, BRITISH ARMY OF THE RHINE, JUNE, 1919

Front Row. Lt. F. S. Vere Barr, Lt. T. Young, Lt. Brooke, M.O., Capt. J. B. Stewart, Capt. G. McualyG., Major F. Eaves, D.S.O., Lt.-Col. J. M. Findlay, D.S.O., Capt. E. R. Saltonstall, M.C. (V.B.), Capt. J. M. Nickoll, Capt. W. S. Kennedy, Lt. Cullen, Lt. W. Miller.

Back Row. 2nd-Lt. J. Telfer (R.S.), ——, and-Lt. T. Lamb, and-Lt. J. S. Caldwell, and-Lt. W. Patterson, and-H. N. C. Thomson, ——, and-Lt. W. Macrae, D.C.M. (G.H.), and-Lt. Cairney, ——, ——.

(Capt. W. B. Dalrymple, M.C. and Quarter-Master, *absent*)

APPENDICES

NOTE

Unfortunately Appendices II and V cannot be considered accurate or complete, as the records concerning casualties and honours are not reliable. It should be noted, however, that these appendices include casualties or honours affecting personnel with, and attached to, the battalion from other units. On the other hand, there is no record of casualties or honours in the case of personnel of the 8th attached to other units or formations, sometimes in a different War area.

Appendix VII, however, contains the names of *all* officers originally of the 8th who were killed. As will be noticed, more than half of these made the great sacrifice *away* from the battalion. It also gives the names of certain Other Ranks attached or transferred to the 8th from other units. It is compiled from the Official List of Cameronians who died in the War, which is presumably as accurate as possible.

J. M. F.

APPENDIX I

Roll of Officers, by Companies, who embarked with the battalion on 17th May, 1915, for Gallipoli.

BATTALION HEAD-QUARTERS

Lieut.-Colonel H. Monteith Hannan.
Major J. M. Findlay.
Captain C. J. Bramwell—*Adjutant.*
Captain A. Bankier Sloan, R.A.M.C.
—*Medical Officer.*
Lieut. and Q.M. H. Bowen.
Lieut. E. Maclay—*Machine-gun Officer.*
2nd-Lieut. T. Stout—*Signalling Officer.*
2nd-Lieut. W. D. Hannan—*Transport Officer.*

No. 1 COMPANY

Captain H. A. MacLehose.
Captain C. J. C. Mowat.
Lieut. A. D. Templeton.
Lieut. G. A. C. Moore.
2nd-Lieut. J. Wood Scott.
2nd-Lieut. O. T. Sloan.

No. 2 COMPANY

Captain J. M. Boyd.
Captain W. Campbell Church.
Lieut. W. N. Sloan.
2nd-Lieut. T. L. Tillie.
2nd-Lieut. R. M. Pattison.

No. 3 COMPANY

Captain C. Dunn Macindoe.
Captain R. C. B. Macindoe.
Lieut. R. Humble.
Lieut. D. S. Carson.
2nd-Lieut. A. F. Rogers.
2nd-Lieut. R. B. H. Robertson.

No. 4 COMPANY

Major R. N. Coulson.
Captain E. T. Young.
Lieut. J. T. Findlay.
Lieut. Hew McCowan.
2nd-Lieut. W. S. Maclay.

Captains A. S. L. Young and W. T. Law were on Brigade Staff in May, 1915—the former then transferred to 2/8th Scottish Rifles, and never served with the battalion, being eventually sent to the 1st Battalion in France. The latter served as Staff Captain with the 156th Brigade until early in 1917, when he was promoted to Major and D.A.A.G. of the Mounted Division, British Army in Palestine. Just prior to our embarkation too, Captain J. W. H. Pattison was appointed Brigade Machine-Gun Officer, a position which ere long became an important command in the Brigade (a Brigade machine-gun company being formed consisting of 4 sections of 4 machine-guns each) and becoming a Major's command. Despite ill-health Major Pattison remained at his post until the spring of 1917, when he was invalided home. 2nd-Lieut. A. R. Tillie ere embarkation was transferred to the Flying Corps, and was killed early in the war, and 2nd-Lieut. G. H. Crichton, owing to ill-health, went to the 2/8th.

Four officers, not in the photograph facing p. 16, joined before we left for Gallipoli, 2nd-Lieuts. A. F. Rogers, R. B. H. Robertson, O. T. Sloan, and R. M. Pattison.

APPENDIX II

SCHEDULE OF CASUALTIES WITH THE BATTALION

Date.	Action.	Killed, Missing, or Died of Wounds.		Wounded.	
		Officers.	Other Ranks.	Officers.	Other Ranks.
22/28 June, 1915 {	Third Battle of } Krithia .. }	14	334	11	114
15 Nov., 1915 ..	G. 11 System ..	—	—	—	—
4/5 August, 1916 ..	Romani	1	16	2	15
15/19 April, 1917..	Second Gaza ..	2	47	9	144
June/July, 1917 ..	Apex, &c. ..	1	13	—	20
1/5 Nov., 1917 ..	Third Gaza ..	3	43	4	112
11 Nov., 1917 ..	Burkah	1	18	3	61
21/25 Nov., 1917..	Neby Samwil ..	—	17	3	80
26 Nov., 1917 ..	Beit Sira	—	3	1	8
22/24 Dec., 1917 ..	Auja, Ballutah ..	—	1	1	6
29 July, 1918 ..	Beugneux ..	2	32	10	129
2 August, 1918 ..	,, ..	—	—	—	55
19 August, 1918 ..	Belgium, Ypres ..	1	42	7	234
2 Sept., 1918 {	Belgium, Kemmel } and Wytschaete }	—	—	2	83
October, 1918 ..	Belgium, Gheluwe	1	14	2	112
October, 1918 ..	Belgium, Anseghem	1	17	1	53
November, 1918 ..	Halluin	1	3	—	66
		28	600	56	1292
			Total	1976	

12th July and 15th Nov., 1915.   No note of casualties available.

APPENDIX III

ACCOUNT OF ACTION AT ROMANI, 4/5th AUGUST, 1916
BY OFFICER COMMANDING, 5th R.S.F.

(1) To give a lucid explanation as to the course of events it is necessary to briefly refer to the position held by the British forces prior to the action. The left of the British line rested on the strongly entrenched camp of Mahemdiya, on the shore of the Mediterranean, and from thence ran practically due south for a distance of 4 miles to Katib Gannit, and from thence almost due west for a distance of 1½ miles towards Etmaler. The whole front was composed of a chain of fortified works, prepared for all round defence and each wired in, but with the exception of the works situated north of Kilo 41, which were in advanced stage of construction, the remainder may be said to have been in only a half-finished state, and some were not even that.

The line of Works south of Kilo 41, and as far west as Work 21, were on the summits of insignificant sand-dunes, from which a considerable field of fire and view for distances up to roughly one mile were obtainable, while behind them there rose abruptly a long clearly defined line of heights on an average 200 to 250 feet high, in which the highest point is Katib Gannit. This latter point in particular, and various other points on the high ground to which I refer, were valuable as points of observation, and being entrenched at intervals may be said to have formed a second line of defence, or could have been so used in the event of the first line (the line of Works) being carried. It is, however, with the first line that we are now principally concerned, and a brief reference to the Works west of No. 21 Work is necessary. These were three in number, and, as shown on the map,[1] were situated on high ground covering the southern flank of the British forces in Romani.

It is interesting to note that it was only on the urgent representation of the Brigadier-General commanding 155th Infantry Brigade that Works 21a and 22a were constructed just prior to the engagement, Work 22a taking the place of Work 22, which had been constructed on low ground and possessed every possible military defect. There is no possible doubt that the construction at the last minute of Works 21a and 22a played a very big part in the active operations of the 4th and 5th August, and their value must be discussed under two different paragraphs.

(2) Firstly, their construction denied the high ground on which they now stand to the enemy, who would have occupied it and have rendered untenable the whole of the 155th Brigade area, which can be roughly defined as the ground enclosed by the following points, viz. Anzac Post–Katib Gannit–Work 22.

The loss of such ground, if such had occurred, would have been extremely serious, and the whole of the centre and right of the British position would have been in peril. Further, any counter-attack made over such ground (and such must have been made if the enemy had gained possession of the heights on which 21a and 22a stand) would have been costly in the extreme and doubtful in results.

[1] See p. 71.

(3) Secondly, Work 22a formed, and proved later that it formed, a most valuable pivot of manœuvre. The left of the British counter-attack, delivered on the evening of the 4th August, pivoted on this Work, and from this Work the covering fire of Maxims, Lewis guns, and rifles assisted the advance of the 156th Infantry Brigade in greater measure than they are probably aware of. It is therefore interesting to record that to the foresight and initiative of a Brigade Commander subsequent success was principally due.

(4) *Nature of Ground in Vicinity of Works.*—(a) The ground east of Works 2, 3, 4, and 5, consists of gently undulating sand-dunes, thickly covered with mounds of varying height and size, on which camel thorn or some other kind of shrub grows. Dead ground and natural cover therefore existed in plenty, and of both the enemy took full and skilful advantage during his advance from Bir Abu Hambra.

(b) In a south-easterly direction opposite part of Work No. 2 and Works Nos. 1 and 21, the ground was of a similar nature, though cover in the form of sand mounds was not so marked.

(c) Opposite Works 21a and 22a the ground was more open in the immediate vicinity of the Works, but 900 yards distant and south of No. 22a there rises a long clearly defined scrub-covered ridge, known as Wellington Ridge, which commands the Work, and on and behind which the Turks had by 9 a.m. on the 4th massed at least 2500 men. Before passing on to details of the action reference must be made to three points. That by G.H.Q. orders

(5) (a) Linking up works by wire entanglement was forbidden;

(b) Sand mounds were on no account to be levelled or removed in the vicinity of Works;

(c) The Works were constructed on the assumption that no high-explosive shell fire would or could be brought to bear on them.

As regards (a), practically at the last moment permission to link up by wire was obtained. The wiring was, by the evening of the 4th, well advanced, and this alone prevented the enemy breaking through in large numbers during the night of 4/5th August. As regards (b), clearing was resorted to by my orders, but time admitted of very little of this being done. In consequence of non-clearing the enemy were able to establish themselves within 100 yards of some Works, and actually reach and cut wire connecting some of them. As regards (c), high-explosive shell fire was intense, and caused nearly all the casualties sustained in the redoubts.

(6) *Preliminary Operations.*—For some days prior to the 4th August, the enemy in strength, estimated at some 9000, with guns, were known to be holding an entrenched line some five miles east and south-east of Romani. The Anzac Division was in touch day and night with them, but it was not definitely known until late in the evening of 3/4th August that the Turks were advancing and forcing the Australians and New Zealanders back upon our positions. The latter fell back very skilfully all through the night, retiring westwards across the southern front of our position, closely followed up by the enemy, and by daylight on 4th August had retired to the western slopes of Wellington Ridge, and farther to the south-west, and from these positions they were forced to retire still farther later in the day.

(7) *The Action.*—At 11.30 p.m. on the 3rd August rifle fire was audible in a south-easterly direction, gradually becoming more distinct as time went on and travelling westwards, thereby indicating the advance of the Turks and the gradual retirement of the Australians and New Zealanders opposing them. Garrisons of all posts stood to arms. At 12.45 a.m. on the 4th August the flashes of the rifles of both friend and foe were distinctly visible from Works 21 and No. 1, at a distance of 1700 yards to a mile and in a southerly direction, but so far not a shot had been fired from any of

our Works. By 3 a.m. the enemy on our southern flank had made considerable progress westwards, and had forced our mounted troops back on to Wellington Ridge, and were in occupation of all the sand-hills and dales south of Work 21a and south by east of 22a. Stray bullets were now finding their way into and over Works 21a and No. 1. At dawn, 4.45 a.m., on the 4th an Australian patrol passed through our lines at No. 4 Work, and reported the presence of large numbers of the enemy in Bir Abu Hambra. A few minutes later large numbers were observed moving towards our eastern line of Works, their right moving on No. 5 Work, and the action commenced.

By now it was clear daylight, and the Turkish artillery opened fire with field guns, 5.9-inch Austrian howitzers firing high explosive, and heavy bombing by three German aeroplanes. At the outset the Works did not receive much of the bombardment, which for the most part was directed on Strong Point and the ground to the west and north-west of it. The shooting was accurate and good. At about 7 a.m., however, the Austrian gunners shortened their ranges and turned all their attention to Works No. 3, 4, 5, and 6, the latter, however, not being held by this battalion. These Works sustained an intense bombardment for three hours, during which time many casualties were sustained and the Works damaged.

Under cover of this bombardment the Turkish infantry advanced from Abu Hambra, and, making full and skilful use of all existing cover, established their firing line along the whole front from opposite No. 5 Work to a point opposite No. 2. Not that this had been accomplished by them without considerable losses, for Maxim guns, Lewis guns, and rifles had taken their toll, the shooting of all being very accurate and admirably controlled, and throughout the remainder of the day it is doubtful whether any Turk got nearer than 200 yards to any of the above-mentioned Works, but between Works Nos. 2 and 3 some more venturesome than the rest managed to reach the long stretch of wire connecting these posts and cut it in one place. They were detected, however, by a few riflemen stationed on Katib Gannit, and were forced to abandon the attempt after suffering loss. At about 12 noon the Turkish artillery turned their guns on Works No. 2, No. 1, No. 21, and 21a, but the fire was not so intense, and was more in the nature of intermittent fire which resulted in small damage to both Works and men, but which was maintained off and on for the greater part of the afternoon. Along our eastern front line the Turkish infantry had advanced to within 200 yards of our redoubt line, and here they were well held by our fire which was extremely effective, and from 10 a.m. onwards the fire fight was conducted on our side mainly by special marksmen and snipers and Maxim and Lewis guns, the combination of which at once established a definite fire superiority and caused almost a cessation of the enemy's rifle fire on this front for the rest of the day. At intervals, but at long range, large and favourable targets offered themselves to our Lewis gunners, and of these the fullest advantage was taken.

It is now necessary to refer briefly to events on our southern and south-west front. At no time during the action did Turkish infantry approach nearer to Works 1, 21, and 21a than 200 yards, and it can safely be said that none of these Works were threatened with infantry attack. Their fire, however, especially that of the Brigade Maxim guns, two of which were situated in each Work, did good execution, notably on hostile infantry 1500 yards south-west of No. 21a, and on enemy infantry and a field battery situated some 1600 yards south by west and south-west of Works 21 and 1 respectively. As dusk approached the counter-offensive by the 156th Infantry Brigade, its left pivoting on Work 22a and its right in touch with the 42nd Division advancing eastwards from the direction of Mount Meredith, began to develop, and by dark the 156th Infantry

Brigade were in possession of the western half of Wellington Ridge, where they dug-in on a line running south-west from No. 22a Work. From this line they did not advance till dawn on the 5th August. At dusk the orders were issued to all Post Commandants to send out listening patrols to take up positions along the wire entanglements which connected the redoubts. These patrols all moved into position without incident, except those which left No. 3 Post to take position halfway towards No. 2. After proceeding for some 300 yards figures were observed just on the western side of the wire, and on Lieut. Kerr, who was in command, lighting a Very light, it was seen that some thirty of the enemy had succeeded in cutting a way through the wire; about this time too, two sharp explosions had been observed in the wire between the Works 2 and 3, and it was subsequently discovered that these were explosions of gun cotton used to destroy the wire. Lieut. Kerr with his party with the aid of the light given by more Very lights which he put up, opened a heavy fire on the enemy, causing them some loss, and then withdrew to No. 3 Work and reported. In consequence of his report machine-gun fire was at once opened along the front of the wire from Works 2 and 3, and shrapnel was also burst to the front of it, and there is little doubt that few, if any, Turks made any further attempt to get through; the few, however, who had penetrated subsequently showed that they still could sting, for when at 9 p.m. an officer's patrol sent out from No. 3 arrived in the vicinity of the place where they had been previously observed, they opened fire, killing Lieut. Findlay and Sergeant Flett of the Cyclist Company. By dawn of the 5th inst., however, they had retired, and the Turk remained on the westward side of the ridge. At some other places, notably at between Works 4 and 5, and at Work 5 itself, the Turks had made not ineffectual attempts to cut the wire during the night, but in no case did they succeed in getting through. Dawn of the 5th August revealed the following situation:

On the southern flank the enemy retired eastwards, with the 156th Brigade following up slowly. On the eastern front Turks in some strength still ensconced behind cover within 250 yards of Works 4, 3, and 2, the rifle fire nowhere of great volume. At about 7.30 a.m. Turks could be seen retiring from the front of No. 2 Work, and it appeared that they were in full retreat in every direction.

At 8.45 a.m. the enemy hoisted the white flag at a point 250 yards east of Work No. 3, and surrendered to us to the number of 2 officers and 117 other ranks, of whom some 12 were wounded. It may now be said that for us the action of Romani was over. The Turks skilfully withdrew, pursued by our mounted forces, but nowhere did their retreat develop into a rout, and a strong rear-guard in position at Oghratina effectually held our pursuing forces at bay for the remainder of the 5th August, and indeed during the two following days.

(8) The enemy's losses amounted to 3930 wounded and unwounded prisoners, of whom some 20 were German machine-gunners, 4 mountain guns, 6 machine-guns, and about 1,000,000 rounds S.A.A. Their loss in killed was heavy, and though not definitely known, is estimated at about 600, of which some 350 fell in front of our Works. It is also known that they evacuated some 1200 wounded from Katia on the night of the 4/5th August, and there must have been many more. It is a matter of extreme regret that no counter-attack was launched by our forces on Bir Abu Hambra and to the south of that oasis on the morning of the 5th August. If such had been attempted (and troops were available with which to make it), it is obvious that many hundreds of prisoners would have been taken, for at this period, viz. the early hours of the 5th August, the Turkish infantry had been on the move and fighting for over 36 hours, had exhausted all their water, and had no further stomach for the fight. Moreover, the assistance which

could and would have been given in the form of fire from our redoubt line, would have facilitated any offensive movement directed on Abu Hambra from the north. A golden opportunity was thereby lost. None the less the enemy suffered a severe defeat, due not so much to our tactics or strategy, but to the fact that a blazing sun, lack of water, and deep sand all contributed to leaving him spent and exhausted at the very moment he got to grips with us.

APPENDIX IV

LETTER OF THANKS FROM GENERAL HARE OF THE 54TH DIVISION

" Please convey to my old comrades and fellow-countrymen of the Scottish Rifle Brigade my heartfelt thanks for the great part they have played in the late battle. The gallantry with which they captured their objectives and held them under several days of heavy shelling adds to the reputation they earned in the Gallipoli peninsula. Tell them that it has been a great pleasure to me to renew our old acquaintance, and to have them under me, especially now that the Brigade includes Battalions from Edinburgh and Leith, it is 'just like being at hame.'

S. W. HARE,
Major-General."

8th November, 1917.

APPENDIX V

HONOURS

D.S.O.

Lieut.-Colonel J. M. Findlay.
Lieut.-Colonel R. N. Coulson.

BAR TO D.S.O.

Lieut.-Colonel J. M. Findlay, D.S.O.
A/Lieut.-Colonel R. D. Hunter, D.S.O. (attached).

M.C.

Captain J. A. Anderson.
Captain Sir A. S. Bilsland, Bart.
Captain F. W. Clark, R.A.M.C.
Captain W. Whigham Ferguson.
Captain C. E. Findlay.
Captain W. D. Hannan.
Captain J. J. M'Combie.
Lieut. R. J. Allan.
Lieut. J. S. M. Aucott.
Lieut. F. V. S. Barr.
Lieut. A. Begg.
Lieut. H. G. Carswell.
Lieut. A. F. Grierson.
Lieut. J. E. Lyle.
Lieut. J. S. Ralston.
Lieut. J. H. Souter.
and others.

D.F.C.

Lieut. J. S. Ralston, M.C.

BAR TO M.C.

Captain A/Major G. R. V. Hume-Gore, M.C., Gordons (attached).
Captain W. Whigham Ferguson, M.C.
Captain J. J. M'Combie, M.C.
Lieut. J. S. M. Aucott, M.C.

O.B.E.

Lieut.-Colonel D. S. Carson.

M.B.E.

Lieut. A S. Cameron.

D.C.M.

C.S.M. J. Buchanan.
C.S.M. P. Campbell.
C.S.M. F. Curtis.
C.S.M. Donald Hunter.
Sergeant W. Bond.
Sergeant J. Gilmour.
Sergeant R. Hargreaves.
Sergeant W. Leitch.
L/Sergeant M. N. Cavanagh.
L/Corporal A. Dunning.
L/Corporal A. Muir.
L/Corporal W. Reid.
L/Corporal W. J. Walker.
Private J. Cavanagh.
Private W. Rennie.
Private J. Skirving.

M.M.

Sergeant A. E. Brown.
Sergeant H. Buick.
Sergeant W. G. Charlton.
Sergeant C. Daly.
Sergeant J. Glencross.
Sergeant R. Litterick.
Sergeant D. M'Dowall.
Sergeant W. Mackenzie.
Sergeant F. Partington.
Sergeant H. Ralston.
Sergeant J. Watson.
A/Sergeant R. Wylie.
Corporal W. Gillan.
Corporal J. Howe.
L/Corporal C. Ramage.
Private W. H. Black.
Private W. Caskie.
Private P. Cassidy.
Private W. Gowanlock.
Private D. M'Dougall.
Private W. Mackenzie.
Private L. Morgan.
Private F. Murphy.
Private R. Napier.
Private J. Nelson.
Private A. O'Hara.
Private T. Ripley.
Private A. Stewart.
Private W. Wallis.

MENTIONED IN DISPATCHES

	Times
Lieut.-Colonel R. N. Coulson, D.S.O.	2
Lieut.-Colonel J. M. Findlay, D.S.O.	4
Lieut.-Colonel R. D. Hunter, D.S.O.	3
Major D. S. Carson	2
Major Hume-Gore, M.C.	2
Captain E. R. Boyd	1
Captain C. J. Bramwell	1
Captain F. W. Clark, R.A.M.C.	1
Captain W. D. Dulieu	2
Captain W. W. Ferguson	1
Captain C. E. Findlay	1
Captain W. D. Hannan	1
Captain A. B. Sloan, R.A.M.C.	2

	Times
Lieut. and Q.M. H. Bowen	2
Lieut. J. M. Nicholl	1
A/R.S.M. A. Drummond	1
C.S.M. C. S. Murray	1
Sergeant D. Learmouth	1
Sergeant H. Ralston, M.M.	1
Sergeant J. Watson	1
L/Corporal A. Muir	1
Private P. Bonnar	1
Private J. Duff	1
Private T. Woods	1

Mentioned in Army Corps Orders for Act of Gallantry not under Fire

Private T. Calder.
Private R. Macnamara.

FOREIGN ORDERS

FRENCH
LEGION OF HONOUR
(Chevalier)

Lieut.-Colonel J. M. Findlay, D.S.O.

CROIX DE GUERRE (avec palmes)

Lieut.-Colonel R. N. Coulson, D.S.O.
Lieut.-Colonel J. M. Findlay, D.S.O.
Major G. R. V. Hume-Gore, M.C.
Captain W. W. Ferguson, M.C.

CROIX DE GUERRE (Silver Star)

Lieut. A. F. Grierson, M.C.
Lieut. J. J. M'Combie, M.C.
2nd-Lieut. F. S. V. Barr, M.C.

Bronze Star

C.Q.M.S. J. Glencross, M.M.
Sergeant H. Buick, M.M.

Sergeant F. Partington, M.M.
Corporal W. Gillan, M.M.
Corporal J. Howe.
L/Corporal W. Wallis, M.M.
Private R. Napier.

MÉDAILLE MILITAIRE

Corporal J. Howe.
Private R. Napier, M.M.

BELGIAN
CROIX DE LÉOPOLD
(Chevalier)

Lieut.-Colonel R. D. Hunter, D.S.O.

CROIX DE GUERRE (avec palmes)

Lieut.-Colonel R. D. Hunter, D.S.O.

CROIX DE GUERRE (avec Étoile)

Corporal A. Ferguson.
Private T. Ripley.

APPENDIX VI

2/8th BATTALION CAMERONIANS (SCOTTISH RIFLES)

When the Second or Reserve Battalions, as they were first officially known, of the Territorial Force were formed, the Cameronian Brigade was not included in the scheme. One result of this was that when a short time afterwards instructions were received to form reserve battalions in this Brigade also, a large number of officers and men who had previously served in the 8th, and who would have been ready to join, were found to be enrolled in Kitchener's Army; the Chamber of Commerce Battalion alone having absorbed more than half a dozen old 8th officers.

On 25th September, 1914, Major A. D. Ker, T.D., Second in Command of the 8th Battalion, was appointed to command the reserve battalion with the rank of Lieut.-Colonel. Captain J. R. Johnston, in charge of Head-quarters at Glasgow, became Adjutant, and William Wilson, from Brigade Head-quarters, Quartermaster. The nucleus of the battalion was ready to hand in the home-service company of the 8th housed in the model lodging at Falkirk under Captain A. S. L. Young, with 2nd-Lieuts. J. E. Bannen, K. B. Craigie, W. W. Ferguson, A. H. Crawford, J. S. M. Aucott, A. D. Cameron, and W. J. Aitken. This company remained at Falkirk, while recruiting was started at Glasgow with the following officers: Captains G. B. Cree, W. E. F. Macmillan, C. T. Burns, J. P. Cuthbert, N. Caw, D. S. Arthur, and J. K. M. Wylie; Lieut. E. R. Boyd; 2nd-Lieuts. W. A. Boyd, R. S. Cree, N. M. R. Smith, C. E. Findlay, J. A. MacLaren, A. S. Bilsland, L. S. Watson, G. H. Moir, and D. J. C. M'Cowan, with Dr. H. A. M'Lean as Medical Officer. Later enrolments in 1915 were F. W. J. Burns, J. M. Nicholl, W. Dow, A. MacDougall, G. T. Cairns, and F. H. Blackie. The staff consisted of Sergeant-Major F. Parris, Q.M.S. J. Barr, and Sergeant-Cook J. Shaw, with assistance in the Orderly Room from Mr. Blench, bandmaster, who, in the absence of a band to train, volunteered for this work.

Training was carried on during the winter in the Alexandra Park and at Riddrie, the members of the battalion living in their own homes. Several visits were made to Glasgow by the band of the 1/8th to help in recruiting, and owing to the generosity of Colonel W. R. Maxwell, V.D., Honorary Colonel, who provided the pipes, a most efficient pipe band, under Pipe-Major M'Dougall, was formed.

In January, 1915, Colonel J. L. C. Campbell (late R.E.) was appointed Brigadier, and along with Colonel Blair (Lowland Reserve Division) inspected the battalion on 30th January.

On 9th March the battalion moved to Kilmarnock and occupied the Loanhead School and other halls. There it was joined by the home service company from Falkirk, with the officers mentioned above, and also Lieut. G. H. Crichton (Captain, 1st July). On 1st April Captains J. R. Johnston and A. S. L. Young were promoted to Major, the former becoming Second in Command, and the latter taking his place as Adjutant. Training was carried on at the Kilmarnock Golf Course and the grounds of The Dean, and route-marches and night-marches were regularly undertaken.

During all this period the 2/8th continued at intervals to send drafts to the first line, and transferred in all nearly 1000 men.

On 17th May the 1/8th left Falkirk for Gallipoli, and on the following day the 2/8th entrained for Glasgow, attended a review on Glasgow Green of the second-line battalions of the Division by H.M. the King, and proceeded to Falkirk, where it took over the quarters vacated by the 1/8th. The Head-quarters of the Brigade also at this time moved from Glasgow to Falkirk, the Brigadier appointing as his Staff Captain, Captain J. P. Cuthbert of the 2/8th.

Soon after arrival at Falkirk a detachment was sent to Portobello for dock defence. This was intended to consist only of those who had not signed for service abroad, but as the number of such was considerably less than the number required, the balance had to be made up from foreign-service men. The latter rejoined the battalion in a week or two, while the remainder, with other similar units, formed a provisional battalion at Leith and Granton.

On 23rd June the battalion left Falkirk and marched to Birkhill Camp, Cambusbarron, Stirling, where it remained under canvas till 4th October. The news of the death of Lieut.-Colonel H. M. Hannan, and later, of so many officers and men of the 1/8th at Gallipoli, profoundly affected everyone. A Memorial Service at Glasgow Cathedral to Lieut.-Colonel Hannan was attended by as many officers as could obtain leave for the purpose. Hopes were entertained by most of a chance of service abroad, and several communications were received detailing the number of different ranks required, but these always concluded by insisting on the observance of a War Office letter which forbade the decreasing of the numbers of the various ranks below a certain point, thus limiting the possible foreign drafts to a minimum. The reason of this was that at that time it was intended that the second-line Divisions would go abroad as a unit. As many officers as possible within the limits of this restriction, went abroad to join the first line.

During its stay at Cambusbarron the battalion went through the musketry course, and took part in a night attack and defence scheme in the newly-formed school of bombing. Much interest was shown in the instruction in riding of a detachment of the third-line transport section by Lieut. J. M. Nicholl, who had temporarily succeeded Lieut. A. S. Bilsland as Transport-Officer.

On 4th October the Brigade marched from Cambusbarron to Lochgelly, camping for one night en route at Bogside Farm, the battalion distinguishing itself by arriving without one man having fallen out. The object of this move was to fence round the trenches previously dug by the H.L.I. Reserve Brigade. On 10th October they left Lochgelly, marching by night to Doni-bristle, thence to Bogside Farm, and on 12th October the 2/8th arrived at Tillicoultry (the remainder of the Brigade returning to Stirling), and was billeted at the Devonside Mills. Here it remained till 22nd November, when it marched back to Stirling, where Lieut.-Colonel Ker handed over his command to Lieut.-Colonel Benzie, the 2/5th and 2/8th being amalgamated on the reorganization of the Brigade.

3/8th BATTALION CAMERONIANS (SCOTTISH RIFLES)

The third line came into existence in May, 1915, just as the first line was leaving for overseas, as a recruiting, training, and draft-producing unit for the first and second lines. The name was subsequently changed to the 8th Reserve Battalion Scottish Rifles, though it was familiarly known throughout its existence, and will be best remembered, as the 3/8th.

Originally a Major's Command, it was after a few months raised to a Lieut.-Colonel's Command, with the usual full establishment, and in addition a large number of supernumerary officers were carried for instruction and training.   Many of these officers became instructors at various schools of training, such as musketry, bombing, signalling, &c., and several were selected as instructors to the 3rd Line Lowland Division, of which the battalion formed a part.   A large proportion of these officers eventually went to other battalions than their own line, many of whom gained distinctions and honours.

The early training of the battalion took place in Glasgow, the men living in their own homes and receiving in addition to their pay a subsistence allowance for themselves and their families.   Recruiting, rather slow at first, improved greatly by early autumn, before leaving Glasgow.   The battalion was fortunate in having a number of officers with previous service, and were also fortunate in getting a number of ex-regular non-commissioned officers, whose experience was most helpful in carrying on the work of a new battalion.

It is right and proper to place on record that through the generosity of Mr. Halley and Mr. Arthur Young (an old officer) the battalion was provided with bagpipes and pipers' uniform, while our Honorary Colonel and several old officers helped with subscriptions to smooth many difficulties in the early stages.

On 18th November, 1915, the battalion, under the command of Lieut.-Colonel J. M. Hannan, proceeded to the North Camp, Ripon, where the command of the Division was given over by Colonel Sir R. C. Mackenzie to Colonel the Hon. W. G. Hepburn-Scott (now Lord Polwarth).   The move was beneficial in many ways.   The training was under the Ripon Training Centre, and there were many facilities for the training of officers and N.C.Os. at York, Strensall, Otley, Oxford, Cambridge, and other places.

The battalion moved on 12th April, 1916, to Catterick Camp, Richmond, where the training was conducted under the Catterick Training Centre. In July a visit was paid to the camp by the Lord Provost of Glasgow and members of the Territorial Force Association, who were entertained to lunch by the officers of the battalion.

It is interesting to note that the Commanding Officer, Second in Command, and the Adjutant, Lieut.-Colonel James M. Hannan, Major David S. Arthur, M.C., and Captain Wilfred S. Sloan, respectively, were all sons of old officers of the battalion, and that the post of Quartermaster was filled by Captain and Quartermaster D. M. Pincock, whose regimental record dated from 1884.

The 31st August, 1916, saw the end of this battalion, as on 1st September it was amalgamated with the 5th, 6th, and 7th Reserve Battalions, which became, and were known until the end of the war as, the 5th (Reserve) Battalion Scottish Rifles.

APPENDIX VII

8TH BN. THE CAMERONIANS (SCOTTISH RIFLES)

EXPLANATION OF ABBREVIATIONS

"b."	..	..	"born."	"d. of w."	.. "died of wounds."
"e."	..	..	"enlisted."	"k. in a."	.. "killed in action."
"d."	..	..	"died."	"F. & F."	.. "France & Flanders (including Italy)."

N.B.—When the place of enlistment is followed by the name of another place in brackets, the latter represents the deceased soldier's place of residence.

OFFICERS DIED IN THE WAR

Hannan, Henry Monteith, Lt.-Col., k. in a., 21/6/15.
Bramwell, Charles Guy, Capt., k. in a., 28/6/15.
Church, William Campbell, Capt., k. in a., 28/6/15.
Cree, Robert Scott, Capt., d. of w., 14/11/17.
Hannan, William David, M.C., Capt., k. in a., 14/10/18.
Harvey, Alec Wright, Capt., d. of w., 27/3/18 (in Ger. hands).
MacDougall, Archibald, Lt. (A/Capt.), k. in a., 31/10/18.
Macindoe, Cecil Alexander Dunn, Capt., k. in a., 28/6/15.
Macindoe, Ronald Christian Black, Capt., k. in a., 28/6/15.
Mowat, Charles James Carlton, Capt., k. in a., 28/6/15.
Tillie, Arnold Reid, Capt., k. in a., 11/5/16 (and R.F.C.).
Blackie, Frank Herndon, Lt., k. in a., 11/4/18.
Bowen, Henry, Lt. & Qr.-Mr., k. in a., 21/5/17.
Cairns, George Thomas, Lt., k. in a., 30/7/18.
Findlay, John Tulloch, Lt., k. in a. 28/6/15.
Gilmour, James, Lt., k. in a., 30/3/18.
Keith, Patrick Hay, Lt., k. in a., 15/6/15.
McCowan, Hew, Lt., k. in a., 28/6/15.
Moore, Gerald Alexander Clifford, Lt., d. of w., 11/7/15.
Neilson, John Towers, Lt., k. in a., 2/11/17.
Sloan, Wilfred Scott, Lt., k. in a., 28/4/17.
Stout, Jnr., Thomas, Lt., k. in a., 28/6/15.
Templeton, Archibald Douglas, Lt., k. in a., 28/6/15.
Thom, Laurence Wilson, Lt., d. of w., 21/4/17.
Watson, Laurence Stuart, Lt., k. in a., 29/7/18.
Allan, Robert, 2/Lt., k. in a., 23/4/17.

Benzie, William Gardner, 2/Lt., d. of w., 10/4/17.
Birrell, William Henry, 2/Lt., d. of w., 20/9/18.
Blair, John, 2/Lt., d. of w., 16/6/18.
Calderwood, William Sewell, 2/Lt., k. in a., 31/7/17.
Campbell, James, 2/Lt., d. of w., 23/7/18.
Conochie, Robert Pollock, 2/Lt., k. in a., 19/5/18.
Dinwoodie, David Wallace, 2/Lt., k. in a., 19/4/17.
Dow, Walter, 2/Lt., k. in a., 19/12/15.
Dunn, Herbert, 2/Lt., died, 25/10/15.
Edwards, Norman Roy, 2/Lt., k. in a., 19/4/17.
France, John Galbraith, 2/Lt., k. in a., 12/4/17.
Gemmell, Cecil Woodburn, 2/Lt., k. in a., 24/4/17.
Johnston, Robert Neilson, 2/Lt., k. in a., 22/7/16.
Lugton, George Deane, 2/Lt., k. in a., 30/11/17.
Macdonald, Charles Gordon, 2/Lt., k. in a., 15/6/15
Mackenzie, Francis Edgar, 2/Lt., k. in a., 23/4/17.
Maclay, William Strang, 2/Lt., d. of w., 25/6/15.
MacLeod, Victor Charles Augustus, 2/Lt., k. in a., 18/7/17.
Macmillan, John, 2/Lt., d. of w., 24/9/18.
Miller, Harold Patterson, 2/Lt., d. of w., 27/4/18.
Mitchell, Frank Kinniburgh, 2/Lt., k. in a., 8/5/18.
Muirhead, John Ritchie, 2/Lt., k. in a., 20/10/18.
Murray, James McMillan, 2/Lt., k. in a., 24/6/17.
Oliver, George Eric, 2/Lt., d. of w., 31/7/17.
Palmer, Bertie William, 2/Lt., d. of w., 25/8/18.
Paterson, James, 2/Lt., d. of w., 20/9/17.

Pattison, Robert Macfie, 2/Lt., k. in a., 28/6/15.
Patton, David, 2/Lt., d. of w., 11/2/18.
Pitt, Douglas, 2/Lt., k. in a., 31/7/17.
Pryce, Alfred Owen Challoner, 2/Lt., k. in a., 14/4/18
Robertson, Robert Bruce Hope, 2/Lt., k. in a., 28/6/15.
Scott, James Wood, 2/Lt., k. in a., 28/6/15.

Stewart, William Marshall, 2/Lt., k. in a., 24/3/17.
Vass, Thomas McKenzie, 2/Lt., k. in a., 4/5/18.
Wells, Henry Frederick, 2/Lt., k. in a., 21/9/18.
Whitelaw, Thomas Mitchell, 2/Lt., d. of w., 29/5/18.
Wilson, Michael Connal, 2/Lt., k. in a., 20/7/16.

OTHER RANKS DIED IN THE WAR

Adam, John B., b. Paisley, e. Maryhill, Glasgow, 203031, Pte., d. of w., F. & F., 1/8/18, formerly S/16690, A. & S. H.
Airth, William, e. Glasgow, 9750, Pte.. k. in a., Gallipoli, 28/6/15.
Aitchison, J., e. Bellshill, 291637 Pte., d., Egypt, 6/11/17.
Aitken, Alexander, b. Eastwood, Renfrew, e. Glasgow, 291125, Pte., k. in a., Egypt, 19/4/17.
Alexander, Andrew, b. Leith, e. Leith, 34065, Pte., k. in a., Egypt, 2/11/17.
Anderson, James, b. Strabane. Co. Antrim, e. Glasgow, 33715, Pte., k. in a., Egypt, 2/11/17.
Anderson, James, b. Cambusnethan Lanark, e. Lanark (Wishaw), 241512, Pte., k. in a., F. & F., 14/10/18, formerly 8080, H.L.I.
Arthur, William John, b. Belfast, e. Glasgow, 28811, Pte., d., F. & F., 27/10/18.
Askew, George Francis, b. Lancaster, e. Glasgow, 9395, Pte., k. in a., Gallipoli, 28/6/15.
Bain, Peter, b. Calton, Glasgow, e. Glasgow, 9568, L/Cpl., k. in a., Gallipoli, 28/6/15.
Bain, William, e. Glasgow, 1017, Pte., k. in a., Egypt, 4/8/16.
Baird, William, b. Milton, Glasgow, e. Glasgow, 8997, Pte., k. in a., Gallipoli, 28/6/15.
Ballantyne, Thomas, e. Glasgow, 26, Pte., k. in a., Gallipoli, 28/6/15.
Banks, George, e. Glasgow, 256, Pte. k. in a., Gallipoli, 28/6/15.
Barclay, Thomas, b. Barony, Glasgow, e. Glasgow, 8853, A/Cpl., k. in a., Gallipoli, 28/6/15.
Barker, James, e. Glasgow, 9659, Pte., k. in a., Gallipoli, 28/6/15.
Barr, Joseph, b. Blantyre, Lanark, e. Hamilton, 203937, Pte., d. of w., Egypt, 11/12/17
Barrett, Reginald, b. Oundle, Northants, . e. Peterborough, 33562, Pte., k. in a., Egypt, 22/11/17, formerly 108142, R.A.S.C.
Barron, John G., b. Glasgow, e. Yorkhill, Glasgow, 37687, Pte. k. in a., F. & F., 1/8/18, formerly 1971, R.A.M.C.
Baxter, William, e. Glasgow. 9938, Pte., d. of w., Gallipoli, 21/6/15.
Baxter, William, e. Glasgow, 291247, Pte., k. in a., Egypt, 19/4/17.
Bell, John, e. Lanark (Crawford), 241509, Pte., d. of w., Egypt, 2/11/17, formerly 8074, H.L.I.
Bell, Kenneth, b. Alvabank, e. Falkirk, 9722, Pte., k. in a., Gallipoli, 28/6/15.

Bell, Richard, b. Elderslie, Renfrew, e. Glasgow, 8799, Pte., k. in a., Gallipoli 28/6/15.
Bethune, Peter, b. Barony, Glasgow, e. Glasgow, 9458, Pte., k. in a., Egypt, 4/8/16.
Beveridge, Charles, b. Dollar, Clackmannan, e. Glasgow, 9109. Cpl., k. in a., Gallipoli 28/6/15.
Biggs, John A., b. Dennistoun, Glasgow, e. Falkirk, 512, Pte., k. in a., Gallipoli, 28/6/15.
Biggs, William Edwin, b. Dennistoun, Glasgow, e. Glasgow, 9397. L/Sgt., k. in a., Gallipoli, 28/6/15.
Black, Alexander McLeod, e. Glasgow, 291101, Pte., k. in a., Egypt, 2/11/17.
Black, George, b. Nairn, e. Glasgow, 9198, Pte., k. in a., Gallipoli, 28/6/15.
Black, Robert, b. Cambuslang, Lanark, e. Glasgow, 7947, Pte., k. in a., Gallipoli, 28/6/15.
Black, Walter H., e. Glasgow, 290625, Pte., d. of w., F. & F., 29/10/18, M.M.
Blair, Alexander R., b. Greenock, e. Glasgow, 291489, Sgt., k. in a., Egypt, 2/11/17.
Boal, William, b. Barony, Glasgow, e. Glasgow, 290106, A/Sgt., k. in a., Egypt, 12/11/17.
Bogie, John, e. Glasgow, 9889, Pte., k. in a., Gallipoli, 28/6/15.
Borland, George, b. Barony, Glasgow, e. Glasgow, 290163, Pte., k. in a., Egypt, 22/11/17.
Borland, Robert, b. Barony, Glasgow, e. Glasgow, 9411, Pte., k. in a., Gallipoli, 28/6/15.
Bowie, George, e. Glasgow, 113, Pte., k. in a., Gallipoli, 28/6/15.
Boyd, James, b. Barony, Glasgow, e. Glasgow, 9233, Pte., k. in a., Gallipoli, 28/6/15.
Boyle, James, b. Barony, Glasgow, e. Glasgow, 9264, Pte., k. in a., Gallipoli, 28/6/15.
Brady, Thomas, e. Glasgow, 2, Pte., k. in a., Gallipoli, 28/6/15.
Brash, David, b. Cowcaddens, Glasgow, e. Glasgow, 537, Pte., k. in a., Gallipoli, 28/6/15.
Brown, Arthur Edward, b. Portsmouth, e. London, 201346, Sgt., d. of w., F. & F., 17/8/18, M.M.
Brown, Forbes Jardine, b. Barony, Glasgow, e. Glasgow, 9059, Pte., k. in a., Gallipoli, 28/6/15.
Brown, Hamilton Aird, b. St. Quivox, Ayr, e. Ayr, 204037, Pte., d. of w., F. & F., 15/10/18.

Brown, Henry Raeburn, b. Edinburgh, e. Glasgow, 203041, Pte., k. in a., Egypt, 2/11/17, formerly S/16919, A. & S.H.

Brown, James, b. Barony, Glasgow, e. Glasgow, 8749, L/Cpl., k. in a., Gallipoli, 28/6/15.

Brown, James Vance, e. Glasgow, 420, Pte., d., Gallipoli, 29/10/15.

Brown, Joseph Anderson, b. Edinburgh, e. Glasgow, 9136, Pte., k. in a., Gallipoli, 12/7/15.

Brown, Richard, b. New Stevenston, Lanark, e. Hamilton, 33656, Pte., d. of w., Egypt, 3/11/17.

Brown, William, b. Edinburgh, e. Edinburgh, 33712, Pte., k. in a., F. & F., 29.7 18.

Brown, William R., b. Glasgow, e. Glasgow, 290139, Pte., k. in a., Egypt, 24/11/17.

Brown, William. b. Lintrathen, Forfar, e. Kirriemuir, 291529, Pte., k. in a., F. & F., 29/7/18.

Buchanan, Alexander, e. Glasgow, 9620, Pte., k. in a., Gallipoli, 28/6/15.

Buchanan, John, e. Glasgow, 43286 Pte., k. in a., F. & F., 1/9/18.

Buchanan, Robert, b. Barony, Glasgow, e. Glasgow, 291493, Pte., d. of w., Egypt, 1/5/17.

Buchanan, Thomas, e. Glasgow, 196, Pte., k. in a., Gallipoli, 28/6/15.

Burck, James, b. St. Luke's, London, E.C., e. Stratford, 291567, Cpl., k. in a., Egypt, 29/7/17.

Burden, Hugh, b. Grahamstown, Stirling e. Falkirk, 9723, Pte., k. in a., Gallipoli, 28/6/15.

Burdon, Thomas Rennie, b. Cowlairs, Glasgow, e. Glasgow, 9600, Pte., k. in a., Gallipoli, 28/6/15.

Burke, John, e. Glasgow, 290718, Pte., k. in a., Egypt, 12/11/17.

Burke, William, b. Maryhill, Glasgow, e. Glasgow, 290867, Pte., d. of w., Egypt, 4/11/17.

Burniston, Matthew, e. Glasgow, 67, Pte., k. in a., Gallipoli, 28/6/15.

Burns, James, b. Milton, Glasgow, e. Glasgow, 9417, Sgt., k. in a., Gallipoli, 28/6/15.

Byrne, Rodger, b. Basley, Roscommon, e. Glasgow, 291114, Pte., k. in a., Egypt, 27/10/17.

Cairney, John, b. Barony, Glasgow, e. Glasgow, 8984, Pte., k. in a., Gallipoli, 28/6/15.

Cairns, Francis, e. Glasgow, 194, Pte., k. in a., Gallipoli, 28/6/15.

Calderwood, Andrew, b. Glasgow, e. Stepney, London, 202999, Pte., k. in a., F. & F., 29/7/18, formerly 25091, H.L.I.

Cameron, Donald, b. Calton, Glasgow, e. Glasgow, 9151, Pte., k. in a., Gallipoli, 28/6/15.

Cameron, James, b. Dunfermline, e. Falkirk, 9693, Pte., k. in a., Gallipoli, 28/6/15.

Cameron, Robert, e. Glasgow, 9757, Pte., k. in a., Gallipoli, 28/6/15.

Campbell, John, b. Barony, Glasgow, e. Glasgow, 9251, Pte., k. in a., Gallipoli, 28/6/15.

Campbell, John, b. Beith, Ayr, e. Glasgow (Beith, Ayr), 291106, Pte., d. of. w., F. & F., 11/11/18.

Campbell, John, b. Killin, Perth, e. Perth, (Killin, Perth), 292106, Pte., d., Egypt, 23/4/17, formerly S/16919, R. Scot. Fus.

Campbell, Robert, b. Lanark, e. Glasgow, 9127, Pte., k. in a., Gallipoli, 28/6/15.

Campbell, William, b. St. John's, Glasgow, e. Glasgow, 8125, A/Sgt., k. in a., Gallipoli, 12/7/15.

Campbell, William, e. Glasgow, 87, A/Cpl., k. in a., Gallipoli, 28/6/15.

Campbell, William, b. Barony, Glasgow, e. Glasgow, 291611, Pte., k. in a., F. & F., 31/10/18.

Carlin, William, b. Barony, Glasgow, e. Glasgow, 8986, Pte., k. in a., Gallipoli, 28/6/15.

Carmichael, Donald, e. Glasgow, 79, Pte., k. in a., Gallipoli, 28/6/15.

Carr, William, b. Eastwood, Lanark, e. Yorkhill, Glasgow, 37689, Pte., k. in a., F. & F., 29/7/18, formerly 1990, R.A.M.C.

Carroll, Thomas, b. Cowcaddens, Glasgow, e. Glasgow, 8809 Pte., k. in a., Gallipoli, 28/6/15.

Carroll, William, b. Cowcaddens, Glasgow, e. Glasgow, 8810, Pte., k. in a., Gallipoli, 28/6/15.

Carslaw, William, b. Barony, Glasgow, e. Glasgow, 9282, A/L/Sgt., k. in a., Gallipoli, 28/6/15.

Carter, Joseph, b. St. Mungo, Glasgow, e. Glasgow, 8867, Pte., k. in a., Gallipoli, 28/6/15.

Cassidy, James Cole, b. Hamilton, e. Glasgow (Hamilton), 72, Pte., k. in a., Gallipoli, 28/6/15.

Cassidy, Patrick, b. Barony, Glasgow, e. Glasgow, 9421, Pte., k. in a., Gallipoli, 19/6/15.

Chalmers, Alexander, b. Barony, Glasgow, e. Glasgow, 42578, Pte., k. in a., F. & F., 29/7/18, formerly 376401, R. Scots.

Chalmers, Harry, b. Parkhead, Glasgow, e. Glasgow, 9727, Pte., k. in a., Gallipoli, 28/6/15.

Chalmers, Martin, b. Stevenston, Ayr, e. Glasgow, 8771, Pte., k. in a., Gallipoli, 28/6/15.

Christie, James, b. St. Rollox, Glasgow, e. Glasgow, 8863, Pte., k. in a., Gallipoli. 28/6/15.

Church, Robert, b. Springburn, Glasgow, e. Glasgow, 8634. A/L/Cpl., k. in a., Gallipoli, 28/6/15.

Clark, George Brown, b. Innerleithen, Peebles, e. Glencorse (Innerleithen), 39654, Pte., k. in a., F. & F., 29/7/18.

Clark, Henry, b. Kirkcaldy, e. Glasgow (Kirkcaldy), 115, Pte., k. in a., Gallipoli, 28/6/15.

Clarke, Andrew, e. Glasgow, 290624, A/L/Cpl., d. of w., Egypt, 22/11/17.

Clarkson, Robert, e. Glasgow, 9910, Pte., k. in a., Gallipoli, 28/6/15.

Clough, William, b. Bowling, Yorks, e. Glasgow, 8428, A/Sgt., k. in a., Gallipoli, 28/6/15.

Cochrane, David, b. Barony, Glasgow, e. Glasgow, 9313, Pte., k. in a., Gallipoli, 28/6/15.

Coid, Charles, b. Green Brae, Dumfries, e. Kilmarnock (Dumfries), 620, Pte., d., Egypt, 17/9/16.

Collins, Neil, e. Glasgow, 9940, Pte., k. in a., Gallipoli, 28/6/15.

Collins, Robert, b. Kelvinside, Glasgow, e. Glasgow, 8006, Pte., k. in a., Gallipoli, 28/6/15.

Conner, Martin, b. Barony, Glasgow, e. Glasgow, 9623, Pte., k. in a., Gallipoli, 28/6/15.

Conway, William, b. Calton, Glasgow, e. Glasgow, 9240, A/L/Sgt., k. in a., Gallipoli, 28/6/15.

Cook, Alexander, b. Govan, Glasgow, e. Glasgow, 8968, Pte., d. of w., Gallipoli, 20/12/15.

Cooper, John, b. Barony, Glasgow, e. Glasgow, 9929, Pte., k. in a., Gallipoli, 12/7/15.

Cosans, John, b. Glasgow, e. Glasgow, 290858, Pte., k. in a., Egypt, 22/11/17.

Cowan, Hugh, e. Glasgow, 245, Pte., k. in a., Gallipoli, 28/6/15.

Cowan, Robert, b. Glasgow, e. Glasgow, 276, Pte., k. in a., Gallipoli, 28/6/15.

Cowling, Arthur, e. Bradford, 35958, Pte., k. in a., F. & F., 14/10/18, formerly 42556, Northumberland Fus.

Craig, John, b. Barony, Glasgow, e. Glasgow, 1171, Pte., k. in a., Egypt, 4/8/16.

Craig, John, b. Newmains, Lanark, e. Glasgow, 8907, Pte., k. in a., Gallipoli, 28/6/15.

Craig, Robert, b. Hamilton, e. Hamilton, 35629, Pte., k. in a., F. & F., 29/7/18.

Crawford, James, b. Tillicoultry, e. Kirkcaldy (Tillicoultry), 351, Pte., k. in a., Gallipoli, 28/6/15.

Crawford, John Hunter, b. Maryhill, Glasgow, e. Glasgow, 8952, A/L/Sgt., k. in a., Gallipoli, 28/6/15.

Croll, George, b. Barony, Glasgow, e. Glasgow, 202072, A/L/Cpl. k. in a., Egypt, 24/11/17.

Cumming, Edward, e. Glasgow, 21, Pte., k. in a., Gallipoli, 28/6/15.

Cunningham, Neil, b. Barony, Glasgow e. Glasgow, 33569, Pte., d. at Sea, 4/5/17.

Curley, Patrick, b. Barony, Glasgow, e. Glasgow, 8989, Pte., k. in a., Gallipoli, 28/6/15.

Currie, James, b. Old Monkland, Lanark, e. Coatbridge, Lanark, 26713, Pte., k. in a., F. & F., 29/7/18, formerly 143548, R.F.A.

Curtis, Frederick Charles, b. Bermuda, W. Indies, e. Birmingham, 292002, C.S.M., d. of w., Egypt, 22/11/17.

Dallas, John, e. Glasgow, 290888, Pte., k. in a., Egypt, 2/11/17.

Daly, John, b. Barony Glasgow, e. Glasgow, 9499, Pte., k. in a., Gallipoli, 28/6/15.

Daly, Joseph, b. Barrhead, Renfrew, e. Glasgow, 290072, Pte., k. in a., Egypt, 23/11/17.

Dalziel, Murray, e. Glasgow, 9616, Pte., k. in a., Gallipoli, 28/6/15.

D'Arcy, Miles, b. Maryhill, Glasgow, e. Glasgow, 9461, Pte., k. in a., Gallipoli, 28/6/15.

Day, Peter, b. Edinburgh, e. Edinburgh, 203019, Pte., k. in a., Egypt, 19/4/17, formerly 23893, H.L.I.

Davidson, William, b. Kilmarnock e. Glasgow, 52883, Pte., k. in a., F. & F., 14/10/18.

Dawson, William, b. Strathaven, Lanark, e. Hamilton (Strathaven), 241265, Pte., k. in a., F. & F., 14/10/18.

De Stefano, Peter, b. Paris, e. Edinburgh (Linlithgow), 52945, Pte., k. in a., F. & F., 31/10/18.

Dewar, Robert, b. Glasgow, e. Wishaw Lanark, 52786, Pte., k. in a., F. & F., 16/10/18.

Diamond, James, e. Glasgow, 9833, Pte. k. in a., Gallipoli, 28/6/15.

Dick, James, e. Glasgow (Thornhill, Perth), 143, Pte., k. in a., Gallipoli, 28/6/15.

Dickson, Jack, e. Glasgow, 290432, Pte., k. in a., Egypt, 2/11/17.

Dietrich, Harman Edward, b. Ayr, e. Ayr, 56451, Pte., k. in a., F. & F., 29/7/18, formerly 49517, R. Scots.

Docherty, John, b. Springburn, Glasgow, e. Glasgow, 9097, Pte., k. in a., Gallipoli, 28/6/15.

Docherty, William, b. Dennistoun, Glasgow, e. Glasgow, 454, Pte., d., Egypt, 1/10/16.

Don, William, b. Barony, Glasgow, e. Glasgow, 290112, Pte., d. of w., F. & F., 3/8/18.

Donnelly, Alexander, e. Glasgow, 359 Pte., k. in a., Gallipoli, 28/6/15.

Donnelly, James, e. Glasgow, 9946, Pte., k. in a., Gallipoli, 28/6/15.

Doris, Robert, b. Townhead, Glasgow, e. Glasgow, 476, Pte., k. in a., Gallipoli, 28/6/15.

Dornan, William, b. Broxburn, Linlithgow, e. Broxburn, Linlithgow, 203059, Cpl., k. in a., F. & F., 29/7/18, formerly S/16879, Arg. and Suthd. Highrs.

Drummond, John, b. Sauchie, Clackmannan, e. Glasgow, 9042, Sgt., k. in a., Gallipoli, 28/6/15.

Dunbar, John, b. Dennistoun, Glasgow, e. Glasgow, 480, Pte., k. in a., Gallipoli, 28/6/15.

Dunbar, John, b. Anderston, Glasgow, e. Glasgow, 203001, Pte., k. in a., Egypt, 19/4/17.

Duncan, Charles, b. Maryhill, Glasgow, e. Glasgow, 290866, Pte., k. in a., F. & F., 29/7/18.

Duncan, David, b. Barony, Glasgow, e. Glasgow, 9488, Pte., k. in a., Gallipoli, 15/6/15.

Dunlop, Andrew, e. Glasgow, 291492 Pte., k. in a., Egypt, 24/11/17.

Dunlop, Robert, e. Glasgow, 201475, Pte., k. in a., Egypt, 23/11/17.

Dunning, William, b. Kilbarchan, Renfrew, e. Glasgow, 9050, Pte., k. in a., Gallipoli, 28/6/15.

Eadie, James, b. Anderston, Glasgow, e. Glasgow, 459, Pte., k. in a., Gallipoli 28/6/15.

Edgely, Matthew, b. Woolwich, e. Glasgow, 9003, Pte., k. in a., Gallipoli, 28/6/15.

Edmiston, James, e. Glasgow, 845, Pte., d. of w., Egypt, 4/8/16.

Falls, Andrew, e. Leven, Fife e. Perth, 291509, Pte., d. of w., Egypt, 23/4/17.

Ferguson, Hugh, e. Kilmarnock, Dumbarton, e. Glasgow, 9594, Pte., k. in a., Gallipoli, 28/6/15.

Ferguson, James Irvine, b. Dennistoun, Glasgow, e. Glasgow, 8871, Pte., k. in a., Gallipoli, 28/6/15.

Ferrie, Edward, b. Townhead, Glasgow e. Glasgow, 8838, Cpl., k. in a., Gallipoli, 28/6/15.

Ferrie, John, b. Townhead, Glasgow, e. Glasgow, 9090, Pte., k. in a., Gallipoli, 28/6/15.

Findlay, John, b. Glasgow, e. Glasgow, 201507, Pte., k. in a., F. & F. 29/7/18.

Fitzpatrick, James, b. Maryport, Cumberland, e. Hamilton, 240882, Pte., d. of w., Egypt, 23/4/17.

Fleck, James, b. Townhead, Glasgow, e Glasgow, 8845, Pte., k. in a., Gallipoli, 28/6/15.

Fleming, Samuel, b. Bridgeton, Glasgow, e. Glasgow, 9854, L/Cpl., k. in a., Gallipoli, 28/6/15.

Fleming, William, b. Glasgow, e. Glasgow, 652, Pte., d. of w., Gallipoli, 13/12/15.

Fletcher, MacKnight Cowper, b. Methven, Perth, e. Edinburgh, 56444, Pte., k. in a., F. & F., 29/7/18, formerly 49497, R. Scots.

Flynn, Edward, e. Glasgow, 9787, Pte., k. in a., Gallipoli, 28/6/15.

Ford, Colin, b. Barony, Glasgow, e. Glasgow, 9331, Pte., k. in a., Gallipoli, 28/6/15

Forsyth, William, b. Galston, Ayr, e. Ayr, 56622, Pte., d. of w., F. & F., 10/9/18, formerly 52172, R. Scot. Fus.

Fowler, Robert, b. Sorn, Ayr, e. Ayr, 235429, Pte., d. of w., F. & F., 4/11/18, formerly 7241, R. Scot. Fus.

Foy, Arthur, e. Glasgow, 434, Pte., k. in a., Gallipoli, 28/6/15.

Frame, Robert, b. Boghall, Lanark, e. Carluke, 241450, Pte., k. in a., F. & F. 29/7/18, formerly 7420, H.L.I.

Fraser, George, b. Rogart, Sutherland, e. Fort George (Rogart, Sutherland) 266450. Pte., k. in a., F. & F., 1/8/18.

Fraser, James David, e. Glasgow, 290584, A/Cpl., k. in a., Egypt, 2/11/17.

Fulton, Robert, b. Glasgow, e. Glasgow, 555, Pte., k. in a, Gallipoli, 28/6/15.

Fyfe, Robert Wilson Morrison, b. Glasgow, e. Glasgow, 266383, L/Cpl., d. of w., F. & F., 31/7/18.

Galbraith, James, e. Glasgow, 290436 Pte., k. in a., F. & F., 14/10/18.

Galbraith, Thomas, e. Glasgow, 9855 Pte., k. in a., Gallipoli, 28/6/15.

Gardner, Malcolm, e. Glasgow, 185, Pte, k. in a., Gallipoli, 28/6/15.

Gaughan, John, b. Dunbar, Haddington, e. Edinburgh, (Dunbar), 56448, Pte., k. in a., F. & F., 29/7/18, formerly 49510, R. Scots.

Gebbie, David, b. Springburn, Glasgow, e. Glasgow, 8660, Pte., k. in a., Gallipoli 28/6/15.

Gibson, David, b. Lasswade, Edinburgh, e. Glasgow, 8256, Sgt., k in a., Gallipoli, 28/6/15.

Gibson, Joseph, b. Barony, Glasgow, e. Glasgow, 9387, Pte., k. in a., Gallipoli, 28/6/15.

Gilchrist, William, b. Glasgow, e. Whiteinch, Glasgow, 291411, Pte., k. in a., Egypt, 2/11/17.

Gillespie, William, b. Barony, Glasgow, e. Glasgow, 9094, Pte. k. in a., Gallipoli, 28/6/15.

Glen, Alexander, b. Bathgate, Linlithgow e. Newmains, Lanark, 241444, Pte., k. in a., Egypt, 29/7/17, formerly 7370, H.L.I.

Glencross, James, b. Dumfries, e. Glasgow, 290187. Pte., k. in a., Egypt, 22/11/17.

Glover, Samuel, e. Glasgow, 290420, L/Cpl., d. of w., Egypt, 8/1/18.

Good, Charles, b. Glasgow, e. Glasgow, 200700, Pte., k. in a., Egypt, 2/11/17.

Gordon, Henry, b. Wilton, Roxburgh, e. Hawick, 204034, Pte., d. of. w., F. & F., 30/7/18.

Gordon, James, e. Glasgow, 9867, Pte., k. in a., Gallipoli, 28/6/15.

Gorman, James, b Newtonards, Co. Down, e. Glasgow, 911, Pte., k. in a., Egypt, 10/10/16.

Gove, Robert, b. Glasgow, e. Glasgow, 8649, A/Sgt., k. in a., Gallipoli, 28/6/15.

Gowanlock, Walter, e. Glasgow, 265463, Pte., k. in a., F. & F., 29/7/18, M.M.

Graham, Alexander, e. Glasgow, 9637, Pte., k. in a., Gallipoli, 28/6/15.

Graham, Charles, b. Barony, Glasgow, e. Glasgow, 6751, A/C.S.M., k. in a., Gallipoli, 28/6/15.

Graham, George, b. Barony, Glasgow, e. Glasgow, 9653, Pte., k. in a., Gallipoli, 28/6/15.

Graham, John, b. Glasgow, e. Glasgow, 8169. L/Cpl., k. in a., Gallipoli, 28/6/15.

Graham, Thomas, b. Barony, Glasgow, e. Glasgow. 8882, Pte., k. in a., Gallipoli, 28/6/15.

Graham, William, b. Broughty Ferry, Dundee, e. Glencorse (Broughty Ferry), 56626, Pte., k. in a., F. & F., 7/10/18, formerly 48487, R. Scot. Fus.

Graham, William, e. Glasgow, 899, Pte., Egypt, 23/6/16.

Grant, James McClanaghan, b. St. Quivox, Ayr, e. Ayr (Irvine), 31882, Pte., k. in a., Egypt, 12/11/17.

Gray, Joseph Stuart, b. Glasgow, e. Glasgow 369, Pte., k. in a., Gallipoli, 12/7/15.

Gray, William, b. Barony, Glasgow, e. Glasgow, 9217, Pte., k. in a., Gallipoli 28/6/15.

Gray, William, b. Pilrig, Edinburgh, e. Glasgow, 291477, R.S.M., d. of w., F. & F., 4/8/18.

Green, James, b. Aberdeen, e. Glasgow, 8743, Sgt., k. in a., Gallipoli, 28/6/15.

Greig, David Wright, b. Barony, Glasgow, e. Glasgow, 290210, Pte., k. in a., F. & F., 1/9/18.

Greig, James, e. Glasgow 28, Pte., k. in a., Gallipoli, 28/6/15.

Greig, William Alexander Fraser, b. Edinburgh, e. Edinburgh, 43807, Pte., d. of w., F. & F., 25/10/18.

Hackett, James, b. Tyrone, C. Fermagh, e. Johnstone, Renfrew, 40845 A/L/Cpl., k. in a., F. & F., 2/8/18, formerly 12978, K.O.S.B.

Haddow, Robert, e. Edinburgh, 202987, Pte., k. in a., Egypt, 23/7/17, formerly 24631, H.L.I.

Haldane, James, b. Hamilton, e. Hamilton, 240375, Pte., k. in a., F. & F., 28/9/18.

Halliday, John, b. Falkirk, Stirling, e. Falkirk (Greenhill, Stirling), 9719, Pte., k. in a., Gallipoli, 28/6/15.

Hamilton, Alexander, b. Whitevale, Glasgow, e. Glasgow, 6965, Pte., k. in a., Gallipoli, 28/6/15.

Hannah, James, b. Stonykirk, Wigton, e. Ayr (Stranraer), 37407, Pte., k. in a., F. & F., 29/7/18, formerly 30077, H.L.I.

Hardie, John, b. Edinburgh, e. Glasgow, 7302, Sgt., k. in a., Gallipoli, 28/6/15.

Hargrave, Roberts, b. Holbeck, Leeds, e. York (Leeds), 291571, Pte., k. in a., Egypt, 28/11/17, D.C.M.

Harkins, Robert Campbell, b. Barony, Glasgow, e. Glasgow, 8969, Pte., d. of w., Gallipoli, 8/10/15.

Harkness, James, b. Camlachie, Glasgow, e. Glasgow, 9566, Pte., k. in a., Gallipoli, 28/6/15.

Harper, David, b. Possilpark, Glasgow, e. Glasgow, 415, Pte., k. in a., Gallipoli, 28/6/15.

Harrigan, John Henry, b. Barony, Glasgow, e. Glasgow, 42983, Pte., d. of w., F. & F., 1/10/18, formerly 3029, Lanark Yeo.

Harrison, Hugh, b. Bridgeton, Glasgow, e. Glasgow, 291417, Pte., d. of w., Home, 30/11/18.

Hartin, Alexander, b. Barony, Glasgow, e. Glasgow. 414, Pte., k. in a., Gallipoli, 28/6/15.

Hastie, David, b. Hamilton, e. Hamilton, 240351, A/L/Cpl., k. in a., Egypt, 2/11/17.

Hastings, Robert Carruthers, b. Dumfries, e. Lanark (Dumfries), 41091, Pte., d. of w., F. & F., 17/8/18, formerly 2244, Lanark Yeo.

Hatfield, Fred, b. Dewsbury, Yorks, e. Dewsbury, Yorks, 291630, Pte., d. of w., Egypt, 13/11/17, formerly 26057, Yorks L

Heally, Patrick, e. Glasgow, 747 Pte., d., Gallipoli, 24/10/15.

Heany, Peter, b. Barony, Glasgow, e. Glasgow, 9186, Pte., k. in a., Gallipoli, 28/6/15.

Heath, James, b. Townhead, Glasgow, e. Glasgow, 8861, Pte., k. in a., Gallipoli, 28/6/15.

Heath, Robert, b. Townhead, Glasgow, e. Glasgow, 8868, L/Cpl., k. in a., Gallipoli, 28/6/15.

Henderson, George, b. Calton, Glasgow, e. Glasgow, 9242, Pte., k. in a., Gallipoli, 28/6/15.

Henderson, John, e. Glasgow, 231, Pte., k. in a., Gallipoli, 28/6/15.

Henderson, Samuel Hay, e. Glasgow, 32, Pte., k. in a., Gallipoli, 28/6/15.

Henderson, William, b. Blairgowrie, Perth, e. Glasgow, 135, Pte., k. in a., Gallipoli, 28/6/15.

Hendry, Walter Scott, b. Redgorton, Perth, e. Dundee, 46224, Pte., k. in a., F. & F., 1/9/18, formerly 2898, Lanark Yeo.

Hennety, Joseph, e. Glasgow, 84, Pte., k. in a., Gallipoli, 12/7/15.

Henness, Reginald Campbell, b. Gillingham, Dorset, e. Glasgow, 9303, Pte., k. in a., Gallipoli, 28/6/15.

Heslop, William, b. South Hetton, Durham, e. Houghton-le-Spring, Durham (Newbottle), 46164, Pte., k. in a., F. & F., 29/7/18.

Higgins, James Campbell, b. Kilmarnock, e. Kilmarnock, 56624, Pte., k. in a., F. & F., 14/10/18, formerly 20669, R. Scot. Fus.

Hill, Alfred Charles, b. Camberwell, London, e. Hounslow (London), 291562, Pte., k. in a., F. & F., 29/7/18.

Hirst, Lewis, b. New Mill, Yorks, e. Huddersfield, 41842 Pte., k. in a., F. & F., 14/10/18, formerly 4331, H.L.I.

Hodge, John, b. Muirkirk, Ayr, e. Glasgow (Coatbridge, Lanark), 8698, Sgt., k. in a., Gallipoli, 28/6/15.

Holmes, James, b. Glasgow, e. Glasgow, 9043, Pte., k. in a., Gallipoli, 28/6/15.

Hopper, David, b. Annan, Dumfres, e. Annan, Dumfries, 33659, Pte., k. in a., Egypt, 2/11/17.

Hornshaw, Charles William, b. St. Andrew's, Grimsby, Lincs, e. Grimsby, 291360, Pte., d. of w., F. & F., 3/8/18.

Howard, George, b. Exminster, Devon, e. Exeter, Devon, 37445, Pte., k. in a., F. & F., 29/7/18, formerly 46453, R. Scot. Fus.

Howarth, Albert, b. Rochdale, Lancs, e. Rochdale, Lancs, 38365, Pte., k. in a., F. & F., 28/10/18, formerly 28414, K.O.S.B.

Howitt, Robert, b. Kirkurd, Peebles, e. Glasgow, 37960, Pte., k. in a., F. & F., 29/7/18.

Huie, Robert, e. Glasgow, 9834, Pte., k. in a., Gallipoli, 28/6/15.

Hull, William, b. Glasgow, e. Glasgow, 290857, Pte., k. in a. Egypt, 2/11/17.

Hutchison, Arthur, b. Rugby, e. Glasgow, 464, Pte., k. in a., Gallipoli, 28/6/15.

Hutchinson, Alexander, b. Barony, Glasgow, e. Glasgow, 8431, Pte., k. in a., Gallipoli, 28/6/15.

Hyslop, Robert, b. Durisdeer, Dumfries, e. Glasgow, 201426, Pte., d. of w., Egypt, 22/11/17.

Innes, James, b. Larbert, e. Falkirk, 431, Pte., k. in a., Gallipoli, 28/6/15.

Jackson, William, b. Hamilton, e. Hamilton, 240555, Pte., d. of w., Egypt, 23/4/17.

James, Andrew, b. Barony, Glasgow, e. Glasgow, 8041, L/Sgt., k. in a., Gallipoli, 28/6/15.

James, Robert, b. Hutchesontown, Glasgow, e. Glasgow, 291218, Pte., k. in a., Egypt, 2/11/17.

Jamieson, Daniel, b. Glasgow, e. Glasgow, 9049, L/Cpl, k. in a., Gallipoli, 28/6/15.

Jamieson, George, e. Glasgow, 987, Pte., d. of w., Egypt, 9/8/16.

Jamieson, Henry, b. Barony, Glasgow, e. Glasgow, 8786, Bugler, k. in a., Gallipoli, 28/6/15.

Jamieson, James, b. Dumbarton, e. Glasgow, 33716, Pte., k. in a., Egypt, 2/11/17.

Jamieson, William, b. Barony, Glasgow, e. Glasgow, 9083, Pte., k. in a., Gallipoli, 28/6/15.

Jess, John Swan, b. Portpatrick, Wigton, e. Ayr (Dunragit, Wigton), 38373, Pte. k. in a., F. & F., 1/8/18.

Johnston, Robert, b. Glasgow, e. Glasgow, 9853, Pte., k. in a., Gallipoli, 28/6/15.

Johnstone, Patrick, e. Glasgow, 9651, Pte., k. in a., Gallipoli, 28/6/15.

Johnstone, Robert, b. Easter Whitburn, W. Lothian, e. Armadale, 291627, Pte., d. of w., F. & F., 1/9/18. formerly 2652, R. Scots.

Kay, Walter, b. Lasswade, Edinburgh, e. Bonnyrigg, 203067, Pte., k. in a., Egypt, 2/11/17, formerly S/16900, A. & S.H.

Kee, Thomas, b. Airdrie, Lanark, e. Glasgow (Bishopbriggs), 8927, Pte. k. in a. Gallipoli, 12/7/15.

Keens, George James, b. Enfield, Middx., e. London (Enfield), 291560, A/L/Cpl., d. of w., Egypt, 25/11/17.

Kelly, Francis, b. Calton, Glasgow. e. Glasgow, 290063, Sgt., k. in a., Egypt, 20/7/17.

Kennedy, Alexander, b. Airdrie, Lanark, e. Hamilton (Rosebank, by Carluke), 32932, Pte., k. in a., Egypt, 12/11/17.

Kerr, James, b. Barony, Glasgow, e. Glasgow, 56611, Pte., d. of w., F. & F., 29/9/18, formerly 32104, R. Scot. Fus.

Kerrigan, Andrew, e. Glasgow, 9648, Pte., k. in a., Gallipoli, 28/6/15.

Kidger, Samuel, e. Ilkeston, Derbyshire, 35961, Pte., k. in a., F. & F., 29/7/18, formerly 66491, Yorks L.I.

Kilpatrick, Neil, e. Glasgow, 9839, Pte., k. in a., Gallipoli, 28/6/15.

King, Alexander, b. Kelvinside, Glasgow, e. Glasgow, 9613, A/L/Cpl., d. of w., Gallipoli, 3/7/15.

King, James, b. Barony, Glasgow, e. Glasgow, 8208, Sgt., k. in a., Gallipoli, 28/6/15

Kippen, Andrew, e. Birmingham, 1520, A/L/Cpl, k. in a., F. & F., 29/10/16.

Knowles, Thomas, b. Burnley, Lancs, e. Glasgow, 33705, Pte., k. in a., Egypt, 11/10/17.

Lambie, William, e. Glasgow, 9976, Pte., k. in a., Gallipoli, 28/6/15.

Lamond, John, e. Aberdeen, 52780, Pte., k. in a., F. & F., 14/10/18.

Lamont, William, b. Cargill, Perth, e. Blairgowrie (Coupar Angus), 46201, Pte., k. in a., F. & F., 1/8/18, formerly 23592, H.L.I.

Lang, John, b. Barony, Glasgow, e. Glasgow, 291519, Pte., d. of w., Egypt, 5/11/17.

Lauder, James, b. Dalry, Ayr, e. Glasgow, 32936, Pte., k. in a., Egypt, 2/11/17.

Law, Alexander Pittillo, e. Lanark (Edinburgh), 46170, Pte., k. in a., F. & F., 1/9/18.

Leckie, Thomas, e. Glasgow, 356, Pte., k. in a., Gallipoli, 28/6/15.

Lee, James, b. Barony, Glasgow, e. Glasgow, 291176, Pte., d. of w., F. & F., 23/7/18.

Lees, Joseph, e. Glasgow, 9788, Pte., k. in a., Gallipoli, 28/6/15.

Leighton, John, b. Galltown, Fife, e. Kirkcaldy, 352, Pte., k. in a., Gallipoli, 28/6/15.

Leitch, Andrew, e. Glasgow, 290968, Sgt., k. in a., Egypt, 25/7/17.

Leslie, William, b. Glasgow, e. Ayr, 266460, Pte., d. of w., Egypt, 14/11/17.

Letters, Harry, e. Glasgow, 290923, Pte., d. of w., F. & F., 4/8/18.

Livingstone, Allan, b. Trossachs, Perth, e. Glasgow, 5447, A/L/Cpl., k. in a., Gallipoli, 28/6/15.

Livingstone, James, b. Glasgow, e. Glasgow, 8202, Sgt., k. in a., Gallipoli, 28/6/15.

Lloyd, William, b. Clackmannan, e. Glasgow, 8973, Pte., d., Gallipoli, 17/12/15.

Loan, Andrew, b. Lanark, e. Glasgow, 457, Pte., k. in a., Gallipoli, 28/6/15.

Lockhart, George, b. Perth, West Australia, e. Glasgow, 465, Pte., k. in a., Gallipoli, 28/6/15.

Logan, Hugh, b. Glasgow, e. Glasgow, 9987, Pte., k. in a., Gallipoli, 28/6/15.,

Logan, John, e. Denbeath, Methil, Fife, 9948, Pte., k. in a., Gallipoli, 28/6/15.

Lowdon, John, b. Airlie, Forfar, e. Glasgow (Alyth Perth), 9464, Pte., k. in a., Gallipoli, 28/6/15.

Lyell, Stewart, b. Newheugh, Fife, e. Kinross (Dollar), 203073, Pte., k. in a., Egypt, 2/11/17, formerly S/16667, A. & S.H.

Lynch, Hugh, b. New Monkland, Lanark, e. Airdrie, Lanark, 291579, Pte., k. in a., Egypt, 19/4/17.

Mackel, James, b. Clydebank, Dumbarton, e. Glasgow, 290217, Pte., k. in a., Egypt, 24/11/17.

Main, David, b. Glasgow, e. Glasgow, 500, Pte., d., Gallipoli, 8/11/15.

Marchand, Jesse Walter, e. Glasgow, 9768, Pte., k. in a., Gallipoli, 28/6/15.

Mars, James, e. Glasgow, 202805, A/L/Sgt., k. in a., Egypt, 24/11/17.

Marshall, David Matthew, b. Portobello, e. Edinburgh (Portobello), 35592, Pte., d. of w., F. & F., 25/7/18.

Marshall, William, b. Muravonside, Stirling, e. Falkirk (Stirling), 9718, Pte., k. in a., Gallipoli, 28/6/15.

Martin, Albert, b. Barony, Glasgow, e. Glasgow, 290125, Sgt., k. in a., F. & F., 29/7/18.

Martin, Arthur, e. Glasgow, 290707, Pte., k in a., Egypt, 19/4/17.

Martin, James, e. Glasgow (Paisley), 366, Pte., k. in a., Gallipoli, 28/6/15.

Martin, Murdoch, e. Glasgow, 296, Pte., k. in a., Gallipoli, 28/6/15.

Martin, Thomas, b. Springburn, Glasgow, e. Glasgow, 9257, Pte., k. in a., Gallipoli, 28/6/15.

Mason, James, e. Glasgow, 9689, Pte. k. in a., Gallipoli, 28/6/15.

Matthews, James Richard, b. Birmingham, e. Birmingham, 6617, R.S.M., k. in a., Gallipoli, 28/6/15.

Mechan, James, b. Glasgow, e. Glasgow 8760, Pte., k. in a., Gallipoli, 28/6/15.

Meikle, Alexander, b. Barony, Glasgow, e. Glasgow, 290303, Cpl., k. in a., F & F., 15/10/18.

Meikle, Robert, e. Ayr (Irvine), 238158, Pte., k. in a., F. & F, 28/10/18, formerly 4752, H.L.I.

Middleton, Thomas, b. Yeserley-cum-Whaley, Cheshire, e. Whaley Bridge (Furness Vale), 290221, Pte., d. of w., Egypt, 5/11/17, formerly 57289, A.S.C.

Mill, Peter, b. Edinburgh, e. Edinburgh, 32085, Pte., k. in a., Egypt, 2/11/17.

Miller, James, b. Stirling, e. Stirling, 1355, A/L/Cpl., k. in a., Egypt, 28/10/16.

Miller, William, b. Glasgow, e. Glasgow, 5502, Pte., k. in a., Gallipoli, 28/6/15.

Milligan, Edward, b. Glasgow, e. Glasgow, Pte., k. in a., Gallipoli, 28/6/15.

Mills, Charles, b. Glasgow, e. Perth (Doune), 43763, Pte., k. in a., F. & F., 14/10/18, formerly 31031, R. Scot. Fus.

Mills, William, b. Edinburgh, e. Glasgow, 9072, Pte., k. in a., Gallipoli, 28/6/15.

Milne, Charles, b. Townhead, Glasgow, e. Glasgow, 407, Pte., d. of w., Gallipoli, 3/7/15.

Mitchell, William, b. Govan, Glasgow, e. Glasgow, 9225, A/L/Cpl., k. in a., Gallipoli, 28/6/15.

Moir, James, e. Glasgow, 569, Pte., k. in a., Gallipoli, 28/6/15.

Monaghan, Daniel, e. Glasgow, 291270, Pte., d. of w., Egypt, 26/11/17.

Monaghan, John, b. Paisley, e. Paisley, 203076, Pte., k. in a., Egypt, 19/4/17, formerly S/16668, Arg. & Suthd. High.

Moonan, Richard, e. Glasgow, 321, Pte., k. in a., Gallipoli. 28/6/15.

Mooney, James, b. Glasgow, e. Glasgow, 290762, Pte., d. of w., F. & F., 20/10/18.

Mooney, John Francis, e. Glasgow, 566, Pte., k. in a., Gallipoli, 12/7/15.

Moore, Henry, b. Hamilton, e. Glasgow, 9428, L/Sgt., k. in a., Gallipoli, 28/6/15.

Moran, Thomas, b. Barony, Glasgow, e. Glasgow, 290117, Pte., d. of w., Home, 9/9/18.

Morrell. Ernest, b. Harrogate, e. Stockton-on-Tees (Harrogate), 2011853, Pte., k. in a., F. & F., 14/10/18, formerly 27796 W. Yorks Regt.

Morrison, Thomas Webster, b. Portsey, Banff, e. Edinburgh (Leith), 56597, Pte., d. of w., F. & F., 3/10/18, formerly 51975, R. Scots.

Morrison, John, e. Glasgow, 202747, Pte., k. in a., Egypt, 12/11/17.

Morrow, Thomas, b. Barony, Glasgow, e. Glasgow, 33116, Pte., d. of w., Egypt, 13/11/17.

Mulholland, James, e. Glasgow,642, Pte., k. in a., Gallipoli, 1/1/16.

Mundy, Edward, b. Barony, Glasgow, e. Glasgow, 8892, Pte., k. in a., Gallipoli, 12/7/15.

Munro, James, e. Glasgow, 252, Pte., k. in a., Gallipoli, 28/6/15.

Munro, William, e. Glasgow, 363, Pte., k. in a., Gallipoli, 28/6/15.

Murdoch, Gavin, b. Govan, Glasgow, e. Glasgow, 9291, Pte., k. in a., Gallipoli, 28/6/15.

Murdoch, James, e. Glasgow, 388, Pte., k. in a., Gallipoli, 28/6/15.

Murdoch, Ronald, b. Dennistoun, Glasgow, e. Glasgow, 8849, Pte., k. in a., Gallipoli, 28/6/15.

Murdoch, William, b. Dennistoun, Glasgow, e. Glasgow, 9074, Pte., k. in a., Gallipoli, 28/6/15.

Murphy, Patrick, b. Barony, Glasgow, e. Glasgow, 9504, Pte., k. in a., Gallipoli, 28/6/15.

Murray, James, e. Glasgow, 9728, Pte., d. of w., Gallipoli, 28/6/15.

Macindoe, James, b. Barony, Glasgow, e. Glasgow, 290091, L/Sgt., k. in a., F. & F., 29/7/18.

MacKay, George, b. Milton, Glasgow, e. Glasgow, 8359, Pte., k. in a., Gallipoli, 28/6/15.

Mackay, James, b. Wick, Caithness, e. Glasgow, 8835, L/Cpl., k. in a., Gallipoli, 28/6/15.

Mackay, John, e. Glasgow, 290549, A/Cpl., k. in a., Gallipoli, 28/6/15.

MacKinnon, Alexander, e. Glasgow, 105, Pte., k. in a., Gallipoli, 28/6/15.

Maclaren, Robert, b. Comrie, Perth, e. Glasgow, 201374, L/Cpl., k. in a., F. & F., 28/9/18.

Macleod, Neil Macleod, b. Springburn, Glasgow, e. Glasgow, 8033, L/Cpl., k. in a., Gallipoli, 12/7/15.

McAllister, David, b. Barony Glasgow, e. Glasgow, 9239, Pte., k. in a., Gallipoli, 15/6/15.

McAllister, James, e. Glasgow, 103, Pte. k. in a., Gallipoli, 28/6/15.

McAninch, Peter, b. Busby, Renfrew, e. Glasgow, 291308, Pte., k. in a., Egypt, 24/11/17.

McBride, William, b. Barony, Glasgow, e Glasgow, 290099, L/Cpl., k. in a., F. & F., 14/10/18.

McCamley, John, b. Barony, Glasgow, e. Glasgow, 56607, Pte., d. of w., F. & F., 15/10/18, formerly 52017, R. Scots.

McCandlish, Peter, e. Glasgow, 9817, Pte., k. in a., Gallipoli, 28/6/15.

McCann, George, e. Glasgow, 9835, Pte., k. in a., Gallipoli, 28/6/15.

McCann, William, b. Wishaw, e. Lanark (Whifflet), 241532, Pte., k. in a., Egypt, 2/11/17, formerly 8766, H.L.I.

McCleavy, John, e. Glasgow, 36, Pte. k. in a., Gallipoli, 28/6/15.

McClelland, Gavin, b. Hamilton, e. Hamilton, 35570, Pte., d. of w., F. & F., 3/8/18.

McClune, David, b. Elderslie, Ayr, e. Glasgow, 9166, Pte., k. in a., Gallipoli, 28/6/15.

McColl, Joseph, e. Glasgow, 290948, Cpl., d. of w., Egypt, 19/4/17.

McColl, Neil, e. Glasgow, 290663, L/Cpl. k. in a., Egypt. 28/11/17.

McCorkle, James, b. Barony, Glasgow, e. Glasgow, 56440, Pte., k. in a., F. & F., 29/7/18, formerly 49492, R. Scots.

McCormick, Robert, b. Renfrew, e. Stirling (Renfrew), 203085, Pte., d. of w., Egypt, 15/4/17, formerly S/16970, Arg. & Suthd. High.

McCrae, John, b. Barony, Glasgow, e. Glasgow, 290083, Pte., k. in a., Egypt, 2/11/17.

McCreadie, Adam, e. Glasgow, 128, Pte., k. in a., Gallipoli, 28/6/15.

McCrorie, John, b. Dennistoun, Glasgow, e Glasgow, 9027, Pte., k. in a·, Gallipoli, 28/6/15.

McCrorie, Peter, b. Bridgeton, Glasgow, e. Glasgow, 9018, Pte., k. in a., Gallipoli, 28/6/15.

McCulloch, Alexander, e. Glasgow, 106, Pte., k. in a., Gallipoli, 28/6/15.

McCulloch, Robert, b. Barony, Glasgow, e. Glasgow, 9424, Cpl., k. in a., Gallipoli, 28/6/15.

McCurdie, Robert, b. Falkirk, e. Falkirk (Stirling), 9747, Pte., k. in a., 28/6/15.

McDermott, James, b. Barony, Glasgow, e. Glasgow, 291608, Pte., k. in a., Egypt, 19/4/17.

McDiarmid, James, b. Barony, Glasgow, e. Glasgow, 9405, Pte., k. in a., Gallipoli, 28/6/15.

McDonald, Alexander, b. Bowling, Dumbarton, e. Dumbarton, 291416, Pte., d., Home, 13/6/18, formerly 6301, R. Scots Greys.

McDonald, James, b. Hawick, e. Glasgow, 290127, Pte., d. of w., Egypt, 26/4/17.

McDonald, John, b. Dunalister, Perth, e. Glasgow, 9100, L/Cpl., d. of w., Gallipoli, 28/6/15.

McDonald, John, e. Glasgow, 290444, Pte.,
k. in a., F. & F. 29/7/18.
McDowall, Hugh, b. Paisley, 203088, Pte.,
k. in a., F. & F., 31/10/18, formerly
S/16850, Arg. & Suthd. High.
McDowall, Hugh Shanks, b. Milton,
Glasgow, e. Glasgow, 238146, Pte., k. in
a., F. & F., 2/9/18, formerly 3115, H.L.I.
McEwen, John Mair, b. Stewarton, Ayr,
e Glencorse (Winchburgh, West Lothian),
42989, Pte., k. in a., F. & F., 14/10/18.
McEwen, Joseph A., b Glasgow, e.
Glasgow, 265096, Cpl., k. in a., F. & F.,
14/10/18.
McFarlane, Robert, b. Anderston, Glas-
gow,, e. Glasgow, 462, Pte., k. in a., Gal-
lipoli, 28/6/15.
McGarvie, Adam, b. Springburn, Glasgow,
e. Glasgow, 9085, Pte., d. of w., Gallipoli,
25/8/15.
McGhee, Charles, e. Glasgow 290920,
Pte., k. in a., Egypt, 2/11/17.
McGhee, John, e. Glasgow, 140, Pte., k.
in a., Gallipoli, 28/6/15.
McGinley, John, e. Glasgow, 440 Pte.,
k. in a., Gallipoli, 28/6/15,
McGinty, Patrick, e. Glasgow, 9733, Pte.,
k. in a., Gallipoli, 28/6/15.
McGowan, Owen, b. Govan, Glasgow, e.
Glasgow, 56561, Pte., k. in a., F. & F.,
31/10/18, formerly 33268, R. Scots.
McGrath, Bernard, e. Glasgow, 9912, Pte.,
k. in a., Gallipoli, 28/6/15.
McGrath, Patrick, e. Glasgow, 416, Pte,
k. in a., Gallipoli, 28/6/15.
McGraw, Hugh, e. Glasgow, 9708, Pte.,
k. in a., Gallipoli, 28/6/15.
McGregor, Alexander, b. Bonhill, Dum-
barton, e. Dumbarton, 203082, Pte., k.
in a., F. & F, 31/10/18, formerly S/16708,
Arg. & Suthd. High.
McGregor, William, b. Townhead, Glas-
gow, e. Glasgow, 181, Pte., k. in a., Galli-
poli, 28/6/15.
McGuckien, James, b. Bridgeton, Glas-
gow, e. Glasgow, 203002, Pte., k. in a.,
Egypt, 2/11/17.
McGuigan, Robert, e. Glasgow, 287,
L/Cpl., k. in a., Gallipoli, 28/6/15.
McGuigan, Thomas, e. Glasgow, 9758,
Pte., k. in a., Gallipoli, 28/6/15.
McInally, Hugh, e. Glasgow (Cambus-
lang), 9917, Pte., k. in a., Gallipoli,
28/6/15.
McIntee, Owen, b. Bridgeton, Glasgow, e.
Glasgow, 9892, Pte., k. in a., Gallipoli,
28/6/15.
McIntyre, John, b. Springburn, Glasgow,
e. Glasgow, 8083, Pte., k. in a., Gallipoli
28/6/15.
McIntyre, William George, b. Ander-
ston, Glasgow, e. Glasgow, 8860, Pte., d.
of w., Gallipoli, 28/6/15.
McIver, Evander Kenneth, e. Glasgow,
290934, L/Sgt., F. & F., 20/10/18.
McIver, John, b. Oban, Argyll, e. Glasgow, 8937, Pte., k. in a., Gallipoli,
28/6/15.
McKay, James, b. Port Dundas, Glasgow,
e. Glasgow, 493, Pte., k. in a., Gallipoli,
28/6/15.
McKay, Samuel, e. Glasgow, 316, Pte.,
k. in a., Gallipoli, 28 /6/15.
McKay, Samuel, e. Glasgow 411, Pte.,
d. of w., Egypt, 4/8/16.
McKean, Wilson, b. Govan, Glasgow, e.

Glasgow, 9469, Pte., k. in a., Gallipoli,
28/6/15.
McKenzie, Daniel, e. Kilmarnock (Salt-
coats, Ayr), 235422, Pte., d. of w., F. &
F., 29/10/18, formerly 8742, R. Scot. Fus.
McKenzie, Hugh, b. Barony, Glasgow, e.
Glasgow, 291135, Pte., k. in a., F. & F.,
31/10/18.
McKenzie, Kenneth, b. Barony, Glasgow,
e. Glasgow, 291618. Pte., d. of w., F. & F.,
11/8/18.
McKinlay, James, e. Glasgow, 9782, Pte.
d of w., Gallipoli 20/10/15.
McKinnie, James, b. Longriggend, Lanark,
e. Edinburgh, 42734, Pte., At Sea, 3/8/18.
McLaughlan, Hugh, b. Helensburgh, e.
Glasgow, 9710, Pte., k. in a., Gallipoli,
28/6/15.
McLaughlin, John, b. Busby, Renfrew,
e. Glasgow, 8779, Bugler, k. in a., Gallipoli, 28/6/15.
McLean, Archibald, b. Townhead, Glasgow, e. Glasgow, 505, Pte., k. in a., Gallipoli, 28/6/15.
McLean, James, e. Glasgow, 290467, Pte.,
k. in a., Egypt, 2/11/17.
McLean, Thomas, b. Cumnock, Ayr, e.
Berwick-on-Tweed (Thornhill), 37565,
Pte., k. in a., F. & F, 29/7/18, formerly
46445, R. Scot. Fus.
McLellan, Donald, b. Barony, Glasgow,
e. Glasgow, 290240, Pte., k. in a., F. & F.,
29/7/18.
McLelland, William, b. Barony, Glasgow,
e. Glasgow, 290128, Pte., k. in a., F. & F.,
29/7/18.
McLeod, John, b. Barony, Glasgow, e.
Glasgow, 9194, Pte., k. in a., Gallipoli,
28/6/15.
McLuckie, James, e. Partick, Glasgow,
23043, Pte., k. in a., Egypt, 12/11/17.
McMahon, Patrick, e. Glasgow, 9755,
Pte., k. in a., Gallipoli, 28/6/15.
McMahon, Thomas, b. Belfast, e. Glasgow, 9238, Pte., k. in a., Gallipoli,
30/11/15.
McMahon, Thomas, b. Barony, Glasgow,
e. Glasgow, 9764, Pte. k. in a., Gallipoli,
28/6/15.
McMath, Daniel, e. Glasgow, 9673. Pte.,
k. in a., Gallipoli, 28/6/15.
McMeeking, Hugh, b. Sorbie, Wigtown,
e. Glasgow, 7874, Sgt., k. in a., Gallipoli,
28/6/15.
McMeeking, William, b. Sorbie, Wig-
town, e. Glasgow, 7873, C.Q.M.S., d. of
w., Gallipoli, 30/6/15.
McMillan, John, b. Govan, Glasgow, e.
Glasgow, 1054, Pte., d. of w., Egypt,
4/8/16.
McMinn, John, b. Barony, Glasgow, e.
Glasgow, 291422, Pte., d., F. & F.,
7/11/18.
McNaught, John, b. Maryhill, Glasgow,
e. Glasgow, 8614, Pte., d., Gallipoli,
20/9/15.
McNaughton, William, e. Glasgow, 362,
Pte., k. in a., Gallipoli, 28/6/15.
McNeil, Alexander, b. Kirkcaldy, e. Glasgow, 8009, Pte., k. in a., Gallipoli, 29/6/15.
McNeil, George, b. Anderston, Glasgow
e. Glasgow, 8731, Pte., k. in a., Gallipoli
28/6/15.
McParlane, James, b. Barony, Glasgow,
e. Glasgow, 291145, Pte., k. in a., F. & F.,
1/9/18.

McPhee, Archibald, b. Hutchesontown, Glasgow, e. Glasgow, 266471, Pte., d. of w., Egypt, 3/11/17.

McPherson, Angus, b. Camlachie, Lanark, e. Glasgow, 9642, Pte., k in a., Gallipoli, 28/6/15.

McPherson, John, b. Cowcaddens, Glasgow, e. Glasgow, 8286, Pte., k. in a., Gallipoli, 28/6/15.

McPherson, John, e. Glasgow, 9702, Cpl., k. in a., Gallipoli, 28/6/15.

McPhillips, James, b. Hutchesontown, Glasgow, 6944, Sgt., k. in a., Gallipoli, 28/6/15.

McQueen, Robert, b. Barony, Glasgow, e. Glasgow, 8823, Cpl., k. in a., Gallipoli, 28/6/15.

McTaggart, Duncan, b. Barony, Glasgow, e. Glasgow, 9202, Pte., k. in a., Gallipoli. 28/6/15.

McVay, Robert, b. Glasgow, e. Glasgow, 477, A/L/Sgt., k. in a., Gallipoli, 28/6/15.

McWilliam, George, b. Barony, Glasgow, e. Glasgow, 203087, Pte., d. of w., Egypt, 19/4/17, formerly S/16902, A. & S.H.

McWilliam, John, b. Liverpool, e. Glasgow, 9319, Cpl., k. in a., Gallipoli, 28/6/15.

Nairn, John, b. Old Kilpatrick, Dumbarton, e. Glasgow (Stewarton, Ayr), 9591, Pte., k. in a., Gallipoli, 28/6/15.

Naylor, Arthur, e. Glasgow, 290407, Pte., k. in a., Egypt, 19/4/17.

Neilson, Hugh, b. Biggar, Lanark, e. Hamilton (Lamington, Lanark), 37268, Pte., d., Egypt, 18/12/17.

Neilson, William, e. Glasgow, 200905, Pte., d. of w., Egypt, 26/4/17.

Neish, Robert, b Glasgow, e Glasgow, 9564, Pte., k. in a., Gallipoli, 28/6/15.

Nelson, David, b Anderston, Glasgow, e. Glasgow, 9618, Pte., k. in a., Gallipoli, 12/7/15.

Nelson, James, e. Glasgow, 290402, Pte., d. of w., Egypt, 20/4/17.

Nesbitt, Thomas John, b. Richhill, Co. Armagh, e. Glasgow, 292009, Pte., k. in a., Egypt, 2/11/17.

Nicholson, William, e. Glasgow, 9886, Pte., k. in a., Gallipoli, 28/6/15.

Nicol, John, b. Barony, Glasgow, e. Glasgow, 8919, Pte., k. in a., Egypt, 4/8/19.

Niven, James, e. Glasgow, 670, Pte., d. of w., Egypt, 4/8/16.

Nixon, Herbert, b. Newcastle, Staffs, e. Glasgow, 291177, Pte., k. in a., Egypt, 12/11/17.

O'Connor, John, b. Barony, Glasgow, e. Glasgow, 9326, Pte., k. in a., Gallipoli, 28/6/15.

O'Donnell, Patrick, b. Ringsend, Dublin, e. Glasgow, 1043, Pte., d. of w., Egypt, 4/8/16.

Oliver, Hugh Ross, b. Hawick. Roxburgh e Hawick, 204033, Pte., k. in a., Egypt, 23/11/17.

O'Neil, Patrick, b. Glasgow, e. Glasgow, 291204, Pte., k. in a., F. & F., 1/8/18.

O'Neill, Hendry, e. Glasgow, 372, Pte., k. in a., Gallipoli, 28/6/15.

Orr, David, b. Carnwath, Lanark, e. Hamilton (Wilsontown), 52782, Pte., k. in a., F. & F., 31/10/18.

Orr, Robert, e. Glasgow, 693, Pte., k. in a., Gallipoli, 15/11/15.

Owens, David Arthur Ernest, b. Newington, Midlothian, e. Edinburgh, 42738, Pte., k. in a., F. & F., 29/7/18, formerly 43842, H.L.J.

Park, Robert, b. Barony, Glasgow, e. Glasgow, 9029, Pte., d. of w., Gallipoli, 19/12/15.

Park, William, b. Townhead. Glasgow, e. Glasgow, 8859, Pte., k. in a., Gallipoli, 28/6/15.

Paterson, James, e. Glasgow, 43782, Pte., k. in a., F. & F., 22/9/18, formerly 33040, H.L.I.

Paterson, Thomas James, b. Holytown, Lanark, e. Motherwell (Holytown), 46217, Pte., k. in a., F. & F., 29/7/18, formerly 2878, Lanark Yeo.

Paterson, William, b. Barony, Glasgow, e. Glasgow, 9279, Pte., d. of w., Egypt, 4/8/16.

Paton, Archibald, b. Duddingston, Midlothian, e. Leith (Portobello), 291338, Pte., d. of w., Egypt, 4/11/17.

Patrick, Robert, b. Springburn, Glasgow, e. Glasgow, 8704, Pte., k. in a., Gallipoli, 28/6/15.

Pattison, Joseph, b. Glasgow, e. Glasgow, 393, Pte., k. in a., Gallipoli, 28/6/15.

Pencovich, Michael, b. Barony, Glasgow, e. Glasgow, 9276, Pte., k. in a., Gallipoli, 28/6/15.

Peoples, Samuel, e. Glasgow, 9628, Pte., k. in a., Gallipoli, 28/6/15.

Pettigrew, James, b. Glasgow, e. Glasgow, 9388, Pte., k. in a., Gallipoli, 28/6/15.

Phillip, Michael, e. Glasgow, 9791, Pte., k. in a., Gallipoli, 28/6/15.

Poliskes, Klemis, b. Suwalki, Russia, e. Glencorse (Newton Grange, Midlothian), 36636, Pte., k. in a., F. & F., 28/9/18.

Priestley, John, b. Brookfield, Renfrew, e. Kilbarchan, (Auchenblae, Kincardine), 203028, Pte., d. of w., Egypt, 23/11/17, formerly S/16831, A. & S.H.

Pryer, John, b. Limehouse, London, e. Stratford (Stepney, E.), 291564, Pte., k. in a., F. & F., 29/7/18.

Pryke, George Henry, b. Enfield, Middx., e. London (Eastbourne, Sussex), 9019 Sgt., k. in a., F. & F., 1/8/18.

Pultney, James, e. Glasgow, 9844, Pte., d. of w., Egypt, 4/8/16.

Quigg, Harry, e. Glasgow, 290854, Pte., k. in a., F. & F., 29/7/18.

Rainey, James, e. Glasgow, 290563, Pte., k. in a., F. & F., 29/7/18.

Ralston, Hugh, b. Coatbridge, Lanark, e. Hamilton (Coatbridge), 291420, C.S.M., k. in a., F. & F., 29/7/18, M.M.

Ramage, Arthur, b. Possilpark, Glasgow, e. Glasgow, 7392, Cpl., k. in a., Gallipoli. 28/6/15.

Rankin, Alexander, b. Barony, Glasgow, e. Glasgow, 8656, L/Cpl., k. in a., Gallipoli, 28/6/15.

Rankin, James, b. Bridgeton, Glasgow, e. Glasgow, 9325, Pte., k. in a., Gallipoli, 28/6/15.

Rashley, Sidney James, b. Clerkenwell London, e. Stratford, 1448, Cpl., k. in a., Egypt, 4/8/16.

Redburn, John, e. Glasgow, 290719 Pte., k. in a., Egypt, 12/11/17.

Reid, Andrew Ramsay, b. Springburn Glasgow, e. Glasgow, 9086, Pte., k. in a., Gallipoli, 28/6/15.

Reid, Samuel, b. Barony, Glasgow, e. Glasgow, 291547, Pte., k. in a., Egypt, 25/7/17.

Reid, Walker James, b. Nairn, e. Nairn, 18728, A/Sgt., d. of w., F. & F., 3/8/18, formerly 34414, R.A.M.C., D.C.M.

Reid, William, b. Townhead, Glasgow, e. Glasgow, 9562, L/Cpl., k. in a., Gallipoli, 28/6/15.

Rennie, William, b. Barony, Glasgow, e. Glasgow, 9295, Pte., k. in a., Gallipoli, 28/6/15.

Rice, Charles Jack, b. Govan, Glasgow, e. Glasgow, 203607, Cpl., k. in a., Egypt, 2/11/17.

Richardson, Thomas, b. Leith, 291593, Pte., k. in a., Egypt, 22/11/17.

Richardson, Thomas Purves, e. Edinburgh, 42751, Pte., k. in a., F. & F., 29/7/18.

Riley, Thomas, b. Sandiacre, Derby, e. Nottingham, 291368, Pte., k. in a., F. & F., 29/7/18.

Roach, John, b. Bridgeton, Glasgow, e. Glasgow, 9473, Pte., k. in a., Gallipoli, 28/6/15.

Robb, Robert, b. Townhead, Glasgow, e. Glasgow, 9419, Pte., d. of w., Gallipoli, 28/6/15.

Roberts, Matthew, e. Glasgow, 230, Pte., k. in a., Gallipoli, 28/6/15.

Roberton, Albert, b. Barony, Glasgow, e. Glasgow, 290169, Cpl., k. in a., F. & F., 29/7/18.

Robertson, George, b. Maryhill, Glasgow, e. Glasgow, 12524, Cpl., k. in a., F. & F., 29/7/18.

Robertson, George Stalker, b. Kincardine, e. Cathcart, Glasgow, 203104, A/L/Cpl., k. in a., Egypt 12/11/17, formerly S/17005, Arg. & Suth. High.

Robertson, John, e. Glasgow, 522, Pte., d. of w., Gallipoli, 4/7/15.

Robertson, John, e. Glasgow, 558, Pte., d. of w., Egypt, 11/8/16.

Robertson, John, b. Barony, Glasgow, e. Glasgow, 8983, Pte., k. in a., Gallipoli, 28/6/15.

Robertson, John, e. Glasgow, 290551, Pte., k. in a., Egypt, 2/11/17.

Robertson, Nelson, b. Edinburgh, e. Edinburgh, 28831, Pte., k. in a., F. & F., 29/7/18.

Robertson, Robert, b. Townhead, Glasgow, e. Glagow, 475, Pte., k. in a., Gallipoli, 28/6/15.

Robertson, William, e. Glasgow, 9916, Pte., k. in a., Gallipoli, 28/6/15.

Roe, James, b. St. Rollox, Glasgow, e. Glasgow, 9302, Pte., k. in a., Gallipoli, 28/6/15.

Ronalds, Joseph, e. Glasgow, 258, Pte., k. in a., Gallipoli, 28/6/15.

Rose, William, b. Barony, Glasgow, e. Glasgow, 9500, L/Cpl., k. in a., Gallipoli, 28/6/15.

Ross, Charles, b. Govan, Glasgow, e. Glasgow, 291141, Pte., k. in a., Egypt, 29/7/18.

Ross, Donald, b. Cowlairs, Glasgow, e. Glasgow, 9436, Cpl., k. in a., Gallipoli, 28/6/15.

Ross, John, b. Barony, Glasgow, e. Glasgow, 9509, L/Cpl., k. in a., Gallipoli, 28/6/15.

Ross, William, b. Auchterarder, Perth, e.

Falkirk, 203101, Pte., d. of w., Egypt, 25/11/17, formerly S/16890, Arg. & Suth. High.

Rothney, John, e. Glasgow, 290944, Pte., d. of w., Egypt, 10/11/17.

Rule, William, b. Tradeston, Glasgow, e. Glasgow, 8465, L/Sgt., k. in a., Gallipoli, 28/6/15.

Rutherford, Samuel, b. Govan, Glasgow, e. Glasgow, 9000, L/Cpl., k. in a., Gallipoli, 28/6/15.

Sands, George, b. Glasgow, e. Glasgow, 42748, Pte, k. in a., F. & F., 29/7/18.

Sands, John, b. Glasgow, e. Glasgow, 42749, Pte., k. in a., F. & F., 29/7/18.

Scahill, Peter, b. St. Rollox, Glasgow, e. Glasgow, 9880, Pte., k. in a., Gallipoli, 28/6/15.

Scobie, William, b. Glasgow, e. Glasgow, 291232, Pte., k. in a., F. & F., 29/7/18.

Scott, George, b. Glasgow, e. Glasgow, 9890, Pte., k. in a., Gallipoli, 28/6/15.

Scott, James, b. Barony, Glasgow, e. Glasgow, 9340, Pte., k. in a., Gallipoli, 28/6/15.

Scott, James, e. Kirkcaldy (Alloa), 9837, Pte., k. in a., Gallipoli, 28/6/15.

Scott, James, b. Dundee, e. Glasgow, 290165, Pte., k. in a., Egypt, 21/12/17.

Semple, William Cochrane, b. Strathaven, Lanark, e. Hamilton (Strathaven), 240911, Pte., k. in a., Egypt, 29/7/17.

Shannon, Daniel, b. Glasgow, e. Glasgow, 9297, Pte., k. in a., Gallipoli, 28/6/15.

Shannon, Thomas, b. Glasgow, e. Glasgow, 42, Pte., k. in a., Gallipoli, 12/7/15.

Sharp, Hugh, e. Glasgow, 201623, Pte, k, in a., Egypt. 25/7/17.

Sharples, Thomas, b. Chorley, Lancs e. Chorley, Lancs, 22512, L/Sgt., d., Egypt, 28/5/18.

Shearlaw, Dugald, b. Gourock, Renfrew, e. Glasgow, 1271, Pte., d. of w., Egypt, 4/8/16.

Sheerin, John, b. Glasgow, e. Glasgow, 9517, Pte., k. in a., Gallipoli, 28/6/15.

Sheriff, John, b. Glasgow, e. Glasgow, 8996, Cpl., k. in a., Gallipoli, 28/6/15.

Shields, James, e. Glasgow, 9871, Pte., k. in a., Gallipoli, 28/6/15.

Shilling, Albert, b. Southport, Lancs, e. Oswestry (Southport), 33573, Pte., k. in a., Egypt, 2/11/17, formerly T/4/197880, R.A.S.C.

Shirlaw, William, e. Glasgow, 290973, Pte., k. in a., F. & F., 29/7/18.

Simpson, John, b. Glasgow, e. Glasgow, 7423, L/Cpl., k. in a., Gallipoli, 28/6/15.

Sinclair, James, b. Glasgow, e. Glasgow, 8741, Pte., k. in a., Gallipoli, 28/6/15.

Sinclair, James Mitchell, b. Cockpen, Midlothian, e. Edinburgh, 45508, Pte., d. of w., F. & F., 26/10/18.

Skelley, John, b. Ayr, e. Glasgow 9335, L/Cpl., k. in a., Gallipoli, 28/6/15.

Sloway, James, b. Glasgow, e. Hamilton (Netherburn, Lanark), 31711, Pte., k. in a. Egypt, 2/11/17.

Smith, Alexander, b. Glasgow, e. Glasgow, 8454, A/Sgt., k. in a., Gallipoli, 28/6/15.

Smith, George, b. Glasgow, e. Glasgow, 8121, A/Sgt., k. in a., Gallipoli, 28/6/15.

Smith, George, b. Glasgow, e. Glasgow, 9360, Pte., k. in a., Gallipoli, 28/6/15.

Smith, William, b. Piershill, Edinburgh, e. Edinburgh, 37284, Pte., k. in a., F. & F., 29/7/18.
Sneddon, Malcolm, e. Glasgow, 12, Pte., k. in a., Gallipoli, 28/6/15.
Soutar, William, e. Glasgow, 9646, Pte., k. in a., Gallipoli, 28/6/15.
Sproul, Alexander, b. Middlesbrough, Yorks, e. Middlesbrough, Yorks, 238143, Pte., k. in a., F. & F., 16/10/18, formerly 4879 Yorks Regt.
Stark, George, b. Glasgow, e. Glasgow, 8841, Pte., k. in a., Gallipoli, 28/6/15.
Stears, Henry, b. St. George's, London, e. Glasgow, 8509. Pte., k. in a., Gallipoli, 28/6/15.
Steel, Robert, b. Polmont, Stirling, e. Glasgow, 9175, A/L/Cpl., k. in a., Gallipoli, 28/6/15.
Steel, William, e. Glasgow, 9877, Pte., k. in a., Gallipoli, 28/6/15.
Stevenson, Hugh, b. Glasgow, e. Glasgow, 9399, Pte., k. in a., Gallipoli, 28/6/15.
Stevenson, John, b. Glasgow, e. Glasgow (Paisley), 9932, Pte., k. in a., Gallipoli, 28/6/15.
Stevenson, Robert, e. Glasgow, 9635, Pte., k. in a., Gallipoli, 28/6/15.
Stewart, Alexander, b. Glasgow, e. Glasgow, 290770, Pte., k. in a., F. & F., 29/7/18.
Stewart, Archibald, b. Barrhead, Renfrew, e. Stirling (Barrhead), 46192, Pte., k. in a., F. & F., 29/7/18, formerly 2544, Lothians and Border Horse.
Stewart, Charles, e. Glasgow 83, Pte., k. in a., Gallipoli, 28/6/15.
Stewart, David, e. Glasgow, 3, Pte., k. in a., Gallipoli, 28/6/15.
Stewart, John, e. Glasgow, 395, Pte., k. in a., Gallipoli, 28/6/15.
Stewart, Joseph, b. Glasgow, e. Glasgow, 290268, Pte., k. in a., Egypt, 22/11/17.
Stobo, Samuel, e. Glasgow, 290827, Pte., k. in a., F. & F., 1/8/18.
Storran, John, b. Kirkcaldy, e. Glasgow (Kircaldy), 9875, Pte., k. in a., Gallipoli. 28/6/15.
Strain, John, e. Glasgow, 153, Pte., k. in a., Gallipoli, 28/6/15.
Strain, Robert, b. Glasgow, e. Partick, Glasgow, 203016, Pte., k. in a., Egypt, 29/7/17, formerly 24181, H.L.I.
Sutherland, John Robert, b. Rogart, Sutherlandshire, e. Partick, Glasgow, 36189, Pte., k in a., F. & F., 7/10/18.
Swan, Robert, e. Glasgow, 40694, Pte., k. in a., F. & F., 1/8/18.
Sweeney, Thomas, b. Glasgow, e. Glasgow, 8981, Pte., k in a., Gallipoli, 28/6/15.
Taylor, Andrew, b. Glasgow, e. Glasgow, 581, Pte., k. in a., Gallipoli, 28/6/15.
Taylor, George, b. Dublin, e. Glasgow, 290893, Pte., d. of w., Egypt, 13/11/17.
Taylor, Henry, b. Glasgow, e. Glasgow, 290249, L/Cpl., k. in a., Egypt, 19/4/17.
Taylor, William Dick, b. Glasgow, e. Glasgow, 8713, A/Cpl., k. in a., Gallipoli, 28/6/15.
Teale, Harold, b. Lanark, e. Glasgow, 8776, A/Cpl., d. of w., Gallipoli, 28/6/15.
Teehan, James, b. Glasgow, e. Glasgow, 8921, Pte., k. in a., Gallipoli, 28/6/15.
Templeton, Robert, e. Coatbridge,

Lanark, 202969, Pte., k. in a., F. & F, 29/7/18.
Third, Charles McGilvary, b. Longside, Aberdeen, e. Glasgow (Peterhead, Aberdeen), 11136, Pte., k. in a., F. & F., 29/7/18, M.M.
Thompson, James Marshall, b Glasgow, e. Glasgow, 9084, Pte., k. in a., Gallipoli, 28/6/15.
Thomson, Alexander, b. Glasgow e. Glasgow, 8728, Pte., k. in a., Gallipoli, 28/6/15.
Thomson, Alexander, e. Glasgow, 290479, Pte., k. in a., Egypt, 19/4/17.
Thomson, David, b. Glasgow, e. Glasgow, 7728, L/Cpl., k. in a., Gallipoli, 28/6/15.
Thomson, James Robert, e. Aberdeen, 42586, Pte., k. in a., F. & F., 29/7/18, formerly S/14230, Gor. High.
Thomson, Joseph, b. Glasgow, e. Glasgow, 9243, Pte., k. in a., Gallipoli, 28/6/15.
Thomson, Neil, b. Greenock, Renfrew, e. Greenock, 37272, Pte., k. in a., F. & F., 29/7/18.
Thomson, Neil McArthur, b. Rutherglen, Lanark, e. Rutherglen, 46227, Pte., k. in a., F. & F. 2/9/18, formerly 35608, Lanark Yeo.
Thomson, Robert, b. Glasgow, e. Glasgow, 6746, Pte., k. in a., Gallipoli, 28/6/15.
Tinney, James, b. Glasgow, e. Glasgow, 8875, Pte., k. in a., Gallipoli, 28/6/15.
Trotter, William, b. Corstorphine, Edinburgh, e. Edinburgh (Winchburgh), 42752, Pte., k. in a., F. & F., 29/7/18, formerly 2/40101, H.L.I.
Turner, Robert, e. Glasgow, 290702, Pte., d., Egypt, 29/9/17.
Tyre, William, b. Rothesay, Bute, e. Glasgow, 9597, Pte., k. in a., Gallipoli, 28/6/15.
Walker, William, b. Paisley, e. Glasgow, 8802, A/Cpl., k. in a., Gallipoli, 28/6/15.
Wallace, Christopher, e. Glasgow, 81, Pte., k. in a., Gallipoli, 28/6/15.
Walls, William, b. Glasgow, e. Glasgow, 8850, Pte., k. in a., Gallipoli, 28/6/15.
Wardlaw, Robert, b. Leith, e. Glasgow, 9548, Pte., k. in a., Gallipoli, 28/6/15.
Ware, Thomas, b. St. Jude's, Gloucester, e. Bristol, 291565, L/Cpl., d. of w., Egypt, 5/5/17, formerly 8008, Northumberland Fus.
Waugh, Herbert, e. Glasgow, 9896, Pte., k. in a., Gallipoli, 28/6/15.
Webster, Alexander, b. Paisley, e. Glasgow, 8717, Pte., k. in a., Gallipoli, 28/6/15.
Weir, John, b. Lochee, Dundee, e. Glasgow, 58, Pte., k. in a., Gallipoli, 28/6/15.
Welsh, Thomas, b. Renfrew, e. Glasgow, 8157, Pte., k. in a., Gallipoli, 28/6/15.
White, William, e. Glasgow, 42966, Pte., k. in a., F. & F., 29/7/18.
Whitelaw, Robert, b. Glasgow, e. Glasgow, 8923, Pte., k. in a., Gallipoli, 28/6/15.
Whittam, John William, e. Burnley, Lancs, 291377, Pte., k. in a., Egypt, 24/11/17.
Wignall, George, b. Garston, Lancs, e. Liverpool (Garston, Lancs), 40014, Pte., d., Egypt, 20/10/17.
Wilkie, Gilbert, b. Falkirk, Stirling, e. Glasgow (Falkirk), 291123, L/Cpl., F. & F., 24/5/18.

Wilkinson, John, b. Glasgow, e. Glasgow, 9245, Pte., d. of w., Gallipoli, 30/6/15.

Williams, George, e. Glasgow, 643, Pte., d. of w., Egypt, 4/8/16.

Williamson, Hugh, b. Townhead, Glasgow, e. Glasgow, 290195, Pte., d. of w., F. & F., 29/7/18.

Wilson, Andrew, b. Glasgow, e. Hamilton (Airdrie), 42756, Pte., k. in a., F. & F., 29/7/18.

Wilson, Edward, b. St. Rollox, Glasgow, e. Glasgow, 7867, Cpl., k. in a., Gallipoli, 28/6/15.

Wilson, James Reid, b. Glasgow, e. Glasgow, 9034, L/Cpl., k. in a., Gallipoli, 28/6/15.

Wilson, William, b. Glasgow, e. Glasgow, 9228, Pte. k. in a., Gallipoli, 28/6/15.

Wilson, William, b. Barony, Glasgow, e. Glasgow, 9478, Cpl., k. in a., Gallipoli, 28/6/15.

Wilson, William Urie Brown, b. Glasgow, e. Glasgow, 42755, Pte., k. in a., F. & F., 29/7/18.

Winning, Andrew, b. Glasgow, e. Glasgow, 291028, Pte., k. in a., Egypt, 23/11/17.

Winning, John, b. Calton, Glasgow, e. Glasgow, 203017, Pte., d. of w., Egypt, 30/7/17, formerly 25001, H.L.I.

Wylie, John, b Barony, Glasgow, e. Glasgow, 9223, Pte., k. in a., Gallipoli, 28/6/15.

Yates, Joseph, b. Blackburn, Lancs, e. Preston (Blackburn), 291599, Pte., k. in a., Egypt, 24/11/17.

Young, James Stewart, e. Glasgow, 9953, Pte., k. in a., Gallipoli, 28/6/15.

Young, Peter Dunlop, b. Kilsyth, Stirling, e. Ayr, 42574, Pte., k. in a., F. & F., 31/10/18.

Young, Thomas, b. Blairgowrie, Perth, e. Glasgow, 244, Pte., k. in a., Gallipoli, 28/6/15.

Youngson, William, b. Aberdeen, e. Glasgow (Bo'ness, W. Lothian), 291470, Pte., k. in a., F. & F., 31/10/18.

APPENDIX VIII

A Trench Mortar Battery was formed by the battalion while at Kantara in 1916. It consisted of two officers, Lieuts. A. C. Sharp and D. H. Begg, and 30 other ranks. After some preliminary training in Egypt, it was sent to Mesopotamia, where it served with distinction throughout the campaign. It retained its identity until the end of the War.

APPENDIX IX

CORRESPONDENCE WITH H. W. NEVINSON

H. W. Nevinson, Esq.,
4 Downside Crescent,
London, N.W. 3,
England.

6th June, 1919.

8th Scottish Rifles, 186th Brigade, 52nd Division.

" Sir,

" I have just read your book *The Dardanelles Campaign.* I have also seen Captain Campbell's article in the *Bulletin* dated 18th April, 1919, and a reply thereto of yours in the *Scots Pictorial* of 24th May, 1919. It is unnecessary for me to go into the details which Captain Campbell gives in the *Bulletin* save to say that, as far as my battalion is concerned, the losses he gives for the action on 28th June, 1915, are correct. I quote them again:

	Officers.	Other Ranks.	Total.
Killed (or missing and never found)	13	334	347
Wounded	11	114	125
			472

One officer and 29 men answered roll-call next morning.

" I write to you because I temporarily commanded the battalion on the date in question (the then Commanding Officer having been killed four days previously), and because the words you use on page 185, ' The 7th and 8th Scottish Rifles entirely failed to advance ', have filled those that are left of us in the battalion, and the relatives of the fallen, with bitter resentment. The implication that the battalion did not go over the top is absolutely untrue, glaringly at variance with the facts and the casualties incurred, and is a gross calumny on the memory of the gallant men who fell. You will, I am sure, understand this very natural feeling, and while acknowledging your readiness to correct the error [1] by rewriting the passage referred to, amongst others, for future editions, I think you will agree that this cannot be regarded in any way as an apology. Mere self-respect necessitates such corrections. For obvious reasons I hope that your book will go into a second and further editions, but meantime the first edition is being read and nothing has been done to rectify the undeserved slur which you have cast upon the honour of fallen men. I think that a correcting slip should be inserted in all existing unsold copies of the first edition, and a letter of apology from you pointing this out should be published in the *Times, Glasgow Herald, Glasgow News,* and the *Bulletin.* I quite understand how mistakes in accuracy and in justice can arise, but when these

[1] *Vide Scots Pictorial* of 24th May, 1919.

do occur, and particularly when they reflect upon men's honour, as in the passage referred to, the very least that an author can do is to make the fullest reparation he can.

Yours truly,

J. M. FINDLAY,

Lt.-Col. Commanding 1/8 Scottish Rifles, British Army of the Rhine."

4 Downside Crescent, N.W. 3.
June 12/19.

" Sir,

" Many thanks for your letter of the 6th, and for the suggestion it contains.

" I have just finished the revision of my book on the Dardanelles Campaign in accordance with new information sent me by many officers and men. As I said in my letters to the *Bulletin* and *Scots Pictorial*, I have re-written the passage to which you refer, and as the correction is now in type, I have asked my publishers to include this page in the text of the remaining copies of the present edition, together with two or three other corrections where injustice has unwittingly been done.

" I think you will agree that this is a better method than the insertion of slips, which leave the original text standing.

" If they agree to my proposal, I can then let the fact be known, as you suggest.

Yours faithfully,

HENRY W. NEVINSON."

Lt.-Colonel J. M. FINDLAY.

17*th June*, 1919.

" HENRY W. NEVINSON, ESQ.,
4 Downside Crescent,
London, N.W. 3.

" Sir,

" I have to thank you for your letter of 12th inst., and I quite agree that the insertion of the whole new page in the text of the remaining copies of the present edition is a better method of correction than the insertion of slips. I should be much obliged if you would inform me that the publishers agree to your proposal, and on what date your letter of apology will appear in the newspapers referred to. May I ask you specifically to refer to this battalion in your letter.

" I thank you for your courtesy, and for the fair-mindedness, which I had no doubt I should receive from you in the matter.

Yours faithfully,

J. M. FINDLAY,

Lt.-Col. Commanding 1/8 Scottish Rifles, British Army of the Rhine."

4 Downside Crescent, N.W. 3.
July 7/19.

" Sir,

" I am glad to be able to tell you that I have now arranged with my publishers to insert a few corrections in the text of the unbound copies of the present edition of my book on the Dardanelles Campaign. Only about 30 bound copies remain, and there are about 300 unbound.

" One of the corrections will of course deal with the point you raised in regard to the 7th and 8th Scottish Rifles.

" I have sent letters upon the subject to the *Times, Glasgow Herald, Glasgow News, Bulletin, Daily News,* and *Manchester Guardian,* and have mentioned the case of your battalion with others.

"The correction is of course rather an expensive thing for me, but I wish I could have done more.

" I will send you a copy of my letter when it appears.

Yours faithfully,

HENRY W. NEVINSON."

Lt.-Colonel J. M. FINDLAY.

From *Glasgow Evening News* of 9th August, 1919.

THE " AMENDE HONORABLE "

When *The Dardanelles Campaign,* by H. W. Nevinson, appeared some months ago, it roused some ire in the breasts of Scottish soldiers of the Lowland Division, who held that their doings were inaccurately represented.

Mr. Nevinson has been influenced to revise his views. He now writes to the Press that " where injustice has unintentionally been done ", alterations will be inserted in all copies of his history still unbound. These corrections concern the doings of the 7th and 8th Scottish Rifles on June 28th, 1915, and part of the Highland Light Infantry Brigade on July 13th.   Good!